Ethics of Coercion and Authority

Ethics of Coercion and Authority: A Philosophical Study of Social Life

Timo Airaksinen

University of Pittsburgh Press

Published by the University of Pittsburgh Press, Pittsburgh, Pa. 15260
Copyright © 1988, University of Pittsburgh Press
All rights reserved
Feffer and Simons, Inc., London
Manufactured in the United States of America

Library of Congress Cataloging-in-Publication Data

Airaksinen, Timo, 1947–
    Ethics of coercion and authority.

    Bibliography: p.
    Includes index.
    1. Social ethics.   2. Power (Social sciences)
3. Violence.   4. Authority.   I. Title.
HM216.A36   1988   303.3   87-35766
IBSN 0-8229-3583-X

Contents

Preface

From a moderately individualist moral point of view, granting the validity of some basic principles of prudential rationality, the question of how to interpret the phenomena of power is interesting. Such interpersonal and structurally determined forces as threats, coercion, deterrence, violence, manipulation, authority, and commands reflect some problematic features of social exchange. Punishment is a familiar philosophical subject. Power, however, is a relatively neglected topic.

Power is a philosophical challenge first as an analytical problem, which demands a more detailed description than that presupposed by vague talk about "forms of power" and its "exercise," and second in the sense that it is difficult to see why any prudent person, conscious of his or her rights and personal goals, could accept certain forms of the exercise of power. The judgment of coercion is easy: threats represent an inherently wicked form of social interaction. But what about authority? Why should anyone surrender his own judgment in prudently serious cases or follow another person's commands in dangerous situations? And if coercion is wrong, what about the right claimed by legitimate states to use force? The state is a power structure that may use drastic methods to assert its institutional rights.

Now, the ultimate question is this: Who are the state agents who wield its power and how can they justify what they are doing? If one cannot understand these agents' "rational" motivation, the state itself cannot be just and justified. No social structure that presupposes individual violation of rights and morality can be acceptable. Individual power wielders must meet a demanding justificatory task indeed, not only in relation to what they do to other people but also in relation to what they must do to themselves. A coercer and a commanding authority seem to violate their own moral autonomy and practical reason. Is such a representative agent so alienated that the state must be called unjust simply because of this agent's role? Therefore, this is a treatise on the limits of the theory of state from an individualist point of view.

My answer to the question posed in the preceding paragraph is that we can avoid the most negative conclusions regarding the legitimacy of state power and its exercise and, by so doing, we come frightfully close to the conclusion that such state agents are in a sense characterized by antiindividualist and collective motives. No power can survive on the grounds of pure prudence, but it is possible to accept some kind of collective authority and its "strong" demands on citizens.

The topic is not a nice one, although it is unavoidable in the present world. There is no excuse for not understanding street violence, organized crime, terrorism, guerilla warfare, sectarian vendettas, state fascism, war, and the legitimate threats issued by "just" states. Power is an ever-present problem, which must not be neglected. It challenges philosophical understanding.

I have been working on this project since 1980, when I first read Steven Lukes's *Power: A Radical View* (1974) and Dennis Wrong's *Power* (1979). Both books are impressive, and they looked important to me, although I soon realized that their sociological approach could not offer the final key to analytical moral and social problems. It took quite a long time before I understood why: the notion of power is so broad that it is almost meaningless. I developed two new approaches: the present softer and more realistic story and also a detailed game theoretic analysis, reported in "Games of Coercion and Power," parts 1 and 2, *European Journal of Political Economy* 2 (1986). Their conclusions agree, but the first motivates the latter, which describes some abstract and formal motivational details and problems. I also refer to my paper "Coercion, Deterrence, and Authority," in *Theory and Decision* 17 (1984), which sketches my whole approach.

I have presented parts of this material in conferences and at universities in Austria, West Germany, the United States, Canada, Iceland, and Sweden. I wish to express my gratitude to all those who have provided support, especially Professor Jay L. Garfield and Dr. Gerald Doherty. Financial support has been provided by the Academy of Finland, Turku University Foundation, Center for Philosophy of Science in Pittsburgh, University of Helsinki, and Tampere Peace Research Institute.

Ethics of Coercion and Authority

1 | Focus on Power

Introduction

We shall study some nonstandard uses of moral language and reasoning—or, as we could also put it, we are interested in some aspects of nonperfect ethics. In a standard perspective such as Kant's, moral inquiry strives, first, to establish the moral ideal and, second, to say something about the necessary and sufficient conditions of the social implementation of this ideal. For instance, Charles Fried opens the introduction to his book *Right and Wrong* as follows: "This is a book about how a moral man lives his life. . . . My central concern is to discern structure and limits in the demands morality makes upon us."[1] My central point will in effect be a reminder in the opposite direction. There is no unique moral man or a single structure of moral demands. Moral reasoning and moral commitments shape our lives in many ways that have little to do with ideal morality.

This is a book about how a person lives his moral life in society, influenced by his moral ideas and challenged by deep conflicts. In social life, the goals of action need not be idealistic to be rational and even moral.

Suppose we argue as follows: Imperfect ethics is used especially in those conflicts in which we do not want to find any cooperative solutions, and such situations in fact occur. A relevant example is crime and its punishment. The state power apparatus is not supposed

3

to reconcile with the criminal. On the contrary, it realizes a more or less violent threat against his person. In this case, the realization of our ethical ideals is doomed to stay "imperfect," even if the act of punishment is regulated by many normative rules and prescriptions. The punishment may be socially just, but nevertheless it implies intended unconditional harm to its victims. Punishment is an area where our social and moral concerns implicitly conflict, so that our moral considerations are made imperfect and, compared to our cooperative ideals, nonstandard. Punishment is a moral enigma exactly because it does not aim at a cooperative solution. However, one may or may not argue that moral ideals are simply fictions.[2] If they are fictions, they still have their important uses in social life and rhetoric. One may act as if one believed that moral ideals are real.

The rest of this introductory section will offer an impression of how we might explain the notion of imperfect ethics from the point of view of conflicts that we either cannot or do not want to resolve. The following paragraphs illustrate the general framework within which the theory of coercion will be developed. I do not think that the correctness of such a framework can be demonstrated in any conclusive manner; but that is not important. What is important is that moral ideas indeed explain our social life even when used without perfect solutions and realized ideals. The following should be read, therefore, as though it were delivered oratio obliqua.

Moral philosophers have worked hard to teach us what we should do and why we should do it. Moral theory has often studied the prospective brighter side of the human world, and it has been supposed that once the good is exposed and offered to us in a palatable manner we shall want to appropriate it. This has not yet happened. The philosophers' work has always been sadly lacking, too. Moral theorists contradict each other and confuse the issues they discuss. Whatever they touch becomes a conceptual mess. The cleanup has been performed by priests, lawyers, politicians and, nowadays, professional bureaucrats. At least they do not hesitate. Neither do they offer much elucidation or argument to support their decisions, advice, and commands.

Philosophers have thought that if their work succeeded the world would be a better place to live in. Perhaps they do not always want to admit this motivation, but why then are they working at all? Yet, while striving toward their chosen ends, they are not committed to religion, social consensus, the state, party programs, or administrative "efficiency." Therefore, philosophers ought not think that if their work succeeded the world would necessarily change into a good place to live in. Philosophical commitments are the commitments of those engaged in scholarly life, which means, again, that they are not interested in such limited and even partisan goals as those others competing in the how-to-live-a-good-life-and-where-to-go-to-get-it race.

Education is sometimes dangerous. The reason is that large-scale educational systems typically serve some basically conservative cultural reproduction processes.[3] Education is always and everywhere a vehicle of socialization. Even such notions as creativity, responsibility, social success, and the good life are defined by the state and are dependent on its cultural domination. I am not saying that this is necessarily bad. If we are not complete anarchists, we certainly realize that organized social life is a desirable thing and certainly something worth preserving. But any given set of actually realizable and formally explicated goals of education are far from such universal ends as the truth or the objectivity of inquiry, which are ideally aimed at by philosophy and the social sciences. Educational authorities necessarily need a well-defined idea of the good life, quite independently of whether they know, or even care about, what they are talking about. Such common fictions as social justice, international peace, and global solidarity with the poor and oppressed seemingly dominate education. Actually, teachers repeat the pleas of the priests, politicians, and bureaucrats. They run an enormous good-life machine, whose grinding mills produce — if they are at all efficient — a string of middle-class mirror images of social reality and sketches of roads to modest utopias. Common to these products is the assumption that we know what a better life would and could be and how that knowledge can be justified and implemented.

Philosophers are employed to produce some minor but important missing parts. They are asked to say, for example, something about whether a fetus is a person when this issue is taken up in the heat of a public debate on abortion. The main part of the normatively relevant work in such a legal battle is done by priests or politicians, depending on the country; but in any case, philosophers are invited to participate. They will show us that a fetus is or isn't a person and how this fact fits into a decisional context where facts with values, right and duty statements, and a logic of practical discourse will yield a proper solution to the potentially divisive issue of abortion.

I am not saying that all this philosophic labor is in vain. My point is not that once the lobbies of medical doctors, lawyers, and priests enter the politicians' premises philosophy will be forgotten. The issue is not that simple. On the contrary, if all these pressure groups share a culture, or at least some aspects of it, so that they are able to discuss the issues sensibly, their background beliefs and logic are partly a product of philosophical tradition. Therefore, even if it is mildly ridiculous to maintain that religious antiabortion groups lobbying against new medical techniques would be impressed by some liberal moral research and theorizing, it is not impossible to think that interest groups mobilized to action in novel and morally pressing social conflicts carry the imprint of philosophy. The issues have been defined for them by their predecessors, among them literary authors, scientists, and philosophers. The created myths are sophisticated enough to make it impossible for their users to claim that the fictions are their own inventions. Their clarity is that of the shared cultural background.

The whole ragged opinion and belief structure floats on mainly because its details are complex and the combinations of meanings deep. No single interest group can dominate the scene by means of claims to unique knowledge or privileged values. The alternatives are far too many and too diverse, so that if no direct external control is exercised, all groups have alternative theories, values, and views by means of which they can go on challenging their opponents. They have also such methodological emergency devices as subjectivism and relativism at their disposal. Any seemingly imminent defeat in rational debate can be duly avoided. The countermove of becoming, say, a relativist will give one time to arrange one's thoughts.

Now, we would indeed come close to cynicism if we said that this is all the philosophers have done. There is more to the picture, of course. The key is that academic philosophy serves the "social life" not only by creating all these varied and incoherent materials. The point is that the philosophers also say that theories are meaningful, that practical logic works, and that human beings can solve normative and theoretical problems. What I mean is this: moral philosophy is supposed to support the view that there are positive values, rights, duties, and virtues, which are somewhat like commodities and available to anyone who earns them. We philosophers allegedly show why one should be moral, what our social duties and proper rights are, and how we decide on a just social order. The basic underlying theme is that the good life can prevail—and there is a definite social order presupposed by this philosophy of social optimism.

One problem will then be forgotten, almost automatically. Why is the world as it is and not exhibiting the signs of realized values and the virtuous life? Our reluctance to take up this question is of course justified if it can be given only the following meaning: if we literally ask why things are as they are, no answer should be expected. But my initial question has a subtler interpretation as well. It can be taken to be the following in the context of the unlimited intentional improvement and change: Why do we think that even if the world is bad it will become better just because we behave in some novel and more laudable ways? This question is not directed at the social world and its characteristics as such but at the context of asking such questions. We postulate a better world. The present world is not important.

Certainly the physical world is unique as it is, and no alternatives make any sense to consider. But the social world can certainly be changed in time, and its future is open. The question in its own context implicitly insists that we change the world in some better direction, toward some broad goals. These goals are then also partially fuzzy. We have no clear consensus as to what they are and what they mean to us. Social reality is disappearing and making room for a fictional idea. Philosophers have given us the sense of direction, and no clear sense of an end point.

Now, all this social optimism may be an ideological mistake, which will lead to greater suffering in the future, in spite of its clever disguise as compassion and social hope. My thesis is that we see (mistakenly) the present state of our social world in terms of a partly but as yet minimally realized fuzzy goal. What we do among the free-for-all ideological battles is the following. Suppose we share some values and premises and a suitable logic. Then we collect facts about our social reality, both scientifically and otherwise, mix them with myths, display the kernel of the consensus of our moral ideals, and conclude that the goals so revealed are absent from our social life-world. We do not want to see reality as it is; we are not facing reality; we are, on the contrary, comparing some limited aspects of the world to a normative idealization.

A moral goal dominates our vision. From everything there is, we pick out only that aspect that can be compared to the moral ideal. Thus a double aspect myopia will result: (1) only part of the possible social object is considered at all; and (2) only some of their possible interpretations will be mentioned. The ironic conclusion is that a slice of actual social life is defective in relation to its ideal measures. But it is the measure that makes it look bad. And as the ideal is, as we hope, reachable, we need not worry. We are going in the right direction.

To recapitulate, we may say that traditional moral philosophy is distorted. Its usefulness and social value is much more limited than we think. Philosophers give us goals and point out the direction toward them. However, the goal is used "backwards"—to identify some interesting aspects of our life-world. Next, we conclude that these aspects are sadly lacking in value. Wickedness and immorality reign freely, as it seems. We naturally decide to start working harder to get away from where we are and toward where we should be—say, a perfectly just liberal social order or, maybe, perfect cooperation among independent nations. This is how an image of progress is created. The problem is that some aspects of the world do not appear in it at all.

Let us take a look at anarchism and exploit the fertile grounds of the conflict theories of human affairs. I shall take up some issues too often excluded from ethics and normative social and political philosophy. I hope to face reality from a traditionally neglected direction: social oppression, alienation, exploitation, coercion, cruelty, and violence. Also, authority must be discussed. These issues have received little attention in ethics because of its internal orientation toward unlimited optimism, according to its social demand. The darker sides of human affairs, like conflicts and oppression, cannot fit our picture of the ideally good life. And while they are practically useful, due to the imperfections of social life, it has appeared advisable to forget them. Conflict-oriented social power is seen simply as something bad. The recommendation is clear: do not practice it. The prediction is then obvious: badness won't survive.

All this is myopic. We must admit that the negative side of human nature is still there and that it is as real as the good in us. I am convinced that there is a dialectical relation between the theories of good and evil. In fact, my project is not very radical: the only thing I want to do is to resist the temptation to identify the proper objects to be studied in moral theory in terms of what a virtuous person, the good life, and a just social order would be. I want to say that those facts that should not be there at all and that are missing in the ideal world are important and perfectly concrete aspects of our lives just now. We ought to study them, not independently of our moral notions, ideals, and utopias, nor of what we hope to realize in this world. An analysis does not entail the moral recommendation of its results. Perhaps what is bad will ultimately disappear, but while it is still with us, let us see how it works and how it influences human action.

Ideas and problems: a summary

Some conflicts can be explained away, but the simplicity of many examples is deeply misleading. The success and stability of interactive strategies is a wide and fascinating topic.[4] The key issue is that quite typically some agents do not want to achieve any cooperative solutions. This entails that these agents do not universalize their practical judgments and principles. The circumstances of justice do not always apply, as David Hume thought.

Such conflicts close off most of the standard "ideal" ethics. But it is a fact of life that a stronger agent may start an interaction that is based on coercive power and that implies his initial reluctance to aim at cooperation. And such a decision may be quite sensible, expected, and functionally efficient even in the long run. It may also employ many moral concepts and arguments. The weaker agent may well agree that the strategy is a feasible one, especially if he thinks his subordinate position is a temporal accident and hopes for revenge. Of course, in most cases the weaker agent will support a cooperative mode of interaction, but he may—and he should—realize that the stronger agent is not open to such a suggestion.

I shall start from the notion of personal coercion, by which I mean a violent conflict between a coercer and his victim when both have fairly complete information about each other's descriptive features, preferences, and moral ideas. No cultural or institutional background factors are initially postulated to explain their decisions and strategy choices. This applies, of course, to ethical principles, too. The situation is context free, so to speak.

We must then deal very carefully with the idea of a threat and its relation to offers and rights. We shall also distinguish between several types of coercion, such as deterrence and exploitation. We need a simple and clear analytical framework, which allows us to proceed step by step toward more complex cases. As a methodological tool, I shall use elementary decision theory and game theory.

We are interested in such situations in which the players realize that their conflict is a real and final one. It includes an element of violence. As we shall see, many aspects of coercion are also paradoxical, so that it seems impossible that any rational agent would coerce his weaker opponent. Coercion does not seem to pay off. Still it is a successful, frighteningly efficient, and common method of reaping extra profits. How does one dissolve the paradoxes?

My argument will be along the following lines: coercion as a context-free game is not a sensible form of human interaction at all. It is paradoxical. Only in some special cases can it work. Yet its appeal is much wider than its problematic conditions of application suggest. We need a social context in order to understand coercion. This context is formed by cultural rules and ultimately by an institutionalized framework. Examples are the Mafia and the police force. Both use explicit, well-defined, and personally neutral threats.

The last condition, the impersonality of threats, is a key to their systematic success. Coercive policies thereby become possible. This fact—that coercion is rationally efficient only if institutionalized—substantiates my claim that the "harder" aspects of social power indeed deserve careful study. The point is that if coercion and related policies are universally and unequivocally wrong, no state can be justified. We might maintain that the use of threats is in principle unjustifiable. This is certainly too simple. For instance, despite its great difficulties, the theory of punishment is not an automatic failure. It deserves our attention. Coercion can be legitimated.

We shall study the complicated issues of justifying a state and the ideas of punitive and corrective justice. The state deters, coerces, and punishes its own citizens; it also protects them against domestic and foreign conflicts. What justifies this controversial work? It seems clear that the idea of a legitimized authority must be introduced and analyzed. Only if the citizens admit that the coercive state agents have some kind of normative authority to do what they are doing can we suppose, first, that the citizens will obey them and, second, that the state agents find their own work acceptable.

Of course, the parties are sometimes in diametrically opposed positions as to law enforcement measures. We are working under the theoretical postulates of a conflict theory, anyway. Therefore, we can suppose that the motivational ideas and ideologies of the coercive agents and their object persons will often be different, a fact implied by the possibility of the breakdown of authority.

I shall argue that the two parties need different justifications for their respective policies, if they are each rational agents. The position of institutional coercive agents is especially tricky, because their actions are performed under conditions that in context-free cases are irrational. The rather peculiar demands of this normatively "constructive" social context must be studied carefully. We have here an example of "imperfect ethics": moral reasoning makes a system of conflicts possible. Ethics does not settle such conflicts.

I shall then take up the issue of the two sets of rationality postulates. It seems intuitively obvious that a deep but controlled conflict implies the players' mutually different moral ideologies; otherwise, the conflict would either be resolved more easily or it would degenerate into actual violence. I shall try to show why the coercer must be a duty-oriented person. And that implies both that he understands what authority is and that he is capable of seeing his own fate in a larger social frame than his own expected utility distribution. The whole issue of the justification of the state revolves around these issues. We must ask whether the institutional demands on coercive agents are so strong that no rational agent will be able to meet them. And if there is no way of making these demands personally acceptable, we must conclude that the state cannot be justified. Its functions are based on impossible prescriptions. Its power functions cannot be grounded.

Let me say something about the victims of coercive policies and measures before I return to the all-important issue of justification. Ideal victims are, from the point of view of, say, the state, conscientious utilitarians in the narrow economic sense. If they make their decisions about how to react to coercive threats on the basis of their own rational calculations of expected utilities, they will offer only minimal resistance to a stronger coercer. But if the victims emphasize, say, their liberties and rights against coercive institutions, they will become very difficult to handle by means of threats. Such subjects will tolerate losses in terms of utilities, and if a threat influences their utilities, it will now become largely inefficient.

Therefore, if all social agents are deontologically oriented decision makers, coercive policies may have no bite. Thus coercion will either disappear as impractical or degenerate into mere violence; that is, threats will be realized randomly. Moreover, such a fact is knowable in advance. This implies that even if, say, punishment is needed, it cannot be used systematically; and if punishment is required for fairness' sake, it cannot fulfill its purpose as a policy. Fairness implies impartiality and systematic application of rules. The state in such circumstances lacks its justification. And second, where violence reigns, we should draw the same pessimistic conclusion: certainly violence as a goal is unacceptable. If violence leads nowhere, it cannot be used.

Let us now go back to some of the broader aspects of the justification of the state. Notice that I am not saying that I actually want to justify the state as we know it in the modern world. My purposes are rather negative. I am saying merely that the use of an institutional coercive apparatus is a necessary condition of the existence of the state. Therefore, if this condition cannot be understood at least in one plausible way, so that it becomes acceptable in moral terms, the state will fail to be justified. I am working at the level of some interesting and certainly tricky necessary conditions.

Another thing worth our explicit attention is this: it is true that coercion in its social context is a problematic constituent of a just preventive and corrective policy. As we shall see, our understanding of the rational motivation of a coercive agent requires quite a complicated theoretical framework, and we must introduce technical ideas and employ some problematic moral terms and notions. I am not saying that coercive policies could not be understood in other, and perhaps simpler, ways. I offer my own theory for consideration and claim that it satisfies our basic and common intuitions to the effect that the state, as we citizens know it, is prima facie justifiable.

Perhaps a simpler and more convincing account of coercion can be found. Perhaps we will say that the account is so complex that it can be used to indicate in an indirect way that the state is *not* justified. Indeed, it is perfectly sensible to suggest that the demands on coercive, rational agents, as I describe them, are too strict to be realistically satisfiable (of course, we insist now on the use of real-life social and psychological data, learnable principles of rationality, as well as ideas of their implementation).

I am arguing that coercive policies are needed; some individual agents must be available to apply them against some other agents; and these coercers must validly justify their own actions to themselves. However, coercion is an intrinsically paradoxical strategy of interaction, and thus it is very difficult to see it as rationally acceptable; but it is true that everything is in some sense "justifiable." We can always stretch our imagination, invent new concepts, and modify normative theories here and there, and even make the very criteria of justification flexible. Yet, some alleged justifications seem to be better than others. And it is true that nothing at all is "justifiable." Just as we can construct a tentative justification for something, we can equally well produce the relevant negative conclusions. If we assume an absolutely rigid and demanding ideal standpoint, and nothing short of the City of God will emerge as a rationally acceptable place.

Therefore, I cannot even hope to produce an unequivocally clear justification of the hard cases. What I can do is to offer an account of the state in normative terms and then display the results of the analysis together with their evaluation so that everyone may judge the results and view them against the background of his or her pet theories and intuitions. I shall present my own view of the rather dark and violent side of the imperfectly organized human interaction, but I do not draw any final conclusions. Someone may suggest a more convincing positive/negative case; again others may find my attempted justification an actual refutation of the idea of the state. Another may want to offer direct and independent anarchist arguments.

I am ready to conjecture that, in spite of all the attention that has been directed toward the authoritative power apparatus of the state, the real problem of punitive and corrective justice has not been fully understood. Law enforcement has been a common topic of discussion. Some deficiencies have prevailed, however. It has not been emphasized that a judge is never a hangman, nor is a high-ranking army officer out there in the trenches shooting at the enemy. And yet, when we discuss authority and social power, we have almost invariably adopted the point of view of the judge, the lawgiver, and the general. They are authorities, and their power and commands flow downward along a typically hierarchic structure. Actually, the judge and the general are in no direct conflict with anybody, except perhaps as a result of their own incompetence and less than ideal efficiency. Their duties certainly do not entail violent conflicts with anybody. They are essentially decision makers in an impersonal and authoritative cooperative environment.

I think this fact is very important for the traditional justification of the state power structure. Nevertheless, it leads to a highly misleading picture. Someone must fulfill the orders from above, face to face with the opposition, and we should ask who could rationally accept the role of such a low-level professional executor of commands. We are discussing now the case of real individuals and not abstract social variables. A hangman's work is easy. He swings the rope, gets paid, and goes home. But a field officer is shot at and perhaps tortured when captured. A police officer walking his beat may get orders to charge against a group of mothers, say, demonstrating for children's rights. He may get involved in the beating of people whose motivation to demonstrate he personally admires.

It seems to me that, in many cases, those lowest level positions in a power-wielding structure are personally almost impossibly demanding, if they are described from the standpoint of prudence. One of my basic points is, therefore, that when we study power we cannot focus only on the superior agents. The most intriguing positions are often to be found at the bottom of the pyramid of power. The state power structure cannot be efficient if some agents are not both willing and capable of actually realizing the orders of the upper-level authoritative agents. In order to be there at all, structural power effects imply that some individual agents do obey orders and act against other persons. There is no impersonal coercive power.

There are no relevant changes in the world without individual action in real space and time. But state power implies that its efficient agents identify themselves with the state and forget their own interests.[5] Is it not strange that the social implications of this situation have not been realized in full? Would any rational individual want to act as such a basic level coercive agent? If we answer in the negative, the state is not justified. Accordingly, *the victims of violent coercion are in no special position.* We misjudge the case against coercion if we do not see that rational coercive agents may refuse to serve in their role. Coercion may be unjustifiable even if the victims' claims to nonviolent treatment are refuted.

Finally, for the sake of the argument let us affirm the justice of the state and the social order, minus the position of the lowest level coercers, and pose the problem of the justification of work of those agents in the service of such a state.

Mystifications of power: Hegel to Russell and Giddens

I shall next explain why the term *power* will not be used referentially but only suggestively in the subsequent argument. The reason is that power, in its global meaning and usage, is a mystifying word. It is simply too broad and vague to be useful. The use of the term makes it impossible even to locate the problems that shall occupy us later.

I shall first give an interpretation of a historical theory. I have chosen G. W. F. Hegel. I shall then discuss and criticize Bertrand Russell and some modern theorists who follow his advice.

Let us start from Hegel's *Philosophy of Right* which, according to the liberalist folklore, is the bible of state power and totalitarianism.[6] Thanks to Sir Karl Popper, among others, the popular idea used to be that Hegel shows why state power is more important than any individual rights and political freedom.[7] History was supposed to be the ultimate judge of merit and worth, and any individual should succumb to it without ever getting a chance to assert his or her own individuality and divergent goals. This is certainly not true of Hegel. But it is, nevertheless, quite an accurate description of the contents of his book to say that Hegel distinguishes between two separate realms of imperfect moral behavior and social life: civil society and the state. No ideal principles of ethics may be implemented, but social practice is the only judge of right and wrong. The former realm — civil society — is the place where individual needs are satisfied, and the latter—the state—is a political controlling body that dominates all social life, with good reason.

We should take a somewhat closer look at the *Philosophy of Right*. It was, after all, thought to justify state power and, moreover, it includes a sharp separation between the source of power and its objects—that is, foreign and domestic enemies and resisters. Rather surprisingly, Hegel is unable to deal with the problems of actually wielding state power against some individual agents. His conceptual apparatus is simply too thin for that. It also seems to me that Hegel's failure in identifying and dealing with this problem is symptomatic of the theories of many later thinkers. If the existence and the legitimacy of state power is recognized at all, it is simply seen as having some kind of miraculous effect on its resisting and reluctant object persons. Alternatively, it has been thought that the "victims" will yield to mere authority, so that coercion is hardly needed at all. This latter postulate is, however, much too strong. It makes social theory look like a poor fiction. Even Hegel himself recognizes that some people tend to fight back.

Once we have dealt with Hegel, we shall be ready to see that the conceptual key to our inability to deal with coercion in any illuminating way is our tendency to speak only of "power." This word means so many things that such a small item as coercion is left out of sight. This is what I mean by mystification: a global approach distorts important local details.

Let us now turn to the actual arguments of Hegel's *Philosophy of Right*. Its blueprint is clear and clean: ethical life, which is life according to some actually implemented principles of social justice and value, consists of the family, civil society, and the state. The family does not interest us now, except to the extent that its external appearance is constituted by family property and that the head of the family represents the unit in the competitive life of the civil society. The latter realm is where individual needs are created, satisfied, and fortified with an ever-growing set of social and artificial desires. It is the laissez-faire economy of the classical liberalists, like Adam Smith, J. B. Sey, and David Ricardo, whom Hegel faithfully mentions by name. Economic life exemplifies the categories of natural rights and laws, especially those of property rights, but also of contracts in their various forms. And of course the ideas of wrong, fraud, and crime are present. Civil society must be understood in terms of certain conceptual categories, but as such these categories are devoid of any effect in the sense that their conditions of implementation may well be absent. Agents may intend to make contracts, but—it should be asked—what makes a contract successful? And when and how is this going to happen? The logic of contracts calls for the actually existing historical conditions of civil society and the state.

Certainly, the "invisible hand" has much work to do in Hegel's description of economic life. Free competition and the openness of economic struggle seem to take care of the continuity and the security of property and contracts. This is not what interests us. We need to discover the breakdown points in this spontaneous adaptation of economic competition to the categories of natural rights and laws.

Two types of difficulties emerge. First, there are wrongdoing and crime as normal systemic properties of economic life; as Hegel writes, "Crime is contingency as subjective willing of evil, and this is what the universal authority must prevent or bring to justice. . . . There is . . . no inherent line of distinction between what is and what is not injurious, even where crime is concerned. . . . These details are determined by custom."[8] Accordingly, crime is an easy and rather common thing, and police action is needed to control it. The natural category of crime comes into being when someone wills it, but no natural way of determining exactly what is a crime can be found.

Second, some system-external, unpredictable, and dysfunctional sources of social unrest exist. Hegel's very interesting discussion of poverty is what I have in mind: the social system and its economy produce a biased distribution of wealth and privileges, so that some people are left on their own. They form a rabble of paupers devoid of all personal honor, sense of virtue, or respect for law. Hegel writes:

> The public authority takes the place of the family where the poor are concerned in respect not only of their immediate want but also of laziness of disposition, malignity, and the other vices which arise out of their plight and their sense of wrong.
>
> In this way there is born in the rabble the evil of lacking self-respect enough to secure subsistence by its own labor and yet at the same time of claiming to receive subsistence as its right.[9]

Hegel indicates that police are needed not only against crime but also against possible social rebellion—that is, against a kind of internal political enemy. The poor are waging a war against the rich, and although it may look like crime its actual bases are much deeper. Crime is just a subjective act of will. The rebellion of the poor is based on their "sense of wrong."

My point is this: in Hegel's theory it is quite clear that the police have not too tough a time against criminals, whose problem is mainly the weakness of will. The poor, however, are desperate, hopeless (Hegel is quite clear about this), and their moral views are different from those of the police and the public authority. This is a structurally meaningful conflict. The result may be violence, and the government's possible recipe is to make the poor emigrate.[10] I cannot help admiring Hegel's social realism and his prophetic insights into the future development of the emerging nineteenth-century industrialized societies.

The next step is to observe that civil society—and not the state—incorporates courts of justice, public authority, and the police. This might look somewhat surprising if we think of civil society as a mere economic organization. Certainly the police force is part of the state, especially because Hegel does not have in mind anything like what Nozick in *Anarchy, State, and Utopia* much later called "dominant protective associations."[11] Protection is not a private business for Hegel. The norms and interests of police work are "universal."

I understand his decision to speak about the police within the framework of civil society in the following way. The police and the administration of justice are certainly a state business, in the sense that their power and legitimization are rooted in the state, but their effects are seen and their actions felt only within civil society. The state controls its private citizens by means of law courts and the police. And because their effects are what count in the area of need satisfaction and subjective freedom, that is where the theoretical account of the police and the public authority belongs.

Hegel's state is a constitutional monarchy, with some democratic undercurrents. Therefore, the police force is an institution grounded in the constitution of the state and ultimately administered by state officials and bureaucrats. The picture we see before us is the following one: civil society is not a permanent equilibrium but has both subjective and functional unstabilizing factors. These are controlled by means of the police *within* civil society, where the effects are felt; yet, the behavior and effectiveness of the police is grounded in the state constitution. Their moral code of relevant duties must be radically different from the egoism of any free satisfier of needs. We should now ask how we can understand, first, the requirements demanded from such state power wielders and, second, who those agents are who are recruited to serve in the police force and in the army.

Police business may look rather innocent in the *Philosophy of Right*. This attitude changes radically when we start studying the army and its important role as a representative of state power against an external enemy. There are internal enemies as well, namely the poor, but they can hardly be a match for the police and the resources of a full-fledged state. Police action need not look too demanding. But the army demands everything. Foreign enemies are prepared to fight, and they are equipped to do so. But once we have checked the "official" demands on professional soldiers as state agents, we can also appreciate more those potential dangers and difficulties that the police meet while acting against, say, some ruthless and immoral mobs. It seems that individual police officers accept exactly the same type of risks as professional soldiers, although the respective probabilities of personal disaster are different.

Hegel writes about those who serve in the army as follows (he introduces the idea of a soldier class in section 326): "Sacrifice on behalf of the individuality of the state is the substantial tie between the state and all its members and so is a universal duty. . . . The intrinsic worth of courage . . . is to be found in the genuine, absolute, final end, the sovereignty of the state. The work of courage is to actualize this final end, and the means to this end is the sacrifice of personal actuality."[12]

Hegel is quite clear about the fact that war is the destruction of property and life—it shows the "vanity of temporal goods and concerns"—and he says that no civil society would ever accept such a policy.[13] On the contrary, war is waged to guarantee the state power and its place in world history. Hegel's idea of the state implies that its basis is the citizen's common interest structure and will; it is an "ethical community." Therefore, it is also everyone's duty to support the state by joining the army.

In other words, since no aspect of civilized life can emerge and survive without the state, it is in our joint interest to sacrifice ourselves for it in the case of a global crisis. It cannot survive without sacrifices: if it did not survive, neither would our way of life survive, and thus we should rationally do all we can to support the state. This is true regardless of our own personal fate.

Hegel generously grants us the right to deceive ourselves in these matters, if we feel that such a strategy would make things personally easier to tolerate. The brute fact is, however, that one goes to war in order to die. Hegel writes about rationalization: "the courageous man's inner motive need only be some particular reason or other, and even the actual result of what he does need be present solely to the minds of others and not to his own."[14]

Now, let us make a clear distinction between professional soldiers and police on the one hand and the common soldier on the other. Hegel does not quite see the full import of such a division.[15] To any civilian called to arms because of a special crisis, this terrible personal accident is just bad luck. He has his rights against the state, and therefore he has also the duties he must now satisfy.[16] He may well think that it is his patriotic, perfectly valid, and binding duty to join in; and it is perfectly excusable if he deceives himself by means of some rationalizing arguments. But the same is not true of a professional soldier. He knows why he originally joined the ranks, what warfare is like, and what his role is supposed to be. According to Hegel, he will be there to die.

My problem is, after reading Hegel, that I do not see that one would feel in the least tempted—except irrationally—to join the army and the police force of a Hegelian state. Hegel is not rewriting the *Republic* of Plato, in which the citizens have their natural places and roles. On the contrary, everyone is, according to Hegel, perfectly free to choose one's own future career according to one's subjective likings.[17] This aspect of subjective freedom is an important part of Hegel's liberalism. (Perhaps the agricultural class is an exception to the rule, but Hegel does not discuss this issue in detail.)[18]

A young man has, thus, two basic alternatives concerning his career choice: to go into business and commerce in a civil society or into the service of the state. Suppose both are equally attractive initial possibilities. But once our young man is employed by the state, he should look around: Is he now in either the army or the police force? If he is, should he not try to leave as soon as possible, immediately after learning the "truth" of the Hegelian state and the requirements of its power? I think he should. As a young professional officer on the lowest rung of the ladder of status and privilege, he takes unreasonable risks. These risks of death and mutilation are unreasonable simply because he has a choice between subjective needs and universal duties. It is not feasible to suggest that self-sacrifice would look initially better than need satisfaction and subjective negative freedom. Only if viewed from the "inside" may the state power structure look like a good place for individual self-realization. But needs belong to everyone. So when a young man makes his decision, he may be supposed to know his own needs and also that they must be suppressed if he goes into the service of the state. But he cannot, as yet, know what the positive motivational aspects of the duties of the state are like. More specifically, he cannot know how easy or difficult it will be to ignore his needs and subjective desires. In other words, a minimax strategist does not choose the army, where the risks are so serious.

Of course, patriotic moral education is normally employed in social life. But since we must still leave the ultimate choice to the individual himself, education does not help. Plain indoctrination is banned from the just social order.

What Hegel is actually showing is how we should think if we are part of the state power machinery, but he does not succeed in showing why a rational individual would ever join in. The duties offered to a candidate are simply outrageously demanding. They make the relevant profession impossible. Of course, if Hegel had recourse to the idea of a hereditary aristocracy, his political theory could be easily saved. The aristocrats' tradition would make them accept the idea of genuine military virtues. But no member of the bourgeoisie would feel the least tempted to follow the call of the state, at least if he were not ruthlessly indoctrinated.

In this way, my conclusion is that Hegel does not succeed even in identifying the problem of why a rational individual would like to join the state's coercive apparatus. State power cannot be rationally grounded, so to speak. There is no one to exercise the supposedly existing power.

I have used this example from the history of philosophy to identify a problem where it first emerges, in the theory of the bourgeois state and its citizens' prudent self-interests, seen at the same time from the point of view of the state's authority and power of self-preservation. The problem is that on this model of the state the requirements of coercion and authority, if they are going to be effective at all, must evidently appear as individually unreasonable obligations. The effective power of the Hegelian state is simply mystical. It cannot be explained. I shall identify one very simple reason why this is so. As I already indicated, the term *power* is too vague and general to be useful in social analysis. For instance, if you want to handle theoretical problems of politics by means of power, how would you explain the Hegelian thesis that state power, which guarantees systemic survival, requires individual sacrifices? In other words, why should professional power wielders willingly suffer extreme personal losses in order to keep the state power intact? Is this not lack of power?

It seems to me that these questions do not allow for simple answers. What follows during the course of the main argument of this book is one possible answer. But before starting to unravel the mysteries of power, let us try to get rid of "power" and see what could replace it.

The grandfather of many books on power is Bertrand Russell's *Power: A New Social Analysis.* Yet its argument is not impressive and the "definition" of power is misleading: "Power may be defined as the production of intended effects."[19] This is an analysis of the *exercise of power* and not of power as such.

The corrected definition is echoed for instance by Dennis Wrong in his *Power: Its Forms, Bases and Uses:* "Power is the *capacity* of some persons to produce intended and foreseen effects on others."[20] Wrong's idea is the prevailing one, and it incorporates tacitly Max Weber's dictum "even against the opposition of others."[21] It seems indeed true that, if we speak about power in general, this is what power is.

However, there is another Russellian idea which must be mentioned: "The laws of social dynamics are—so I shall contend—only capable of being stated in terms of power in its various forms."[22] We have here a very influential double thesis: first, everything in some way connected to action is power and, second, there is a "natural" classification of power, both social and nonsocial. There are said to be some "forms" of power.

Once again, Wrong follows this clue. He tries to provide such a classification and explore its implications. An alternative approach consists of resistance to classification and of an effort to elucidate the broad definition itself. The most successful work in this latter direction is done by Steven Lukes; but technically the most impressive effort is that of Alvin Goldman.[23] These writers, however, do not offer any classificatory schemes, even if they work within the global theory of power.

The general problem is that power is an umbrella concept, covering all the effects of any action. Moreover, all of our resources and capacities are power, so it follows that every person has unlimited and infinite power. And when we try to find a classification that would capture everything in practical life at once, nothing but a conceptual mess is to be expected. For example, look back to our two Russell quotations. They are mutually inconsistent in a rather obvious way: if power implies only intended effects, there is no reason whatever to expect that all the laws of social dynamics could be stated in terms of such a limited idea of power. Social dynamics entail, say, an invisible hand, too. However, the invisible hand certainly excludes all the *intended* effects of actions. Therefore, Russell's idea of social power is even broader than one first supposes.

Let us look at Wrong's "power as capacity." My capacities of thought, invention, and destruction are in principle very great. And in principle I have the power to kill, so that for instance my poor family is at my mercy all the time. If I have the capacity to push the button that launches nuclear missiles toward the "enemy" country, which will then retaliate, I have the power to destroy the world. And I have power over any given person because I can influence his or her behavior: I approach a perfect stranger and say "hello"; she will look at me in amazement—I have changed her behavior, and this shows that I had power over her. She was not going to do anything when she approached me. She reacted against her own will. There was also a conflict between us, simply because it can be verified that she was going to ignore me. Thus my interests and hers clashed. This type of reasoning is trivial, though.

Another philosopher and social scientist who is apparently happy with the general notion of power I have called mystifying is Anthony Giddens. In his book *New Rules of Sociological Method* he writes as follows:

> "Power" in the narrower, relational sense is a property of inter-action, and may be defined as the capability to secure outcomes where the realization of these outcomes depends upon the agency of others.
>
> The reflexive elaboration of frames of meaning is characteristically imbalanced in relation to the possession of power, whether this be a result of the superior linguistic or dialectical skills, . . . authority or "force," etc.[24]

The broad notion of power is too difficult to elucidate. I cannot see how the actionist idea of power, as mentioned in the first paragraph of the quotation, or "the *transformative capacity* of human action,"[25] fits together with the more complex structural idea.

For instance, violent threats or use of force in order to exercise our power are usually far from changing meaning structures. Actions and meanings are different. Yet it is of course true that many aspects of power, such as legitimate authority, are properly structural, meaning related, and dependent on how we perceive reality. Coercive power is different, however. If I have a hidden handgun, it conveys actionist power to me due to the fact that I may be willing to shoot someone. But when a police officer carries a gun, it is also a symbolic token of his authoritative position. His visible gun is effective even if it is unloaded. His power is partly structural, while mine is purely actionist.

In this perspective, it looks rather meaningless to write, as Giddens does in the summary section of his book: "Processes of structuration involve an interplay of meanings, norms and power. These three concepts are analytically equivalent as the 'primitive' terms of social science, and are logically implicated both in the notion of intentional action and that of structure."[26] I think this is supposed to mean that both actions and structures should be explained, at least partly, in terms of power. But if *power* is at the same time both a primitive (unanalyzed) term and more or less indistinguishable from *meaning* and *norm*, I fail to see how we can make sense of the essential difference, as observed above in the first Giddens quotations (at note 24), between the actionist and the structural types of power. How could "intentional action" and "structure" both imply the same notion of power? Moreover, Giddens tries to define power in the Russellian-Weberian way; therefore, *power* cannot be a primitive term.

I hardly need to say more about this global notion of power. An analytical theory of the cluster of powerlike phenomena, interactions, and structures should be provided instead. I shall start from a simple notion of *coercion*, introduce the subcategory of *deterrence*, explain them in terms of *threats* and *offers*, evaluate them in terms of *rights* and *duties*, and proceed by contrasting them to *authority*. I shall try to make sense of certain types of important conflicts.

Actually, there is only one excuse for doing mystifying social philosophy: when we want to sail between social science and literature so that we can capture the imagination and provide new ideas for further study, trying to provide new, convincing, insights and alternative frames of reference in an artistic way. My prime example is Elias Canetti's admirable book *Crowds and Power*, which presents a theory of "power as an ancient disease." It is rich in empirical data, and its explanatory framework is shamelessly crude and fictional.

My own approach will be diametrically different: I shall start from simple elements and try to proceed toward some more dramatic aspects of social conflicts, but no constructivist ever goes very far. It is, however, useful to ask whether we are trying to justify something like Canetti's idea of power: "The Saviour of the World and the Ruler of the World are one and the same person. . . . Paranoia is an *illness of power* in the most literal sense of the words and exploration of this illness uncovers clues to the nature of power clearer and more complete than those which can be obtained in any other way."[27] Perhaps we should ask whether we are dealing with the use and the effects of such madness. Actually, we shall sail between the mystifying and the fictionalized notions of social power, and forget the idea of power as uniquely referring to the social world.

The role of rights

To illustrate the perils of ordinary-language arguments and, more urgently, to eliminate one possible false start from our attempt to understand the ethics of coercion, we turn our attention to C. C.

Ryan's article "The Normative Concept of Coercion."[28] His idea is that coercion is defined within ordinary moral discourse in terms of rights and thus is characterized as intrinsically (im)moral. Coercion is said to entail logically a violation of rights and hence moral failure. We shall return to the subtler and more substantive aspects of this moral problem in due course.

Ryan maintains that it is a confusion to think that A may coerce B not to do, against his (B's) will, something which he had no right to do anyway. This conceptual move, allegedly based on some ordinary-language intuitions, makes coercion a morally negatively loaded concept. According to Ryan, A's coercive efforts are necessarily directed against B, who either has the right to do what he is doing or at least is in a morally neutral starting position. Let us take an example: B is a burglar whom A finds in his home in the middle of the night. A grabs his handgun and threatens to shoot B if he does not leave the house immediately; B flees. Has A coerced B to run away?

Ryan's answer is in the negative.[29] He maintains that "it sounds absurd" to say that (1) John coerced the burglar not to rob his house. It is also absurd to say that (2) John coerced the man not to sell the Brooklyn Bridge to Kalervo. On the other hand, he accepts the following two propositions. (3) The police coerced John to stay in the hospital because he had evidently contracted bubonic plague. (4) The police coerced John not to sell heroin.

Let us keep in mind that Ryan divides rights into two main categories, namely, *capacity rights* and *allowance rights*. This is, of course, a rather demanding technicality in an ordinary-language argument, but let us accept it for the moment. The first type of right, a capacity right, entails the following important feature: "the absence of rights implies here that I am not *capable* of performing the action."[30] Certainly we have no right to sell the bridge—simply because it is not ours. But Ryan also thinks that we are not *capable* of selling it, and therefore it is logically impossible to coerce us not to sell it. We cannot be coerced not to do something we are incapable of doing anyway.

But, it must be asked, is it true that our inability to sell the bridge results from our not having the right to sell property that is not our own? Strangely enough, Ryan fails to see the crucial differences between the following cases: (1) we may sell stolen goods; (2) we may be able to make sense of the proposition that we sell objects like bridges, parks, and streets to private citizens; but (3) we cannot sell the state of Finland to the highest bidder. Ryan plays with the ambiguity between these three cases. We have no right to sell any of the stuff; we can certainly sell stolen goods, but we cannot sell the state of Finland, simply because there is no customary procedure to be followed when we attempt to sell it. It is not quite clear what kind of thing the bridge is taken to be, in the sense that it is both a physical object and a public good. But it is clear enough that a thief can coerce another thief not to sell goods they stole together. The missing right to private ownership in this case does not matter at all.

What the thieves will find themselves incapable of doing, because of their missing rights to the goods, is to sell the goods legally. But we are certainly not interested in the case where a thief tries to get a legally valid deal on stolen goods. Ryan's argument seems to collapse into the triviality of saying that if we have no right we cannot be coerced not to use just this specific right. No normative commitments are needed to define coercion in the present case.

Let us go then to *allowance* rights. Ryan writes: "one can easily imagine a case in which someone is coerced into not selling heroin, but one is hard put to imagine an instance in which one would assert that a person is coerced into not murdering another."[31] Heroin selling, unlike direct physical violence, allegedly does not violate the customer's individual rights. The problem is that Ryan has produced no real argument to back up his statement. He just feels that it sounds very strange to say that (2) John coerced the man not to sell the Brooklyn Bridge but not to say that (4) the police coerced John not to sell heroin. The only hint he gives is that one has a prima facie right to sell things, even heroin, but no right whatsoever either to physically assault a fellowman or to willfully endanger his property.

Coercion is defined by Ryan in such a way that it always presupposes a violation of one's prima facie rights. For critical purposes, I will next present a case in which A coerces B to do something that does not violate B's rights. Take the familiar case of a house robbery. B, the robber, has no right to do what he is doing. Why do we hesitate when we are supposed to say that the legal owner of the home, A, coerces B to flee? As I see it, a perfectly nonnormative explanation may exist: we normally suppose that B wants to escape, and thus he need not be coerced to do so. We include a modest rationality pre-supposition in B's psychology. We suggest that his least harmful action alternative is now a quick escape. He will suffer no loss by doing so. Therefore, one of his alternatives is positive and profitable.

If we play with words, we can also express the same idea by saying that because B escapes anyway he cannot be coerced to escape. No coercive threat is needed, and none exists. And it is after all a popular idea that social life is ordered so that, whenever we do an unlawful thing, we are prone to be punished after we are detected. Therefore, it is also quite natural to expect that B escapes A. He has no reason to resist.

To repeat the main idea: we suppose that B knows both that staying in the house will prove to be harmful to him and that no profitable stealing is possible in the new situation; therefore, he wants to flee and need not be coerced to do so. However, if the police reach B after his million-dollar bank robbery, B has a solid motive to resist arrest, and the police must behave in a genuinely coercive manner. The basic point is that our linguistic habits reflect our commonsense idea that some right violations are prone to be harmful to the violating agent himself and that he normally knows it.

As we shall see later in a greater detail, we must carefully distinguish between *deterrence* and *coercion*, as these two things are really different. Part of Ryan's difficulties results simply from his reluctance to use the term *deterrence*, instead of *coercion*. For instance, although it sounds somewhat strange to say that (2) John coerced the man not to sell the Brooklyn Bridge, it is quite all right to say that (5) John deterred the burglar from robbing his house by pointing his gun. The basic idea here is that John just prevents the robber from creating more harm: John does not want to make the robber do something profitable from John's own point of view. I shall return to these distinctions below, but the main idea should be clear enough: John, by toting a gun, prevents the robbery and also deters the criminal from attacking him. Unlike a mugger, John does not desire any booty from the interaction. According to my basic definition of coercion, John does not coerce, simply because there is no positive booty for him to get. He just wants his house to be without intruders. He also tries to avoid physical harm to himself. If this is called coercion in some essential sense, small wonder that the results feel strange to our ordinary-language intuitions.

My criticism of Ryan's ideas points to the need to do more work in two different directions. First, if the hypothesis to the effect that coercion presupposes the immorality of threats is false, there are justifiable cases of coercive threats. We must pay closer attention to the role of ethical notions in the analysis of coercion. Second, coercion seems to be such a broad concept that its subtypes and their related notions must be analyzed separately. Coercion itself is another umbrella term covering many ways of repressing people's interests, including the essential case as well as cases of deterrence. Threats may do many types of work.

The following is an outline of how to understand some of the most important methodological concepts in the coming chapters.

By *individual rationality* I mean a prudent attitude toward practical questions in which a person follows the laws of logic, takes epistemic evidence and information fully into account, and, most of all, chooses his or her own first preference among all the given alternatives, seen within a reasonably long time span.

By *collective rationality* I mean an analogous extension of the case of individual rationality into collective decisions. These can be best understood in terms of voting procedures, which give us an idea of what it is to choose the jointly best social alternative.

By *moral rationality* I mean the full personal recognition of such prescriptions and values, which logically entails the application of general rules and the acceptance of impersonal notions of norms and values. As we shall be dealing with those cases I called imperfect and nonstandard, I cannot include the full requirement of the universalizability, prescriptivity, and overridingness of moral rationality. Instead, I can say only that a morally rational agent recognizes the fact that moral principles are universal, prescriptive, and overriding but that these conditions apply only to a certain extent—which is more limited than in the ideal case. Yet the application is as strong as we are able to understand and implement. For example, we might apply moral rules only within our families; to us, other people may lack the necessary moral relevancy. The important point is that moral rationality is something more demanding than the mere prudent kind. Nevertheless, moral considerations need not apply independently of their social context.

2 | Threats and Personal Coercion

The psychology of a prudent victim

When we say that an agent, the coercer, coerces another agent, or his victim, to do thing x, we mean that he presents a threat, y, which makes the victim do x. My central suggestion will be that coercion logically entails that whatever the victim does, he will suffer or lose something. But if he does as told, his losses will be smaller. The coercer is supposed to profit from this compliance. There are three main points concerning coercion: (1) the victim will lose whatever he does; and (2) this is because of the coercer's threat; but (3) he can minimize his losses by obeying.

For example: Jack Dillinger threatens a cashier with his gun. She knows that Jack will shoot if he does not get money, but he will leave without shooting if he gets the money. As a prudent person, she will surrender the money. She has avoided the shooting, but all the money has been lost. She minimized her expected harm even if she could not avoid all harm. This is the essence of threats. The situation is threatening when one knows that it is impossible to leave the situation without suffering some personal harm.

I shall elucidate this in what follows, but we must keep these two things in mind. It is exactly this double-loss theory of threats and coercion that helps us understand the messy issues of power exercise from a novel point of view.

31

We shall now deal with two individual agents whose interests conflict within an interactive social situation. Let us study both agents separately and try to check on what grounds they may plan their decisions. We shall then combine our accounts of the coercer and his victim by using an informal game theoretical framework. This will allow us to make sense of the strategic aspects of coercive power. We must, however, be clear as to what psychological and social factors influence an agent's thought and action.

The victim of coercion is threatened by the coercer in a sufficiently severe manner. This pressure is directed against his more or less strong subjective preferences (understood also in terms of expected utilities). We should obviously resist the temptation to characterize the victim immediately as, say, a perfectly rational utility maximizer, even if we used a preference-oriented and broadly utilitarian approach to his decisions. Otherwise, we shall experience two types of theoretical losses. First, we shall be unable to appreciate the extreme nature of the victim's personal situation in the course of full-fledged coercion. In such cases, utility calculations become in a sense nonstandard, as will be argued in due course. Second, the coercer's available threat-related moves become unnaturally restricted, although in real life he may choose to work on the side of such values of the victim that the victim himself does not know or control very well. We should admit that the coercer may exploit the victim's irrationality, in some sense of the term. Both the coercer and the victim may take into account the fact that the victim's utility calculations follow rather different principles in the extreme ends of his utility function. And such end points exist: pleasure and pain have a maximum, even if this maximum seems to have the nature of an extended area more than that of a point. Let me explain these ideas in a more discursive manner.

The basic principle behind the victim's actions is supposed to be such that he will yield to his coercer only if his loss is smaller than the (expected) loss in the case of his resistance; or to put it formally, the threat promises a larger loss than compliance does. The victim gives away his money rather than let the coercer shoot him simply because he can thus minimize the expected subjective loss. It follows that the more valuable the booty is to the victim, the severer the threat the coercer must present, if he is to be successful.

Quite evidently, the coercer must know something about the personal characteristics of the victim, or about his utility function, if the coercer hopes to be an efficient actor. We suppose also that the coercer does not want to make any empty or risky threats. The coercer tries to realize his will, or preferences, against the victim's preferences, but he must keep in mind the fact that the victim's personal psychology may prove to be tricky.

If we recover from the wreck of C. C. Ryan's argument for the normative interpretation of coercion — his example of a coercer who typically threatens a victim who has the right to do what he is doing at the moment — we see clearly enough that the situation is bound to be both surprising and irritating to the victim. His quiet compliance cannot be expected. Perhaps one coerces normally in just those cases where the victim feels that he is entitled to defend himself. At least this idea is supported by the hazy idea of coercion going against one's individual rights. Coercion carries a permanently negative evaluative tag. As such, the tag has only an emotive meaning and is devoid of genuine normative weight, but its very existence is quite sufficient for our present purposes.

The coercer must, therefore, recognize that his victim is going to enter the coercive interaction unwillingly. Moreover, there is no reason to suppose that the degree of resistance, as felt by the victim, is always a direct combination of the two alternative losses he may choose from. The victim may lose his money or suffer a wound, as in the basic mugger example, but the negative value of the whole coercive situation may be much larger than either of the two alternatives or even their sum. What is important here is to see that the *negative value of the situation itself* may be larger than that of the loss of the target booty.

Nevertheless, the value of the intended booty gives us the first minimum estimate of the value of the whole situation, simply because the victim need not lose more than that. I mean that the victim may enter a coercive situation willingly if he gets a future compensation whose value is larger than the smaller of the two expected losses. The victim may be, for example, a police decoy who is supposed to obtain information about the coercer's tactics and as such he needs a compensation exceeding his expected temporary loss; the minimum is the booty.

If a victim thinks that coercion is wrong, dangerous, and extremely irritating, and if the instance of coercion happens to occur in a nasty context, unlike the decoy one, he may well refuse to cooperate with the coercer. It is easy to admit that this will happen to a victim if the value difference between the booty and the realized threat is merely marginal. The larger this difference is, the harder is the victim's decision to neglect his better alternative and to accept the realization of the threat.

Notice also that the idea that a victim could stay away from a coercive situation by simply refusing to communicate is definitely a controversial one. We shall have a chance to return to it. All we need to see now is that, if the intrinsic negative value of coercion is large enough to the victim, he may think that his total rejection of the threat offers him a positive utility difference large enough to justify fully the absorption of the consequences of the realized threat—that it is good to resist. All avoidance methods have similar results, but in the first case the victim closes himself off from the coercer altogether and in the second the victim communicates with him but finds the required forced cooperation intolerably painful. Both strategies are natural; both are used. They are different approaches to the same problem, and their results are roughly similar. The main difference is that a victim who hates all coercion is more difficult to coerce than one who hates only to surrender the booty. Humiliation is more likely to block the response of the former victim. This happens because he may be unwilling even to calculate the sums of his own expected utility, as it would require listening to the coercer's demands.

The victim may perhaps set—at least indirectly—the disvalue of coercion so high it is without limit. At least no a priori utility floor can be set to his relevant negative feelings. This fact suggests a definite difficulty for the coercer: he should know how his victim feels about the threat before it is actually presented. If the coercer does not have this knowledge, his coercive efforts will not be prudently feasible.

Some important consequences follow, especially because we understand that a threat is often, and even typically, applied to a person whom the coercer does not know very well. If the coercer knows the victim on the basis of their earlier contacts and their shared social and cultural background, it is likely that they are able to negotiate some kind of deal and resolve their conflict of interests without drifting as far as threats. Especially if both the coercer and the victim are well informed and prudentially rational agents, as we suppose them to be, it is easy to think that any prior contacts and the possibility of seeing each other's motives in a large enough context facilitate their attempts to find a cooperative solution to their disputes.

So we may well think that coercion takes place only when its importance is further enhanced by the fact that the agents do not understand each other very well, and yet, at least the coercer feels that it is urgent to elicit the reaction in question from the victim. Certainly, he may try to coerce any kind of person, but the practical need for and the importance of coercion is clearly seen when we suppose that the victim has an enigmatic psychological and social background. Coercion is possible between any one coercer and his victim, but it typically replaces other conflict resolution methods when the victim's psychology is not quite transparent to the coercer. In a rather paradoxical fashion, to be successful, the coercer should be well informed even if he need not actually present a threat in such cases.

The point of these considerations is that even if a coercer does not know the victim well, he may still have a good reason to coerce; and because the coercer is prudently rational, he does not want to take any unnecessary risks. Therefore, he uses such threats as can be taken to be both universally disvalued and intrinsically negative, in addition to being easy to plan and cheap to apply.

An optimally effective threat has the following characteristics: it is a threat against any possible victim; it is unpleasant as such and not merely because of its contingent consequences; it is cheap to administer and includes no large-scale planning. By this last item I mean simply that the threat is independent of any special social arrangements and organized action: the efficiency of a threat is badly hampered if the coercer must mobilize other people to accept and administer it. He might then find himself in a new conflict situation, calling for a preliminary exercise of power and even coercion.

Only one natural candidate offers itself to the role of an ideal threat: *violence.* This is a sad but unavoidable conclusion. If we take into consideration all the desiderata of the threats the coercer may use against a resistant and enigmatic person, it is easy to conclude that violence is exactly what a determined coercer will finally use. All people tend to be afraid of violence and the pain it produces. It is also cheap and easy to use, although it tends to be ultimately costly, too.

The coercer should certainly expect resistance. Threats vary according to their purpose, but ultimately both the coercer and the victim know that everyone is afraid of something, and the coercer's best guess of what this might be is some variety of violence. This reaction is simply rooted in our animal nature. Moreover, the variety of the types of violence is large—larger than one usually thinks.

The key idea about violence as a threat is the following: there are things which the victim is afraid of, so that the negative utility value that the victim assigns to threats is actually larger than any possible value of his utility function. Now, this means that such violent threats exemplify a new kind of disvalue. The victim's loss of booty can be of any magnitude in reference to his utility function. But if some violence-related threat is still worse than any of those limited disvalues, it follows that violent threats are not measured on the same scale along with other utilities.

This is exactly what I am suggesting: not all disvalues are measurable in the same Archimedean scale. Some things, like violence, remain outside the ordinary rational, or measurable, preferences. To put it in a picturesque way, we can say that most people have deep-seated, almost morbid, fears whose evaluation is not in line with those ends that are measurable in dollars. Violence and cruelty are such things, and we can understand their role as ultimate threats on this very basis.

We cannot understand human motivation without taking into account our negative emotions, in the sense of aversions. We all have our personal fears and terrors. They may be straightforwardly neurotic phobias, like being unable to even look at a cat. It is typical of these strong negative feelings that they dominate any motivational contexts where they occur. They are outside our reasoned control. This control varies in effectiveness, but the truth is that if we feel fear in the present strong sense, our motivation is at least partially independent of both utility calculations, practical reasoning, and long-term plans of a good life.

The following summary considerations illustrate the irrational side of the victim's resistance. Suppose he values the booty at ten million dollars. This is such a large sum that we might think that the coercer's task is very difficult indeed, as he must then stage a threat in which the victim's expected loss is greater than ten million dollars. What could he do? His task is to get the ten million dollars from the victim without spending too much himself. His violent threat may be cheap to apply, and thus he will use it. But more importantly, the victim may resist in such a stubborn manner that any loss, even one greater than ten million dollars, becomes acceptable to him.

If this is indeed possible and the agent still wants to coerce, he must have at his disposal a threat whose disvalue is independent of the victim's dollar-valued utility function: the victim is now willing to tolerate any dollar losses, and the coercer knows this fact. Violence is such a threat. Let us take a couple of illustrations so that we get a more detailed view of mad threats.

Two illustrations

My first example is the true story of Urbain Grandier, as told by Aldous Huxley in his *The Devils of Loudun*.[1] This is a historical narrative, told in a partly fictionalized form. It illustrates T. C. Schelling's point to the effect that "the threat that compels rather than deters . . . often takes the form of administering punishment *until* the other acts, rather than *if* he acts."[2] Every threat is first an *if* idea, but it may turn later into an *until* idea: gradually increasing threats may look efficient. We shall see, nevertheless, that one cannot always utilize fear and terror in this way, especially if the resistance itself is strongly emotional. The booty may be valued without a limit.

Urbain Grandier was a priest in the first half of the seventeenth century in Loudun, France, who was accused of being a witch, found guilty, tortured, and burned. The case has become famous because of its extraordinary magnitude: the nuns of an Ursuline convent were supposed to be possessed by the devil, with whom Grandier apparently had a pact. A veritable mass hysteria raged around the case, and the exorcism of the nuns revealed strange and horrifying things.

Grandier himself was a brilliant and ambitious man, who did not take the narrow moral constraints of the life of a Catholic priest too seriously. He also desired earthly pleasures and fame. Yet, as

Huxley lets us understand, he was a truly religious man and nothing like an immoral and ruthless egoist. He simply had his own, rather idiosyncratic, view of Catholic morality. Now, Grandier was found guilty of witchcraft by his enemies in the church. Nevertheless, they wanted to get a full confession from him before they finally burned him at stake.

If we look at the situation within a coercive framework, we can say that Grandier was threatened with infinite but gradually increasing pain by his archenemies, especially the tough-minded and determined Father Laubardemont. The three alternatives Grandier had were, first, to confess his pact with the devil; second, not to confess; and, finally, not to allow himself to be coerced. The last possibility is especially pertinent. Actually, he felt that a confession was out of question and, therefore, he had already made his own choice knowing what would follow.

However, it is still unclear to us whether he had chosen not to confess or not to be coerced. I have already indicated that these can be two different alternatives. This means that Grandier may have thought that it was important not to confess because then his relationship to God would be destroyed. This in turn would put his future heavenly life in jeopardy. We may suppose now that straightforward utility calculations can still be used to determine whether temporally restricted maximal pain is more important than eternal life in paradise. The negative value of Laubardemont's booty—confession—is practically infinite to Grandier.

The weak point in this approach to Grandier's decision is that, if he really was a good Christian and entitled to salvation and if his views were independent of the canonical views of the church, it might be possible for him to believe that a white lie in such a pressing situation would not be dangerous, as it is presumably forgivable. In this way, it seems that when Grandier faced the ultimate torture he did not need to believe that to yield to his enemies would carry an outcome whose negative value is larger than that of torture. Grandier was an unconventional and brilliant man, who could have easily avoided the terrible consequences of single-minded fanaticism in this case—as he had been able to do earlier.

The situation really changes once we notice that any confession meant Grandier's personal defeat to Laubardemont, plus the possibility, however small, of eternal condemnation. Yet, once we put together the value of the booty and the disvalue of the coercive situation, we understand why just a man like Grandier resisted Laubardemont's efforts at any cost. His was a creative and strong mind to which unjustifiable coercion is the worst possible thing. There was seemingly nothing Laubardemont could do to break his will, simply because Grandier was not governed by rational utility calculations in terms of expected future pleasure and honor. He was, on the contrary, governed by the idea that to confess was a thing whose intrinsic disvalue was limitlessly large—that is, it was not a true value at all.

Let us consider what possibilities Laubardemont had against Grandier's stubborn will. We shall find out that his available tools were in the end so limited that he had to operate too closely at the level of Grandier's conscious decisions concerning the impossibility of forced cooperation with the coercer—and ultimately of confession. He was unable to stage a superior threat against Grandier's fixed opinion.

First of all, as was typical of the method of interrogating witches, Grandier was shaved of all hair on his body. This is a clever method of psychological manipulation. But then Laubardemont also wanted his fingernails pulled out, which the surgeons on duty strictly refused to do. Thus even this first step toward a maximal threat was prevented by the reluctance of Laubardemont's staff. Why didn't they do it? Huxley suggests, with a novelist's liberty, that the surgeons had some moral qualms against hurting him: "the convicted sorcerer was still a man." This idea is utterly unconvincing. The surgeons probably did not react against the victim's pain. Grandier was prepared for severe torture anyway, and officials at that historical period had apparently no difficulty in accepting the idea. We must think, as it seems to me, that the surgeons saw that pulling out the fingernails was not part of shaving and therefore unlawful or was against the official procedures of this particular stage of interrogation.

Real torture was finally started, and this is what happened. "And when the parson protested yet once more that he was innocent, a sixth wedge was hammered home. . . . From ordinary, the question had reached the traditional limits of extraordinary. The bones of the knees, the shins, the ankles, the feet—all were shattered."[3] Grandier passed out, and his coercer had then to admit he had failed. He had reached his own ultimate limit, and still Grandier had been able to resist confessing. The coercer's methods and resources were inadequate. We may say, even if it sounds almost ridiculous, that the disvalue of obeying was still larger than that of torture. We certainly feel that utility calculations do not really apply, but yet Grandier's decision to resist was just that—a decision.

Grandier's two alternatives were the shame of confession or the victory of staying quiet. He could not save his life, and he would not consider this. Thus, he stayed quiet. In this perspective, Grandier's decision to resist till the bitter end was indeed a conscious and— granting its tradition—a perfectly understandable decision. If it were no decision, we cannot understand why his pain, fear, and panic did not causally bring about a confession. Yet, it was not a decision along the lines of standard utility calculations. It was clear from the beginning that no amount of negative value would change Grandier's behavior.

Notice, however, what the catch of the present argument is: Grandier's fingernails. They were not pulled out. This fact implies that Laubardemont's action arsenal was inherently limited. The results were disastrous. He made his ultimate decisions without any ultimate weapons. The rule to which I am referring now is that a maximal price can be captured only by using a threat that reaches outside the victim's decisions. Laubardemont was constrained by too strict laws and traditions. He could not exploit threats that reached deep enough in this individual case. The key to the most efficient threats is the realization that every person is an individual, and, because no two persons are quite alike, both what we really want and what we really fear are different from person to person. Grandier had his maximum loss at stake, but Laubardemont could not launch a properly individualized threat; hence his failure.

What seems to be the case is that the victim can set the personal disvalue of a coercive situation infinitely high. Nevertheless, some personal threats have an indefinitely negative effect. Not to yield is the victim's conscious decision. Therefore, only if the ultimate threat works independently of the victim's decision have we reason to believe that the threat constitutes the strongest motive to the victim. The roles of the coercer and the victim are, therefore, not symmetrical: the coercer is able to experiment with his threats and to work on the victim's will. The victim stays with his one fixed idea and decision. Ultimately, Grandier could have been coerced to confess.

To substantiate such claims we now turn to George Orwell's fantastic novel *1984*, whose philosophical acumen overcomes its psychological limitations.[4] It is a book on ethics. I shall argue for two claims within the framework of *1984:* (1) the victim's decision to resist at any cost is indeed a decision; but (2) his yielding to the threat is not always a decision. On these grounds, it follows that any victim finally yields; I mean, in principle this is the case.

In the year 1984, Winston Smith was arrested because of his anti-government activities. He was interrogated in prison by Mr. O'Brien. As a dissident, Winston had no hope of personal survival. He knew it. Winston hated the oppressive Big Brother, and he had matured to the point of starting to protest in spite of the fact that he knew it was dangerous and even hopeless.

Just like his Catholic counterpart Laubardemont, O'Brien wanted to get a confession from Winston—that he was wrong, that Big Brother really was good. And he, Winston, should also believe all this. No conditional acceptance of Big Brother was enough. Winston must actually love him. Of course one cannot just decide to believe. Belief change is not a matter of decision. But just this is important: if O'Brien could have made Winston accept a completely new proposition or could have induced a belief in Winston by substituting a repulsive falsehood for a strong commitment, he would have solved Laubardemont's problem. The new belief will make all earlier decisions void.

Winston was ready to risk everything. Now, O'Brien had to convince him that he was wrong. After that, he would be under O'Brien's oppressive control. What happened was that Winston's resistance was broken so that he had to accept the new idea. His old convictions were impossible for him to hold. Grandier, on the contrary, entertained his original belief to the end. Had his ideas changed, he would have confessed—and believed what he said. In fact, this fictional case of extreme coercion is mental manipulation. It changes beliefs.

Orwell makes it quite plain that O'Brien's power was absolute; he needed to consider no aspects of law and legitimacy nor the traditional morality of his position. Neither was he dependent on any personal, management, cost, or resource problems. He also had access to complete information. He was free from all restrictions. O'Brien knew that every victim has his weak point, something he fears extremely, and that thus constitutes the supreme negative element embedded in his belief system. His problem was just to find what it was. After that, the victim was helpless.

The fictional setting makes Orwell's ideas interesting. We see the bare essence of the conflict between the two individuals, Winston and O'Brien. As it is put in *1984:*

> He paused, and went on in a gentler tone: You are improving. Intellectually there is very little wrong with you. It is only emotionally that you have failed to make progress. Tell me, Winston—and remember, no lies; you know that I am always able to detect a lie—tell me, what are your true feelings toward Big Brother? I hate him. You hate him. Good. Then the time has come for you to take the last step. You must love Big Brother. . . . Room 101, he said.[5]

O'Brien continued this exchange by answering Winston's earlier question of what was in room 101. "Room 101 is the worst thing in the world." Yet we cannot find a single thing that is "the worst" for everyone. O'Brien said that the variety was large, from burying alive to some "trivial things," not necessarily fatal.

Room 101 was empty when they entered. Thus the coercive setting could be created anew for any victim: "in your case . . . the worst thing in the world happens to be rats." A small package was carried into the room, and Winston's face was put inside a cage to create the impression that rats would eat up his face. Winston totally collapsed. Although the situation was close to anyone's nightmare, it was Winston's greatest fear. The effect was debilitating, just as in Sigmund Freud's Ratman case. At the end of the novel, Winston loved Big Brother and accepted the fact that his punishment by death would come at some unspecified future moment.

We see that Orwell tells basically the same story as Huxley: their victims have no hope of escaping, but both want to resist the ultimate threat in order to save their most cherished asset, personal integrity. Winston has no chance, because O'Brien's actions were not limited by knowledge, law, organization, customs, or material resources. He knew everything and was therefore able to accomplish everything. Yet Orwell does not evade the question of whether Winston could have successfully resisted; the point is that he had a weakness whose exploitation depended on some contingent factors. If the conditions were right for O'Brien, he would be invariably successful.

Room 101 was empty. Nevertheless, one generic factor remained true. Whatever happened would be violent, at least psychologically. Actually, Winston was saved from the rats, of course; therefore, psychological violence must be the key notion here. We need not speculate too much about whether mere psychological threats might be effective without implying "real" violence. We need say only that if O'Brien's threat worked, it is violent — simply because it worked. I shall argue that if O'Brien did not know Winston completely, the best starting point would have been to explore his reactions toward physical violence and its imagined expressions and results. The key to 101-type threats is in the victim's mind, but its content will be essentially related to violence. Any such strong effects may be said logically to imply violence.

Our animal nature is certainly survival oriented, and the most basic fears tend to grow on that basis. We may, therefore, maintain that once the booty is important enough to both agents the coercer will try to use violence as his final threat. Coercion rests on violence, and we have no reason to believe that a victim could emerge as a winner from a conflict in which his coercer is powerful enough in the Orwellian sense.

It is certainly consoling, and perhaps socially desirable too, to insist that any victim can successfully resist threats if he firmly decides to do so. A more sophisticated variant of the same myth is to say that, if something is important enough to the victim, nothing can take it away from him; which implies of course that, if he yields, the booty was not really so highly valued by him. It is undeniable that no decision is rigidly fixed by any utility distributions. Either agent's actions always have a certain surprise potential. But the truth remains that the coercer will be ultimately successful against all decisions and valuations by the victim if the coercer has no contingent limitations working against his threats. He is then able to gradually diminish the surprise potential by playing his game repeatedly. In this way, the victim's successful resistance against threats is ultimately more a matter of the coercer's weakness than of the victim's independent strength. Humans are vulnerable to the exercise of power, and that is the reason why power is so important an ingredient in social life. But it explains as well the social idea that power should be kept hidden and secret. The realization of its effectiveness is often seen as a virtual invitation to start exercising power. This kind of chastity is, however, a type of bad faith.

This section has described a serious conflict in the state of nature. The next sections will deal with some less serious cases within this same viewpoint. We shall later introduce a social contract, which regulates conflicts and sets some limits on violent threats. Many types of successful threats occur only in an institutionalized social context. This politics of threats is not the only road to success, though. In the last chapters of this book I shall take up some moral problems. Power exercise is always an ethical challenge, too. And moral motivation can make some threats successful as well as allow one to resist coercion. I emphasize that the following considerations of threats presuppose a state of nature.

Freedom of choice and knowledge

We now return to the investigation of "ordinary" coercion. It means that the respective values of the booty and the threat to the coercer and the victim are in line with their other preferences, understood in terms of utilities, or, alternatively, that they do not occupy a place very close to the extreme positive or negative ends of their respective utility functions. It is predictable that this type of case is more straightforward than the extreme cases introduced above. We recall also that in order to be able to speak about coercive threats at all we must suppose that the coercer displays a set of alternative actions to be realized so that whatever the victim does he will actually lose something. The only goal the victim can achieve is the minimization of his expected subjective loss; for instance, his money before bodily health. But if this is to be the case, the coercer must be able to tie him to the coercive situation, which the coercer himself creates. Otherwise the victim will escape. The method of prevention is easy enough: in ordinary mugging cases, the robber simply shoots if one resists or runs away.

The victim's basic motive is that of avoidance, except if the threat is very weak. We then introduce the emotion of fear to block the otherwise logical route to the idea that the victim might in any possible situation have a chance to face and challenge the coercer's threat. However, in many normal and moderately serious cases of coercion, fear is no factor, in spite of the fact that the victim is tied to the situation. We must therefore pay closer attention to his fear-independent alternatives, which are at the same time real choices, that is, they are prima facie open; yet their openness cannot exemplify any true liberty.

It is clear that any efficient act of coercion reduces the victim's personal freedom in the all-important sense that the victim is then unable to set his own goals in such a manner that their realization would be possible or their seeking would be rationally feasible. It is also impossible for the victim even to consider the conformist strategy of adopting the coercer's goals, simply because all these imply his subjective losses.

The victim is not capable of realizing his first preference in coercive interaction, namely, to escape without harm. Yet, he has a real choice between two alternatives, namely, the threat and the booty. This choice implies a surprise potential, as I shall show. In a narrow sense of freedom, the coercer is not able to destroy the victim's freedom completely. Actually, the coercer does not even want to do so, since a coercive demand is typically such that the victim's intentional goal-directed reaction, or action, is necessary for its success. The victim is now required to make an unfree but a typically intentional choice and to act accordingly. Freedom and choice are two different things. The victim has a choice, but he is not free not to choose; a constraint applies to him.

It is instructive to consider here the following case: the coercer tells his victim that if he will not give him a cigarette he will be beaten, but if he gives it he will get a large dollar reward. The coercer makes a combined threat and offer to the victim. It seems that in this case the victim is unfree in the counterfactual and conditional sense that if he wanted not to give the cigarette to the coercer he could not avoid a larger loss to himself (a beating). In this sense, he must give the cigarette. But the force of *must* is now based on the supposition that the victim is a prudent agent. And if he is prudentially rational, he will *want* to give the cigarette to the coercer, simply because he would like to get the large reward. The element of constraint is motivationally redundant in the present context. What the victim is unable to do is to keep the cigarette and not get beaten. Escape is thus his second-best alternative, and its influence on his freedom is negligible. The same is not true of essential coercion, where the victim has two undesirable choices before him: he cannot get his best result (avoidance of the coercer) without experiencing the realized threat.

Notice that some coercive threats do not as such limit the victim's freedom. Suppose a case where a person is hanging from a cliff over a deep valley. Another person demands a price if he saves him. The victim (the cliff-hanger) is coerced by these demands. There is a natural threat to his well being, and the coercer exploits this fact in order to extract a concession. But since the victim's freedom to escape is due to natural causes, this freedom is not limited by the coercer. Such a constraint is the case only if the coercer's action causally creates the victim's initial distress, so that he cannot realize his first choice, escape, without first dealing successfully with the threat.

Offers work in a different way: even if the victim is subjectively unable to avoid accepting a tempting offer, it does not restrict his freedom in any way. Suppose that one gives a workman a choice between hard labor and staying lazy. He prefers the second over the first. Then one adds a good dollar reward to work. Does this restrict his freedom? It is a mistake to claim that the coercer makes the victim unable to stay lazy and also get the money: the victim was not able to stay lazy and get the money before the coercer entered the scene. Money and laziness would indeed be the victim's first choice, should he be in the position to make such a choice. In this sense, a constraint is relative to the actual action alternatives. It seems that in our special context we should understand the victim's freedom not in terms of what he wants, or his preference-ordered choices, but in terms of the real circumstances open to him.

The problem of freedom in coercive interactive situations is treated in an illuminating fashion by J. P. Day.[6] He says, correctly, that the victim's constraint under threat consists of his inability to escape with the booty. It is this combined action that is crucially important. In the case of offers, there is no such combined action whose possibility would have been taken away from the victim. On the contrary, offers create new action possibilities. In sum, threats take away but offers create complex possibilities of action. However, the victim is free to realize any single action he may want or imagine. The key to coercive constraints is the idea of combined actions that become impossible because of threats.

Jack, who is a student, sits in his room. Jill, his teacher comes in and says that she will punish him if he leaves the room before she comes back. Let us suppose that Jack loves to read; is this relevant in relation to Jill's threat? To understand the force of the story, let us compare it to one where Jill locks the door so that Jack will be physically unable to escape, should he wish to do so. In the case of physical constraints, Jack's will, desire, and preference, are clearly irrelevant. What is important is that he is in fact unable to leave the room should he want to. *Freedom* is defined by means of a counterfactual clause. But if the door is open and Jill just threatens Jack by means of a punishment, say, a good old-fashioned whipping, the case just might be different. Indeed, it is different.

Day maintains both that "desire (or will) is irrelevant to liberty"[7] and that our "concept of unfreedom . . . is relative to our idea of the average man or of human nature."[8] This looks patently inconsistent: if Jack is not like the other boys but desires whipping, Jill's intended threat becomes actually an offer. So, if the average man is mentioned, desires are also needed in the definition of freedom of choice. We cannot understand threats without saying clearly what the victim does not like. Therefore, even if Jack loves to study in his room, Jill's threat makes him counterfactually unfree (if he wanted to leave, he couldn't), yet the threat itself is defined by means of preference terms. Whipping is painful to an average person.

For instance, Jack's whipping may either (1) deny his right to physical well being, which he used to have; or (2) create a new possibility of enjoyment—always depending on how Jack happens to think about the case.

As can be guessed, the relation between threats and offers, as it is analyzed in reference to a victim's preferences, may show some rather surprising features. It sounds strange to say that Jack, who loves to be whipped, cannot leave the room without being whipped. Suppose next that a victim hates apples but someone offers them to him. This exchange turns into a threatening one once we suppose that the victim cannot turn down the offer. The apples are, say, thrown into his room and the door is locked. Even if a coercer merely says he will do so, he is still threatening the victim, because if he did not want the apples, he could not do anything about it. In this way, it is important what the victim can or cannot do. Threats cannot be refused. Offers can normally be refused. This is a crucially important feature of them. Unavoidable offers are just threats, and threats form the essence of coercion. It is, however, problematic that offers that we like but cannot turn down restrict our freedom. Should we say that "hard" offers (which cannot be turned down) restrict freedom, but "soft" offers do not? Any unavoidable results are threatening to a person. We now can make a distinction between (1) threats as constraints and (2) threats as motives. The former are anything we cannot avoid. The latter are anything we cannot avoid and also do not like. I shall focus on threats as motives and not as constraints.

Before we leave the present topic, let me clarify the difference between threats and offers in relation to David Miller's ideas. Miller criticizes Day's thesis about the coercive constraint as the prevention of the relevant double action by saying that such an analysis is "too permissive."[9] According to him, "any disadvantageous change in the environment can be described as making some conjunction of actions impossible." Certainly this is false. Miller illustrates his thesis by saying that if Bill gives tomatoes to Mary every day and then suddenly stops and demands money for his tomatoes, Mary would be unable to both keep her money and also have fresh tomatoes. But of course Mary did not have any fresh tomatoes before the first transaction between them. Yet a threat is supposed to take away from the victim an action alternative that he already had; like that of leaving the room and not being whipped. In the tomato case, Mary did not have a chance of getting fresh tomatoes independently of Bill's benevolent action. Therefore, Bill did not take away from her any real action possibility. In other words, if the coercer offers x to the victim and then withdraws his offer, he does not deprive the victim of something relevant to the victim's liberty. If the victim already had the thing offered, the offer is redundant, and if the victim does not have the thing, it cannot be taken away from him. Threats deprive him only of something he has.

In sum, when Miller writes that "there is now a conjunctive action . . . which it is impossible for him to perform",[10] he does not see that he mentions an originally impossible action, which is not made impossible by the other agent. It does not do to say that if Bill withdraws his offer Mary will be unable to get free tomatoes from Bill, for obvious reasons. In order to refute the challenge from the side of offers, we must use a battery of enigmatic concepts. The simplicity of Day's analysis is merely illusory; if this is Miller's point, he is right.

Let me next deal briefly with the problem of how important the concept of freedom is in coercion theory. It does not play a major role, even though it might suggest just the opposite at a glance. The question asked by David Miller is symptomatic of this: "What causal history must an obstacle to action have in order for it to count as a constraint on freedom?"[11] The coercer's causal history, or something sufficiently like it, may be really needed to make sense of our talk about freedom. Yet in such coercive cases as Robert Nozick's slave (see below) and my cliff-hanger, no causal influence by a coercer explains the victims' initial distress that makes the subsequent threat possible. The coercer just exploits some preexisting possibilities, or "coercive circumstances." He need not create the threat. Therefore, no intentional limitation of the victim's freedom occurs. The victim simply has no power to be free, or alternatively, he is in no situation to assert his personal freedom. He is unable to act.

It seems that freedom and liberty need not be used in the analysis and the further moral evaluation of coercion and its social effects. All this is quite intuitive: coercion is supposed to be profitable to the coercer, and this effect can be achieved by many different means. These need not require any intentional limitation of the victims' freedom. At the moment of interaction, the threat does not allow the victim to reach his best alternative, namely, to escape without harm. But the coercer himself need not bring about such a threat. He may exploit certain circumstances.

It is time to change our perspective from that of the victim's to that of the coercer's. When we do this, our most interesting problem switches from that of determining our own preference orders and subjective utility functions to that of how and to what extent another agent can get accurate information about those orders and functions.

We therefore enter the realm of epistemology, since our problems will concern the coercer's knowledge of the victim's psychological mechanisms for evaluating alternatives. And as we know, no one is O'Brien. We always struggle when reactions to novelty are called for. Ordinary decisions are structurally complex, and their most significant features are difficult to identify; those features themselves tend to change over time and during the process of interaction with others. Consensus often eludes us, even if we try to be honest and cooperative. But this last characterization especially cannot be presupposed in the case of coercion; on the contrary, the coercer is bound to find himself working under many uncertainties, especially if we assume that he is not in a position to use strong, fear-based methods.

We know already that the victim has in all nonextreme coercive situations a real choice between two alternatives and that he can avoid the coercer's demands by taking the action that the coercer, correctly or incorrectly, believes is the victim's worse relevant alternative. In some circumstances, the victim's success against coercive power must be based on prima facie irrational decisions: if the victim chooses against the coercer's true belief to the effect that the chosen alternative is the worst one for him subjectively, the victim's irrationality has enabled him to avoid the coercer's grip. In the robbery case, the victim allows himself to be shot. However, he pays a heavy toll, as he has both suffered a net loss and has called his individual rationality into question.

Can irrationality constitute an exercise of freedom of choice and lead to genuine defensive success? Certainly the answer may be in the affirmative only if we find it possible to drop the basic postulate of the victim's prudent rationality, with which we have been working all along. And if the theory allows for the victim's irrationality, it does not seem possible to understand how and in what cases the victim can be coerced. The coercive interaction, however immoral looking it is initially, becomes now a chaos. That is at least a philosophical loss. We cannot understand one important aspect of social life.

The idea of the victim's alleged irrationality can also be expressed this way: if the victim's avoidance of the point and the intention of a coercive effort can be explained by referring to the victim's functionally effective irrationality, then exactly why the victim can act in an irrational manner can be also explained. Irrationality becomes another rational strategy the victim may use. We do not want to lapse into saying anything like this. On the contrary, we want to say both (1) that the victim always has a choice; and (2) that this means that the victim's reaction in some cases will be a genuine surprise to the coercer. We should forget the suggestion that the victim's choices are actually irrational, since we can get the same effect out of the thesis that his actions are fully surprising to the coercer. He does not and cannot know all about his victim anyway, especially because the victim is motivated to deceive him. No human agent is fully predictable on the basis of decision theoretical rationality postulates. Those ideas tend to work only post hoc, or after the dust kicked up by the victim's action has settled. The victim does not choose *because* of his revealed preferences.

Let us formulate the key issue above in the following way: the coercer's limited knowledge is effectively equivalent to the victim's irrationality in choosing an action. The victim's action has its definite surprise potential against the coercer — and actually against anyone who takes the coercer's standpoint. In this way, we can avoid saying that the victim's choice of the (apparently) worst alternative under a coercive threat is a sign of his emerging real irrationality. It may look like irrationality; nevertheless, it signifies a surprise, which is always possible in the case of an action performed by another person.

We are now discussing a conceptual issue and not a mere empirical generalization; this is so because it is impossible to imagine that the coercer could always prevent the victim from reacting against his own revealed preferences — even if the coercer had a sufficiently well-warranted and detailed set of beliefs concerning the victim's preferences and values. The coercer cannot know the victim well enough to fix his personal choices in all new occasions. Knowledge of his earlier actions does not determine, deductively, his present choice. Whatever the victim does, regardless of the surprise it produces, we may still conclude that he is rational even if some preferences have changed from his earlier revealed ones. Therefore, the victim is able to choose in a new situation in relative independence of his earlier revealed preferences and values. (Of course, normally his choices may be predictable quite reliably.)

The main idea is that the coercer has no way of fixing those reactions in advance. The victim may always nullify the coercer's intentions, if he chooses to do so. But this ability to choose means only that the victim may surprise the coercer. Yet the fact that we often are able to assign a high probability to the proposition that the victim will not resist is another matter. We need a name for the victim's unpredictability. We may dub it *surprise irrationality*, or *s-irrationality* for short. A rational victim, if he behaves s-irrationally, cannot be distinguished from an irrational victim in any specific action context. Yet we need not change our view that he really is prudent and rational.

I shall say nothing about the underlying decision mechanism, which in some special cases leads a victim to exercise his s-irrational freedom of choice under coercion. Yet the fact remains that the element of surprise is always possible; perhaps this is what Hegel means when he writes rather enigmatically that "only the will which allows itself to be coerced can in any way be coerced."[12]

Such a proposition is simply false if the victim is prudent and the coercer is omniscient, determined, and rich enough. But this is only a fictionalized limit case. Therefore, Hegel is right if he is taken to mean just that the victim has always his own choice in any moderately demanding coercive situation: he could have changed his relevant preferences, as far as anybody knows. The coercer's chances against such a victim are therefore limited. The victim is an individual whose interests conflict with those of the coercer. Both factors are relevant, *individuality* and *conflict of interests*. A victim is bound to try to reveal as little as possible about his own preferences, plans, and strategies. Moreover, he knows about the coercer's difficulties and does not sympathize with him.

These reflections lead us to the next topic, the nature of the coercer's rational attitude toward the victim and the inevitable epistemic uncertainty under which he must work. I shall suggest that a coercer should be behaviorally rigid. His basic trouble is that he should be ready to realize his threats, even if they are harmful to himself. And his victim should understand that this is so. In fact, it motivates his resistance.

The psychology of a successful coercer

When a coercer presents a threat, it is functionally desirable for the victim to be prudentially rational. He is supposed to minimize his expected losses. My basic idea in what will follow is that the coercer, on the other hand, can afford to be prudent only in exceptional circumstances. Normally, his task requires a simple rigidity of behavior, the counterpart of which we meet in overtly legalistic interpretations of Kantian moral theories. These latter emphasize agents' duties in relative independence of their own personal goals and expected consequences. In fact, consequences should not matter too much to the coercer, for several reasons.

My question is whether in some rather special circumstances the coercer can at the same time be a prudentially rational agent and a fully successful coercer. The argument for such a conclusion must be stated from the beginning. We have already dealt with some aspects of the above query: O'Brien certainly is a coercer who satisfies all the conditions of success. But he is only a fictional character. Laubardemont is a real historical figure, but he was unsuccessful in his attempts to make Grandier confess sorcery. Actually, the fictional case is so plain that we need not waste our time. We saw what an ultimately effective coercive plan requires, but now we must turn to the real-life question of what assets the coercer should have when he meets the victim. The first one, omniscience, looks like an idealization. Yet if we go into details, as I shall do immediately, what emerges is that, although omniscience is an impossibility, it is something any coercer must aim at. This task has some interesting features.

Next, we may say that the coercer's deontic determination must replace knowledge in all those respects in which the relevant knowledge is missing or incomplete. In what follows, my main point is, accordingly, that the coercer cannot formulate his strategies against the victim only on the basis of his knowledge about the effects of his use of resources. He rules out some features of prudentially rational, often typically maximizing, decision making, and instead adopts a firm commitment to pursuing and winning the interactive game he is playing. The victim's psychology diverges from the coercer's well-founded beliefs about it; but the coercer can, and he should, make the victim's efforts to utilize such cognitive deficiencies void. Then he cannot do better than show a rigidly determined face. (We should, of course, distinguish between single and multiple, or iterated, plays of a coercive game.)

The coercer's situation interests us for the following reasons. When he initiates a coercive interaction with the victim, he provides his victim with a limited number of undesirable action alternatives, adding a suitable threat to some of them. The one action alternative that will not trigger the realization of the threat is the alternative the coercer wants. However, in order to be able to squeeze out exactly this response, the coercer must, at least sometimes, act in a rather peculiar manner. He must fix in advance his own reactions to the victim's possible counteractions. This makes the coercer's behavior relatively rigid.

A threat that is realized entails a loss to the coercer. Such a feature belongs to all coercive threats. They are not expressions of aggressive feelings but are rather functional tools. If carrying out the threat will be beneficial to the coercer himself, he would realize it even after his victim's obedient behavior. This increases his net utility. But then the threat could not convince the victim that he should obey. As we know, his original motive is to avoid the realization of the threat. Only mutually risky threats will work properly.

Let us study the simplest case. In paradigmatic cases of coercion, if the victim resists, (1) the coercer is not supposed to be willing to bargain and negotiate with the victim in relation to the realization of his threat; and (2) he will indeed act against the victim's welfare, depending on his reaction, even if the coercer himself cannot profit by realizing the threat. He accepts his own expected loss. These two conditions create the background of all coercion, and they present certain decisional challenges the coercer must meet.

These conditions require, in a general fashion, that the coercer plan the threat carefully enough with respect to his own resources, knowledge, and the preferability of its possible outcomes. That the coercer's preferences and values do not change too much because of the victim's manipulative counterefforts is also presupposed. The coercer should also take care that the victim will not get the idea that he, the coercer, cannot afford to realize the threat because of some expensive consequences.

It is natural in reference to point (1) above to think that the coercer is not open to new suggestions concerning the conduct of the interaction and, moreover, he should not be willing to reconsider or reevaluate his own fate in case he is driven to realize the original threat. We may suppose in relation to point (2) that any threat is at least to some extent costly to the coercer, although ultimately the matter is not quite this simple. Nevertheless, in general a threat cannot be supposed to bring about independent profit. Otherwise, the coercer would present just a fake threat and realize it quickly, to his own profit. Threats are risky to all parties. As we know, the concept of threat logically entails its intrinsic undesirability. Nevertheless, the threat must be such that it can be exploited with profit.

We shall assume the typical behavioral rigidity of the coercer. This follows from point (1) above and constitutes a necessary condition of all successful coercion. This seems to be the case in spite of the undeniable fact that both (1) and (2) allow for degrees. The coercer may be concerned about the victim's suffering, or he may be worried about making himself a murderer; and he may for these reasons make his initial threat somewhat milder. Yet, the more the coercer feels tempted to act in this "soft" direction, the less effective his coercive position becomes. And the more rigidly he sticks to his original plan, the more fully can he utilize his coercive potential. All this presupposes, quite evidently, that the coercer's initial coercive plan is as nearly optimal as his necessarily incomplete information allows, since he may be willing to correct his picture of the present coercive game in the light of new information provided by, say, the victim.

Now, some weakening of the coercer's threat position will follow; but only one condition is crucial: he must avoid a subjective reevaluation of the value of his intended goals and of the costs of their achievement. This aspect of coercion is typical of all conflicts and competitive interactions. It assumes an important role in social and official coercion, where duties are in key positions.

Before I present any technicalities, let us consider the following examples: suppose that a coercer threatens to beat both the victim and his friend if the victim does not tell the location of an old treasure. The victim asks the coercer to let his friend go because she is weak and knows nothing more than the victim, anyway. Now, the coercer may comply if he thinks that the victim does not manipulate him but tells the truth *and* the following is not the case: the victim loves his friend and he is also strongly suicidal. Then, if his friend goes, the victim is not motivated to tell anything. Cooperation with the victim may quite well destroy the coercer's coercive potential completely, or it may prove to be immaterial depending on the victim's psychology, but the coercer cannot know which is the case. My present point should now be clear: coercion is an interactive conflict situation where one agent is in a dominant position, and in order to succeed he should not check and change his action guidelines after the actual coercive interaction has been started. The information requirements for doing so tend to be too demanding. The victim should face only the threat and the prospect of giving away the booty; otherwise he is not coerced.

To continue, let us take a couple of additional simple examples. The victim emphatically reminds the coercer that by shooting him the coercer takes the risk of becoming a murderer, which will mean some frightful personal prospects for the future. If the coercer listens and now starts thinking of these consequences, his position has also weakened considerably. Or the victim tells a lie, saying that he has a concealed weapon which he does not like to use but which now he must use if the coercer does not disappear from the scene immediately. In this latter situation, the coercer must suppress his emergent hesitation and relevant beliefs. He has to refuse to listen to the victim or, equivalently, to offer him an extraneous action alternative. A perfect power wielder would refuse, since the new inputs may alter the decision environment.

We can systematize the considerations above in the following way: let us make a technical difference between such threat positions that are, first, *believable* and, second, *convincing* to the victim. A threat is believable (or the coercer is rigid, as discussed above) if the victim has a sufficient reason to think both (1) that within this interaction there are only the booty and the threat as open alternatives; and (2) that he cannot alter their characteristics through manipulation or bargaining. In other words, the victim admits that the coercer is together with him in a closed interactive situation. If the threat is believable, the victim cannot influence its details or interpretation. Nevertheless, it is still perfectly possible that, after he has accepted the threat as believable, he still thinks that the situation is badly planned. The coercer's personality may be too weak to realize his threat in case he meets resistance. The victim need not mobilize his s-irrationality. This means that a believable threat satisfies some important formal conditions but need not become convincing.

Only if the victim has a sufficient reason to think that the coercer will go on to realize his threat can we say that the threat is convincing. This is a demanding condition. No threat is absolutely convincing, as is easy to see on the basis of similar considerations used in the case of the victim's s-irrationality: the victim cannot know the coercer's preferences so completely that he can be certain that the coercer would not back out of the situation if he, the victim, does not yield. In general, the victim might have trouble in seeing why his coercer would go through with his initial threat. The convincingness of a threat is indeed a matter of degree; but the fact is that, in general, convincingness is a necessary condition of the success of a threat. As I shall show, this simple-looking condition is not at all easy to realize. Coercive policies are difficult to establish.

The coercer's situation is a combination of two decisions. He calculates the increase in the probability of the victim's compliance, given the explicit threat. If the expected utility of the booty to the coercer is larger than the expected loss of presenting an unsuccessful (and realizable) threat, the coercer may then rationally coerce the victim. But there is one further problem here. How is the coercer supposed to estimate the costs of a failure and a realized threat? The coercer must first determine the cost of his threat (say, his risk of capture) should the victim yield. But should the victim resist, the realization of the threat is an absolutely new decision for the coercer. In this situation, the value of the booty does not figure at all. The coercer cannot win anything now, but still the threat will be costly. What should the coercer do? To realize the threat looks like an act of sheer wickedness and unmitigated destructiveness. It is difficult to see why he would realize a threat after his victim proves to be hopelessly stubborn. The threat must be harmful to the power wielder. Therefore he perhaps cannot rationally realize it.

If the victim conceptualizes the coercer's dilemma in this way, he may even think that no threat position is ever fully convincing. He now fails to understand the coercer's commitment to his original, explicit action plan against the victim's interests. It seems strange that the coercer would go on with his threat even after it is clear to him that no profit can be expected from it. The victim, if he reasons in this way, is not going to follow the orders. The threat implies a loss. My question is, Why is it reasonable to suppose that the conditional decision to realize a threat can be grounded prudently? Why should the coercer shoot the resisting victim and no one else?

In sum, a threat is *believable* once it has a fixed form outside of a bargaining context and independent of new information (the coercer is then rigid). A threat is *convincing* whenever the victim has his adequate reasons for thinking that the coercer will indeed realize the threat if the victim does not comply. One striking illustration of a fully convincing threat is a deliberately produced guarantee of the coercer's future behavioral rigidity in the course of continued coercive action. Think of an airplane hijacking in which the coercer starts by killing some passengers in order to prove that he is serious when he says he will destroy the plane and its passengers if he does not receive a ransom. The significance of this gesture is that, as he has now already partly realized his original threat, he has made himself vulnerable to the full punishment if he surrenders to the police. He has thus nothing to lose, and thus his threat becomes fully convincing. He has produced as good a guarantee of his essential rigidity as, in principle, is possible.

This example shows how a coercer can connect the ideas of the *believability* and *convincingness:* the most straightforward method of making a threat convincing is for the coercer to produce an acceptable proof that he is absolutely rigid. (By rigid I mean that the coercer acts in a predetermined manner and, thus, also independently of the consequences of the realized threat.) If he can show to his victim that only two alternative actions are at their disposal, the threat is also convincing.

Another relevant example, considered also by Schelling, mentions a coercer who sets both a deadline for the victim's compliance and a timing device that releases the threat automatically, if needed. Nothing the victim does can change these plans. A new question immediately suggests itself: In what sense is rigidity rational? I go into that below, but first, to recapitulate.

A threat position must be believable and convincing to the victim. This implies that the occurrence of the realized threat is a real possibility on the coercer's part, in spite of the fact that there seem to be no prudent reasons for his keeping to his original action plan, as revealed by his opening moves. On what basis can the victim expect the coercer to go ahead with his threat? If the coercer does not get his booty, would it not automatically be best to leave the victim alone? Recall that the action used to define the threat must not be intrinsically rewarding to the coercer; if that were the case, the coercer would realize his threat independently of his victim's compliance. A robber does not want both money *and* life. Under these conditions, a prudent victim may resist and save at least the booty.

We cannot leave the topic of threats and their convincingness to the victim without taking into account David Gauthier's recent attempt to solve this problem.[13] His basic approach to the proposition that deterrent threats should and can be rational (in the standard utility-maximizing sense) is a novel one. I do not quite agree with Gauthier that his approach clarifies and explains the right things. However, his description of threats and his analysis of the difficulty that a rational coercer should be willing to meet is interesting. Let us concentrate on his solution to the problem.

Gauthier's main point is this. Suppose Jack threatens to shoot Jill if she leaves the room, and he makes it clear that he is going to do so in spite of the fact that he himself is going to suffer a loss by shooting (he hates to shoot people and he is afraid of the police). According to my analysis, Jill will not find Jack's threat position convincing. But according to Gauthier, Jack and Jill may think in the following way: Jack recognizes that Jill's staying in the room is profitable and he predicts according to his knowledge of her psychology that the threat of getting shot will reduce the probability that Jill will leave—and make him shoot. The probability of shooting becomes smaller *because* of the threat of shooting. It may then well happen that the probability of shooting becomes so small that, even if Jack takes this risk into account, he will still find it profitable, or utility maximizing, to adopt this threat. All things considered, Jack can predict that he will profit from his coercive policy decision. Jack's planning becomes at least believable.

Gauthier thinks that Jack makes a maximizing policy decision and that this entails that he is going to shoot Jill if "necessary." When Jill understand this, she will find the threat convincing. Gauthier maintains that, should Jill resist (and this may indeed happen, because Jack's decision is based on probabilities), Jack will shoot and, accordingly, will bring about some unconditional harm to himself. Does this really make sense? Is it rational to shoot Jill simply because the policy of coercing Jill was initially a utility-maximizing one? I do not think so, for the following reason.

Gauthier says that "it is rational to execute an intention if and only if it is utility maximizing to form it."[14] Normally, one should form an intention if and only if it is maximizing to execute it. And the normal order is the right one. We see that this is so when we recognize that Jack can always get a sort of double profit if he does not shoot. First, Jack's threat policy was maximizing, and second, if it fails to develop in the ideal way, Jack can still minimize his loss by not shooting. Let us consider this example: Paavo Nurmi is a famous professional long-distance runner who participates in a rich competition. The winner will get a lot of money, but the last man to cross the finishing line will lose his license. Paavo supports this rule, because he thinks that a keen competition will increase interest in the race and bring him more money. He supports the policy because it maximizes his expected utility. Such a policy is maximizing to form. Should it be followed?

Before the race, Paavo thinks that it is highly unlikely that he will be the last man in the race. But as the end of the race approaches, Paavo notices that he is indeed going to be last. He may, however, give up and step aside, saying that he is injured. This would save the day for him. He understands that the initial policy decision in favor of running was certainly maximizing, even without any consideration of giving up; finishing last was such a remote possibility. But certainly if Paavo finishes the race, he is simply irrational. The loss of his license is an avoidable fate. And if all runners think like Paavo, this is what will happen. All desire more money. They will start because they are self-confident and do not expect to lose. But only the first man will reach the goal. This means that, just like coercion, the race starts well but cannot be concluded properly. David Gauthier does not agree. His view implies that those who start also finish the race.

The same situation occurs if Jill stubbornly resists Jack's threat. Jack can then avoid the worst consequences to himself, and he should do so. Notice that this means that the initial policy decision and its associated threat may well causally influence Jill's position—so much that she becomes more likely to obey Jack's orders. Jill is afraid of Jack and therefore she tends to obey. Although Gauthier shows quite successfully under which formal conditions it is rational to adopt the policy of threat, he does not solve the problem of whether Jack should actually realize the threat. Perhaps he does not pay sufficient attention to Jill's subjective ideas concerning the threat against her.

Jill will change her action plan when she meets Jack's apparently serious threat. She has no way of telling whether Jack is faking. Now, if she thinks that Jack acts under some holistic policies and not under single-action planning, she finds the threat more convincing than if she does not see this. Jack's communicated idea of holistic rationality is self-fulfilling. Jack can convince Jill that he is rigid; therefore, Jill may well change her reaction into a direction that is more favorable to Jack. Gauthier says that in many cases this new attitude will make a coercer successful. He is right. But then the victim must already have a reasonable idea of why a rational coercer would indeed harm himself by realizing his threats. If the victim does not see this point first, the coercer will be in deep trouble. His threat need not then influence the victim's planning to the point that the threat policy becomes maximizing.

We may conclude that, when Gauthier says that a rational agent is the "one who subjects the largest, rather than the smallest, segments of her activity to primary rational scrutiny," he may be wrong.[15] Decisional holism cannot alone entail behavioral rigidity. On the contrary, a coercer plans the whole threat policy taking into account the possibility that he can always slip away from the situation. But it is exactly because his victim tends to understand the uses of escape routes that coercive and deterrent threats are so difficult to be fully convincing, if presented by visibly rational agents.

Force and violence

Before we go on, the relation that coercion and social power in general bear to violence must be taken up and clarified, simply because these two different things are often identified rather uncritically. This is, however, a mistake. Coercion and violence are not one and the same thing. Sometimes they have nothing to do with each other; sometimes coercion uses violence as an operative component of a threat. Confusion about these points still prevails.

For example Michael Taylor writes, "employing force or physical constraint is itself, of course, a relatively straightforward way of getting another person to pursue a course of action he would not otherwise have pursued. . . . No other way of getting others to do things does this. . . . Power, persuasion and the exercise of authority all work on the individual's will . . . without reducing the range of options actually available to him."[16] Taylor maintains mistakenly that the actual use of, say, physical force could make one act intentionally, without working on one's will. Not even violence can work miracles. Thus, "force is the only way of getting people to do things they would not otherwise have done. . . . Because of the coercer's actions, the victim *has no choice*" with respect to the excluded options.[17]

It is easy to see the nature of Taylor's confusion. He thinks that because of the coercer's actual use of force, or violence, the victim is physically unable to do thing x he wants to do. The victim may be locked in a room. Therefore, the victim will do something else, y. But the coercer cannot be said to have made the victim do y. The coercer just prevents the victim from doing x. Certainly, force is a constraint, but that is also true of natural forces, like storms and floods. And we must be clear about the fact that the use of force is now supposed, by Taylor, to be not a threat but an actual action against the victim. In this case, it only blocks his plans. Not until he interprets the forceful act as a kind of implicit threat will he do something new. My conclusion is that if force is not a threat it does not help the coercer to change the victim's action plan. Force just stops the victim. It prevents him from doing something but does not and cannot make him "pursue a course of action." The key to action is always in the will.

Another philosopher who tends to confuse this important issue is Harry Frankfurt. This overstatement is quite well known: "the person who is coerced is *compelled* to do what he does. He has *no choice* but to do it."[18] Three examples follow; two are simple but the third is somewhat trickier. In the first example, suppose Sam goes home and finds a burglar robbing his house. He grabs the man and carries him out. Did Sam coerce him to go out? The answer must be no.

In the second example, suppose some people are convicted and imprisoned because of terrorist acts. They claim to be political prisoners and so demand better treatment and conditions than the other prisoners, who are murderers and the like. Their demand is turned down, and they start a hunger strike. They seem willing to die rather than submit to prison conditions. Because their death would make them political martyrs and create serious mass disturbances among their sympathizers the government orders the prison authorities to force-feed them. As is well known, force-feeding amounts to virtual torture where the victim is not cooperative. Is the situation coercive? More specifically, are the prisoners coerced to eat? Again our answer is no, simply because violence is used without any threat element. The victim is forced to take some food, but this is not coercion.

In the third example, suppose a conflict situation in a strictly theocratic state where the priestly king wants to get rid of a religious and political enemy. This can happen either symbolically or physically, because of the ideological mixture between religion and politics in the country. Hence, if the victim either publicly condemns his own allegedly heretical religious doctrines or dies, his political power would collapse and his earlier achievements would disappear without trace. The victim's power would not exist any more, and the king would get what he desires. A real historical example involves Pope Innocent III and the religious sect of Catharism in thirteenth-century France. The pope's earthly power was severely endangered by the heretics' growing influence in economically and militarily important areas. Moreover, the Cathars were very strict in their loyalty to their own religious ideas, which were both demanding and radically different from Roman Catholic doctrines. Many Cathars had the following pair of alternatives to consider: death or the repudiation of Catharistic doctrines. Both routes led to the total collapse of personal power.

Is this an example of a coercive situation? Notice that we suppose that the victims are tied to their situation and that the coercer demands something that the victims would in no case like to give. But the answer to the question is no, it is not a coercive situation. No threat element occurs. Whatever the victims do, the end result will be of the same negative value to them. We are interested only in situations that imply that the victim's own choices determine what he will actually get, given the limited set of action alternatives, as in our original mugging situation. There he can save his money only if he accepts a beating. It is the function of coercion to provide the coercer with what he wants by means of an unrealized threat; but in our political example, there was no threat at all. If no threat exists, there can be no relevant choice; and if there is no choice it is, accordingly, immaterial what the victim ultimately does. The interaction is best characterized as involving merely force or violence.

We can characterize the concept of violence in the following general way: violence means the use of force so that the likelihood of intended or nonintended personal harm increases. The term *harm* refers to physical harm and to strictly analogical psychological harm, at least in all paradigmatic cases.

Such a definition is certainly problematic, but we need one anyway. In general, I suspect that no real analytic definition can be given, since violence is one of those complex social notions tailor-made for a variety of rhetorical uses. It is many different things, and what one calls violent action may tell as much about the speaker as about his or her objects of interest. For example, war is violent, streets are violent, some horror movies are violent, and some divorces sever the links between parents and children violently. Often, we just proscribe an action or thought by calling it violent. We should, however, take the definition seriously and keep it in mind. Its point is, simply, that violence entails drastic harm to the subject persons.

It is important to see that right violations, injustice, and violence are different things. Rather surprisingly, this has not always been realized. Johan Galtung maintains the opposite.[19] He says that avoidable hunger entails violence, apparently in the same sense as beating and shooting. Robert Audi shows quite nicely why violence and violations are two separate ideas.[20] The negative import of such a failure is that we should resist the idea that right violations license the victim's use of violence, even if genuine violence could be countered with violence. Such a confusion has serious consequences to the justification of counteraction in conflict situations. A violent revenge is a serious matter.

3 | Types and Meaning of Repression

Introduction

Coercion is related to a wider set of repressive methods and results, whose common point is deterrence—the stronger party (the coercer) is able to force his will upon the weaker one (the victim) either directly or in an anticipated way. (In its essential form as described above, coercion always requires an explicit threat.) In our definitions, we must focus on the distinction between threats and offers in relation to the victim's zero-utility baseline. The same construct is also usable in the definition of deterrence. This fact has not always been recognized. Another important distinction is that between causally produced threats and coercive circumstances. This idea provides further depth and interest.

The present set of ideas may look rather formidable, but as we proceed we shall see that the pieces of the puzzle interlock nicely. My key methodological point is that we should always keep in mind the notion of a threat when we try to define coercion and deterrence. Otherwise, the result will be confusion about such constructs as coercive offers and compulsion to act. Repression cannot take place without the proper tools. A coercer cannot repress the victim's preferences, interests, liberties, and right claims without putting some convincing pressure on him. And it seems best to conceptualize this pressure by means of the idea of a threat—understood, of course, in quite an inclusive way.

If we cannot give an analysis of simple and essential coercion, we cannot grasp the respective roles of threats and offers in social life. We end up analyzing institutions like slavery as involving a compulsion indistinguishable from that a butcher uses in raising the price of meat or from that used by an industrialist in making an insulting salary offer. Examples of such potential confusions are easy to find for instance in Harry Frankfurt's paper "Coercion and Moral Responsibility." Luckily, the concept of a threat provides the key to the solution of many of these conceptual problems.

I shall also extend my discussion to simple exploitation. I do not mean the Marxist economic notion but something much simpler: in some cases, the victim is so strongly motivated to get what he desires that the coercer is able to exploit the victim by making an offer that violates the victim's rights (to get a fair offer, for example). This is an extension of the threat-based repressive case, as no real threat occurs and yet the victim's choice is in a way forced. Here I shall use another analytical idea: normal life conditions, which is an application of the idea of a utility baseline. In deciding whether the coercer restricts the victim's freedom, we ask whether the coercer's offer allows the victim to return to normal life and to the initial status quo, or zero-utility level. We need not, however, characterize normal life in full; it is enough if we state what cannot be part of it.

The idea of exploitation helps us understand why coercion is an undesirable and immoral game and see how normative concepts enter into the analysis of social repression. We should distinguish between the senses of such terms as *harm* and *loss*. Sometimes our rights and freedom are violated (harm). Sometimes we suffer a dollar-valued loss. I shall distinguish explicitly whenever necessary. However, we should not turn to ethics too early, as I shall also argue. In the last sections, I shall return to the ideas of freedom and offers and, finally, I shall suggest what is the correct place of rights in our coercive theory. But first we shall study deterrence.

Deterrence

We can distinguish between essential coercion and deterrence in a simple way. (I shall call the agents *coercer* in both cases.) Consider this example: A police officer has arrested a suspect, his victim, and is presently taking him to the police station. The officer prevents the victim's escape, which is the victim's first preference in the situation, by keeping his handgun ready and making it clear to the victim that he is willing to use it, if necessary. The availability of the gun and the officer's intention to use it constitute a deterrent threat.

Notice that the police officer need not say anything; both parties recognize the informal rules of the game, so that the victim knows that his attempted escape would be very dangerous. The officer cannot expect any personal net profit from the situation; he already has his man and he wants to keep the present status quo intact. Certainly it is possible—but not necessary—that the present status quo was created by means of an explicit and occurrent threat, something like saying to the victim that he is going to get shot if he will not put his hands up. This was coercion. However, the act of coercion has now created a status quo, which the power wielder wants to continue till they both come to the police station. There the victim may be put under a new coercive threat, for instance, during interrogation. From the victim's point of view, this new and unavoidable status quo is also undesirable: only the implicit but continuous threat can make the victim follow the officer. Without the threat, the victim's first preference is to escape.

At least two types of deterrent threat can be identified. In our example above, the threat is a preventive warning. The coercer has made it clear to the victim, implicitly or explicitly, that if he does not obey he will get hurt. Now it is also made clear that even if the victim gets hurt he cannot avoid the interrogation. He might go to a hospital for a while, but ultimately he will end up in front of the police and the jury. At least this is the intention behind the original threat. No one wants the officer to kill the escaping victim. That would be unjustifiable punishment on the spot. The expected result of the victim's breaking the short-term status quo is getting hurt, so that the first preference of the victim, escape, becomes a practical impossibility.

This type of deterrent threat is the kind of warning that is also practiced between two nuclear powers: state A threatens state B by making it clear that any political moves that would commit state B to using its nuclear arsenal will result in their first use by A. The idea of this warning is that, even if no booty, or positive increase in expected utility, may result from the use of the bomb, at least the victim cannot complete its plan of striking first or getting some extra profit from blackmail. A warning is a deterrent threat that prevents one party (the victim) from bringing about harm to the party who presents the warning (the coercer).

Another example is a NO TRESPASSING sign, which is supposed to warn possible intruders that a punishment will ensue. In this way, it prevents any harm to the land before it may occur. In comparison to punitive threats, prevention occurs in those cases in which the victim has not yet caused any harm but has already altered the status quo. In this way, a warning prevents harm before it has actually materialized, given that the harm could be predicted to ensue in the absence of the warning. This shows how many sided repressive contexts in social life tend to be.

If we identify a case where harm would be caused by breaking the status quo, we come to a situation where the full harm has already materialized. Here a country has, say, suffered the nuclear strike and hits back in a retaliatory manner. It cannot win anything nor can it repair the status quo, which is now gone for good; but it can show that it was serious about its earlier retaliatory threats. We imagine the victim having said that if it is hit first, it will hit back, just to take revenge. Having announced its second-use strategy, it supposed that this would stop the enemy and make its warlike plans void. In our example, this was a miscalculation. The bomb was used, and the victim retaliated. But in many cases retaliatory threats are successful.

The logic of preventive warnings and retaliations can be stated as follows. When we warn someone, we make clear our intention to harm the person if he assumes a position which is likely to harm us. We present a threat which is independent of the actual harm done to us. We want to guarantee that no harm will ensue, and for this reason we are ready to realize the threat as a precautionary measure. We make access to our property unlawful in order to guarantee our safety. Retaliations are different. Retaliatory threats presuppose that they are realized not before some actual harm has emerged. We announce our intention to punish anyone who, let us say, breaks our windows during a softball game. We believe that this makes the players more careful than they would otherwise be, at the same time allowing them to play ball. In this way, both warnings and retaliations are meant to preserve the status quo. They are deterrent measures.

Let us see next what the difference is between deterrence and essential coercion. The main point of deterrence is, as we recall, that by means of a relevant threat the coercer does not intend to increase his own expected utility over and above the present status quo but merely to prevent the worsening of his initial situation. Let us call this initial utility balance a baseline or floor. Deterrent threats are, accordingly, designed to prevent the coercer from going through the floor because of the opponent's actions.

Deterrence is also a possibly continuous form of interaction between the coercer and his victim, quite unlike essential coercion, which involves the use of an occurrent threat. The point is that, once the deterrent threat is presented or the victim acknowledges its continuous presence by means of some hints, it is supposed to stay effective over the time span of the whole interaction. In our specimen case, once the officer tells the suspect that he is under arrest, the latter need not perceive any further explicit threats. The existence and the presentation of a threat are two different things.

Deterrence does not entail changes; on the contrary, it is stabilizing. The deterrent threat makes the victim omit further actions designed to change the current pattern of exchange. Essential coercion is clearly different: when the coercer presents his threat, he must give some time to the victim to deliberate on his response, but no status quo between the coercer and the victim can be created before the victim has decided. The coercer expects the victim to increase his profit by acting. And once the victim has decided whether to act or not, the situation is fixed. It has no continuity after the victim's decision to obey or oppose the coercer. In deterrence, the victim's decisions presuppose an apparently stable situation, which the coercer may utilize over an extended period of time. If a threat creates the victim's standing attitude of obedience and subservience toward the power wielder, so that the victim will, say, give money to the power wielder without any further occurrent threats, we should say that the victim omits his change of behavior. Deterrence may be exploitative.

Let me illustrate these ideas by means of an example, adopted from Michael Laver's charming book *The Crime Game*.[1] A mobster collects protection money from a local nightclub owner. He gives the coercer money because the coercer has already destroyed a couple of places whose manager tried to resist. These were blatant acts of essential coercion, designed to provide more money for the mob. But now the owner anticipates new acts of violence, and therefore he is willing to make a very unprofitable deal with the mob. He starts paying protection money. The original, duly realized, coercive threats have now been transformed into a deterrent threat, whose effect is to warn the victim against any impulse to resist. In this sense, a status quo, or a utility floor, has been constituted. This floor is built on the victim's well-founded anticipation of violence, even through such a period of time when the coercer does not even express his intention to hurt him. The mobster may look very friendly indeed. And notice that he does not get any extra profit above the baseline. His successfully executed coercive plan created a new, exploitative baseline, profitable to him; and now he need only keep the utility floor intact. This happens by means of the deterrent effect of the victim's subjective idea that the coercer is both willing and capable of realizing his preventive threats. Moreover, he will retaliate if the victim calls the police to stop the collecting of money.

I want to argue that the baseline of deterrence is always relative to a historical social exchange between the coercer and the victim. There is no natural zero-level floor. The floor is what the coercer expects to get. We cannot interpret deterrence and coercion simply by saying that if the coercer gains something he coerces and if he avoids losing something he deters. We must specify this something by focusing on the history of the social exchanges between the coercer and the victim, or their respective reference groups.

The floor is the status quo created through some definite events in the past that explain the present distribution of goals and expectations between the coercer and the victim. This distributive history may or may not contain repressive power and its exercise, such as threats or accidental gains, good or bad fortune, and profits. The historical results may, of course, be strongly biased in favor of, say, the mobster against the club owner. The bias itself and its unfairness have, however, no role when we decide about the proper description of the interaction: the floor is what the coercer may be supposed to get. His expectations, at least if they are epistemically well founded and historically reasonable, are what fix the baseline as that belonging to deterrent contexts.

Another example involves a father whose adult daughter demands much too much of the family property from him. He uses threats to keep their respective financial situation as it has always been. She understands that the threats are continuous. It may happen that no initial explicit threat is needed, as both parties understand that in their culture threats would be issued to counter any extravagant demands that could destabilize the typical distribution of family wealth. Deterrent threats may be purely expected and never actually issued.

If the coercer wants to break the circle of expectations and get even more, he must introduce a new explicit and occurrent threat. To change the status quo, which as such need not imply any stable distribution, he must convey new information to the victim. The coercer himself wants to break the old rule of action, so that the victim's omissions become impossible. This idea of coercion is somewhat troublesome, however, because the coercer may repeat his old warnings. If the floor has already been constantly rising, it may be very difficult to tell whether the repeated threats are in fact deterrent or essentially coercive. Thus it seems that the best test of deterrence is always historical: it should focus on the long-term effects of the coercer's earlier threats against the victim, who is or is not following, against his own will, an already fixed unprofitable distribution rule. One should check whether the victim would not give the coercer what he desires without his explicit and occurrent threat. The only method to do this is to look at their earlier exchanges. Any occurrent-looking threat may in fact be redundant, regardless of its seeming effects. A victim might give more even without the new threat.

The final conceptual problem is that of fines. Suppose the mobster cannot make the owner give him the baseline booty he used to get. Then he informs the owner that next time he must pay a double sum of money, or he will smash the place. The demanded increase is now a kind of fine that the victim must pay in order to compensate for his earlier disobedience. That fine is actually a realized deterrent threat, if we see the whole exchange in its historical perspective. If we look just at their present-moment exchange we should say that the owner is coerced to give the mobster extra money above the baseline. But our case does not exemplify essential coercion. This shows further why the historical perspective is important when we try to understand the relation between implicit deterrent threats and their occurrent and essentially coercive counterparts.

We have seen that deterrence is different from essential coercion and that it gives rise to some interesting problems concerning the baseline distribution of utility between a coercer and his victim. Essential coercion is a means of getting more than the victim expects the coercer to get from him. Another way of putting the same idea is to say that, in the context of deterrence, the coercer knows that he is able to get baseline zero without any new effort, or at least without any new type of effort.

Because deterrent threats are so often latent and rest on a utility floor, they have some interesting motivating long-term effects on the victim. My point is that if a warning threat is effective, like a NO TRESPASSING notice backed by ferocious dogs and guards, the victim will ultimately fail to form an intention to trespass, even if he originally wanted to and would still gain something if he were able to. This never happens in coercion, where we suppose the victim always forms the intention to escape and considers resistance; the coercive situation is new to him. But in deterrence, the status quo might well become subjectively acceptable to the victim, independently of its biased distributive properties, simply because he gets accustomed to its presence. We can then say that he does not form the relevant intention. A victim seems to be more able to ignore an omission than an action proper. Is this irrational? Let us look at this case a little more closely.

Suppose that a person wants to go to town and the only short cut goes through lands where trespassing is strictly forbidden. Certainly he wants to trespass, as that would bring about a considerable net gain in terms of expected utilities, disregarding the guards. But the guards are there, and when he deducts their supposed effect from the utility of the short cut, the result is negative. He will not use the short cut across the land, although he could have gained a lot. But the effect of the guards might be so convincing that he fails to see the point of the counterfactual "I could have gained by going through these lands." He simply thinks that his baseline utility distribution is determined according to the alternative of not using the short cut. If he thinks that the natural way of going to town is to use the longer route, he will not regret traveling round the land.

This is what I mean by saying that the victim does not form an intention: he is fully accustomed to the idea that his zero-utility level, or the floor, is historically defined according to the strains of the longer route. This is an example of a rationally accepted perfect warning, if we mean by perfect that the victim does not feel any regret or remorse because of the implicit threat. Yet, if the victim looks back in history and checks how the floor was originally established, he may see that the short cut was originally used by people like him and the owner has invented the enforcement idea. Therefore, the victim may think that in the normative perspective, he has the right to use the shorter route. He then regrets that he has lost his rights. We shall return to the normative case in due course. Here it is important to notice that if the victim accepts a baseline, this entails that he may or may not regret the warning threats against his welfare and right claims.

A victim may accept a baseline for many reasons. For example, he may want to minimize the waste of mental energy in rebellion against a far superior power. However, if this baseline violates his rights, he may take up the distributive issue. In this latter case, the warnings can only be imperfect. I suggest that even perfect warnings, or those that in fact eliminate regret, are irrational for the victim to accept if they are against his rights. Rightful perfect warnings exist also, of course. Indeed, to law-abiding citizens, the laws of the state need not have any deterrent effect. We accept the authority of the just laws and never consider breaking them. Apparently, if a deterrent threat is implicit and causes no worry or regret and is just, it is no "real" threat. In other words, just and perfect deterrent threats are not repressive. And therefore they do not qualify as real threats. In this respect, deterrence is markedly different from essential coercion, which one always tends to resist. Perfect warnings constitute a limiting case of repression.

The idea of deterrence must be sketched in full view of both the victim's rights and the justice of social conditions. When his rights are violated, he morally should feel himself deterred from doing something that would alter the status quo. Quite evidently, if we are going to understand deterrence, we need to understand right-based motivation in terms of harm. For instance, no behavioral differences may occur between two persons who see the same warning sign and follow it, even if only one accepts the message to be just and is, therefore, not deterred.

Rights, coercive circumstances, and exploitation

A main topic in the theory of coercion concerns its definition in terms of individual moral rights in a form more illuminating than C. C. Ryan's familiar view. Can coercion be defined exclusively in terms of descriptive notions? We already saw that our attempt to draw a conceptual distinction between coercion and deterrence led us first toward a context-relative zero-utility baseline and then toward the use of right-related ideas in connection with perfect warnings. Something similar may be expected to emerge from the analysis of coercion itself.

A good starting point is Robert Nozick's paper "Coercion," which seems to have initiated the discussion concerning rights, floors, and coercion. The debate has spread toward the problems of wage offers and more openly political issues. Let us keep close to analytical topics. We may start from Nozick's statement of the problem and his hint at its solution:

> Thus far we have considered threats as introducing certain deviations from the normal and expected course of events. The question arises as to whether the normal or expected course of events itself can be coercive. Suppose that usually a slave owner beats his slave each morning, for no reason connected with the slave's behavior. Today he says to his slave, "Tomorrow I will not beat you if and only if you now do X." One is tempted to view this as a threat, and one is also tempted to view this as an offer. I attribute these conflicting temptations to the divergence between the normal course of events, in which the slave is beaten each morning, and the (morally) expected course of events, in which he is not. And I suggest that we have here a situation of a threat, and that here the morally expected course of events takes precedence over the normal course of events in assessing whether we have a threat or an offer.[2]

This is a fascinating idea: Nozick seems to maintain that, when we evaluate a seeming offer normatively and in terms of the victim's rights, we may admit that it is in reality a coercive threat. Nevertheless, descriptively speaking it is an offer.

Actually, there are three different issues here: first, the characterization of the relative baseline; second, whether we characterize it descriptively or normatively; and third, whether an important presupposition applies, that is to say, that the social background situation is coercive, so that the coercer's causal influence alone does not create the victim's distressing position. In such a case, the threats are based on the victim's coercer-independent peril, such as the social institution of slavery. It is irrelevant in these circumstances exactly who beats the slave. The circumstances themselves are coercive.

Now, it is easy to see that if we tell Nozick's original story carefully enough, no rights need be mentioned; yet we can conclude that slave owner coerces his slave. Nozick seems to confuse the issue by claiming that the normal and the expected courses of events may fail to be coercive because they contain an offer to the slave—that is, a reduction of expected pain.

I shall argue that (1) Nozick's slave example describes a new case, which is different from my original examples; but (2) the same basic analysis of coercion can be extended to it. In other words, no moral perspective is needed in order to show that the case is coercive.

Suppose the master approaches his slave and says that if the victim performs in a moderately demanding way x he will not get his daily ten lashes. His utility floor is now ten lashes, which is certainly considerably worse than any natural baseline. The victim then calculates his own expected utilities: "I shall get ten lashes if I say no, but if I do x I shall lose only the utility worth of the trouble of doing x, which is much less than the beating." Now, it seems quite clear that in this choice situation the victim recognizes a clear-cut coercive threat even without any reference to his right to physical welfare. He faces a choice situation that corresponds perfectly to our original descriptive definition of coercion. If the victim can get only less pain while successfully avoiding more pain, but cannot avoid all the pain, he is under a coercive threat. In this case, the slave is under a repeatedly occurring threat, so to speak, since whatever losses he may suffer because of a given task must always be compared to the still greater loss of the magnitude of ten lashes, which is the victim's sole alternative.

The Nozickian way of making the victim's situation look as if it included an apparent offer from the coercer is to say that the ten lashes constitute the victim's baseline, which allegedly means that the victim historically expects to get them but subjectively does not accept the fact. He might accept his fate if (1) he is accustomed to beatings and thus will not pay too much attention to them; or (2) he assents to the idea that the coercer has the moral right to beat him.

The victim does not accept the baseline if (1) he hates beatings or (2) he thinks that it is his moral right to avoid them. Expectation and acceptance are two different things. Therefore, if the beating is dropped, he will feel relief, and he will experience a welcome offer, as Nozick thinks. But, although the slave may indeed historically expect to get the ten lashes, he does not accept them, and he is therefore coerced without a trace of an offer in the situation. The lack of acceptance may be based either on the victim's conviction that the coercer has no right to torture him or on the recognition that lashing always hurts terribly. In fact, the right-based analysis is just one way of reaching the key conclusion to the effect that the victim is under a standing coercive threat and has received no offer.

One decisive way of settling this issue is to consider the relation between freedom and coercion. Let us recall that in coercive cases the victim cannot realize his first preference, which is escape from the interaction without suffering any extra loss. This analysis stems from our basic mugger case, but it seems to work also with Nozick's slave example: the slave would like first of all to escape from slavery and its violence. Even if his master would allow him to do x every day and so avoid all beatings, the slave would still like to escape. He does x if and only if he cannot escape. But he does not try to escape, because that would mean beating.

Compare this with the case of a genuine offer: an offer is always the victim's first alternative, so that he would like to get it. An offer does not take away from the victim anything he had earlier. Certainly, the master's proposal does not take anything away from the slave, but it cannot be inferred on this basis alone that the proposal would be an offer. The slave may be happy to receive the proposal but, nevertheless, he would like to avoid the position where the proposal was made. The victim would still escape from the situation, even if nothing is taken away from him by means of the proposal to do x. This entails that the situation is itself coercive and that it cannot be turned into a noncoercive one by any normative or descriptive tricks.

Nozick's misleading formulations rest on his uncritical acceptance of the fact that the socially constituted ten-lash situation could be some kind of utility baseline, which it is not. The purpose of lashing is to make the victim suffer. The main point is that the baseline circumstances should qualify basic and normal life conditions: the normal course of events cannot be intrinsically motivating, like whipping is. Normal life is an equilibrium, or a nonmotivating state.

Alternative x is a (small) loss, and if lashing is not a still greater loss, a prudent victim will simply refuse to act. The coercer is capable of inflicting, and has inflicted, some real harm, which drives the victim to action. It seems, therefore, that we have no hope of making the master's deal with the victim look like a genuine offer. In whatever way we tell the story, the conclusion still seems to be that the victim is facing two negatively loaded alternatives, the worse of which is a standing threat of violence. Even a mugging case could otherwise contain an offer: the robber suggests to his victim that normally people get killed in this part of the city but now the victim is, quite exceptionally, offered his life in exchange for his watch. Is this an offer? The positive utility difference between one's life and one's watch cannot constitute any sufficient condition of offers.

Perhaps the main interest of Nozick's case of coercive social exchange is that it shows how the coercer's and the victim's respective points of view and their explanations of the interaction can be drastically different and asymmetric. We already saw why this exchange is always coercive to the victim. But when we consider the coercer, we can say that to him society's customary and even legal right to beat the slave allows him to maintain that he has subjectively provided an offer to the victim to do x. According to his alternative narrative, there is indeed an offer: for the coercer, ten daily lashes to the victim is the utility floor, and to do x means a relative gain to the victim. According to the coercer, the victim is able to avoid beatings quite cheaply, so that he may expect a gain from their interaction.

This is a very one-sided offer, because the victim cannot accept either alternative as such. Can we always define coercion without referring to normative conflicts and rights?

If we want to see why rights are in some cases necessary when we interpret a social exchange as coercion, we need more subtle examples. They should not refer to the victim's pain, or to anything that is, in principle, impossible to accept subjectively. Pain is always bad, regardless of any legalistic explanations, historical traditions, and normal courses of events.

Let us say, therefore, that normal life is an equilibrium set of conditions that we accept subjectively as our permanent situation and status quo without any obvious—moral or prudent—need to escape from it. It must be both morally acceptable and physically and psychologically tolerable in terms of pain and suffering. I suggest that it might be impossible to determine any historically and culturally nonrelative utility baselines, even if the idea of normal life still makes perfect sense. I also maintain that it is ultimately impossible to define and understand coercion without moral notions: in some cases, circumstances are nonnormal because they are, say, unfair, and not only because they are undesirable to someone.

My main hypothesis is this: a seeming offer is coercive if the victim cannot both return to his normal life and refuse to act. In some cases, however, normative right elements are at stake.

Assume now that salary negotiations take place in an economically depressed society. An industrialist tells a worker that she will get ten dollars per day, even if all other workers doing similar work will get twenty dollars. Otherwise the victim may stay unemployed. Is this an offer or a threat? This may well be a genuine offer—namely, if her normal life includes unemployment. The owner has no moral or other duty to employ her, and she may expect nothing else but unemployment. Life without work is also possible to accept subjectively. (If it is not, this example becomes coercive, just like the slave case.) Even a small salary helps considerably; the victim then need not beg or steal for a living.

A prudent person may herself maintain, however, that because everybody gets a double salary the industrialist is threatening her by unemployment if she will not allow himself to be exploited. Is this a threat simply because the victim has both a bad and a worse alternative, and nothing else, open to her? It is not if (1) the victim can say no to the coercer and then return to her starting point, which is (2) now her normal life. It may be depressing living, but it may not violate her rights; it is not subjectively impossible to accept and it is a perfectly predictable fate in that stage of history. In other words, the victim has a real alternative, that is, the normal life of an unemployed person, and this fact is independent of whether any capitalist is willing to give her work. Of course, the apparent offer is in some sense exploitative, especially if a better salary could be paid. Nevertheless, given that our political and moral theory condemns unemployment as unjustifiable, the victim is coerced. The victim's fate without a job is of negative value to her, and the owner's proposition does not help.

Let us continue this tough-minded story with further stipulations. First, our industrialist actively prevents the worker from getting employment elsewhere by informing other capitalists about the victim's difficult personality. Second, the coercer's private security force does not let the victim leave the factory after she has refused to work for the ten-dollar wage. The interpretation is no longer open to partisan and subjective opinions concerning the fate of those people one sympathizes with; the case is coercive.

In the first situation, we can identify coercion: by accepting the offer the victim will suffer a loss in relation to her expectations, but by refusing to work she will suffer a still greater loss by becoming unable to get any work in the future. Whatever she does, she will lose, as she cannot return to her normal life as an unemployed person who can continue job hunting. Her normal life has been disturbed. This is coercion. Notice that the worker may accept her fate as part of normal life, if she is confused enough. The point is she should not accept it either morally or prudently. The situation violates her rights to fair treatment. It can then be pondered whether the right violation has consequences that are harmful to the victim. Anyway, rights to fair treatment enter the picture here, along with utilities.

In the second situation, the coercer has practically speaking imprisoned the victim within his factory. Forced labor is impossible to accept, as it is always against the victim's liberty. In these conditions, the victim cannot choose any other alternative but serving the coercer or suffering the pain of imprisonment. The threat is now imprisonment, and the coercer's booty is the victim working for him. This is indeed a very clear example of a situation in which one has no recourse to the normal life. Imprisonment in the factory is certainly against her rights and impossible to accept.

My conclusion is that, if unemployment is politically acceptable as normal life, the worker's case is not coercive. If unemployment violates human rights, it cannot be a normal life and constitutes a coercive circumstance. The two stronger versions of the same example combine the considerations of utilitarian harm and rights. Finally, the imprisonment case displays no more coercive circumstances. Unemployment is a general social problem; imprisonment is a clear-cut causal threat. Normative language is needed, though.

Another example that illustrates nicely the relation between offers and threats and also relates them to exploitation is the case of a mountain climber in distress. Social and even natural situations themselves may be coercive, fully independently of the coercer's causal role in framing the threat; such situations exist regardless of the coercer's intentions. So the victim's initial peril need not depend on the coercer's causal influence, in spite of the fact that he threatens the victim.

Suppose that the victim has been climbing in the Alps and has got himself into dire trouble. He is hanging from a cliff two-thousand feet above a rocky valley. An old acquaintance arrives on the scene. This man hates the climber because of some scandal, the revelation of whose details could clear his own reputation should the climber tell the truth. Now, the acquaintance makes an "offer," saying that he will save the climber if he tells the truth first; otherwise he will just walk away. (This presupposes he can recognize the truth.)

Is this an offer or a threat? There is no explicit framing of any threat elements that we can identify, yet the case certainly looks like coercion. The victim must choose between the genuine loss of falling and the apparently smaller loss of humiliation. Yet the coercer is in no way causally responsible for this nasty predicament. The coercer has not formulated any threats, as he has not brought about any changes in the original circumstances in which the victim is involved. He may well say that he is not threatening the victim as he is simply making him an offer and is quite willing to leave him in his present position. The victim's counterargument is, of course, that the refusal to help him will causally contribute to his plunge into the valley. The coercer would not be detached from the course of events.

It seems best to call this case coercive, simply because it satisfies the utility distribution requirements and because the victim has no recourse to his normal life. Hanging on a cliff and falling to his death is no baseline source of utilities. It is simply an exceptional natural accident. An offer implies either a profit or a return to normal life. The mountain climber cannot do either: he either will fall or he will suffer humiliation. Any talk about offers is misleading. But so also is any talk about exploitation (see below), although a little less so. Less misleading is talk about coercion. The only problem is that the coercer has not created the original situation. He need not issue any explicit threats. But as the utility distribution is structurally similar to that of the artificial coercer-made threats, we may call this coercion.

It should also be noticed that, if the coercer lets the victim fall to his death, he is just as morally culpable as if he had killed the victim. This is not just a case of letting die, because he has actively approached the victim, talked to him, and made a proposal to save him, should the victim fulfill some rather repulsive preconditions. The coercer has decided not to save him if the victim does not agree to his conditions. He actively participates in the process.

Finally, notice that this cliff-hanging case is just the same as Nozick's slave case, if the institution of slavery is such that all the slaves of all the masters are always and automatically beaten. Our individual master has not created the institution and he cannot stop its practices. He perhaps has nothing to do with the actual violence. He just witnesses at a distance how the life of the institution goes on, and he thinks that he may present an "offer" to one of his slaves. But just like falling from a cliff, the ten lashes are never part of normal life, and thus the two cases share the characteristic of being coercive. A coercer's causal responsibility for the threat element is not a necessary condition of coercion. The industrialist did not create unemployment either. However, someone must exploit the unfavorable circumstances before a case of coercion can be detected.

Next, let us consider exploitation: we shall see why and how rights enter the picture. Suppose an anthropologist has been planning for a long time a trip to an exotic country and has committed herself both personally and professionally to her important trip. She hates the idea of being forced to return without good results. Then she meets the governor of the country; he has a legal right to grant or refuse her permission to enter. The governor is a nasty person and, knowing her situation, he considers either a very high dollar price or a perverse sexual act in exchange for the visa. The anthropologist's motive to continue the trip is now to be weighted against the price of the visa, as expensive as it is.

It seems that two kinds of considerations are relevant here. If the governor demands a dollar price, she may then calculate whether her motive to continue is so strong that it is still more important than the price of the visa. Here is a possible case of simple exploitation without any coercive overtones; the victim may refuse and go home and return to her normal life. It is also questionable whether the governor would be violating the moral rights of some foreigner whose plans he cannot understand if he demands a high dollar price for his visa, to which he has the legal right anyway. This situation has its exploitative features, but it is also a typical bargaining situation, where both opponents weigh their respective demand and supply characteristics against the other's potential contributions. And certainly the victim should have known, as an anthropologist, that a trip to that exotic country would not be easy. An escape route should have been left open.

Everything changes drastically when we look at the governor's attempt to get the victim to perform a perverse sexual act. The governor has no moral right to insist on this. Although he may or may not have a legal duty not to do it, the moral side of the issue is clear. He acts against the anthropologist's moral rights, and so she may find it impossible to estimate the dollar value of her scientific plans in comparison to her sexual aversions. It is an impossible decision. Her original plans drive her forward; her feelings of shame and humiliation hold her back. It is her choice, granted the knowledge that she can return to her normal life and work and at the same time realizing that her moral rights are not respected.

Even if the victim cannot make any dollar estimations, she may still succumb to the temptation to agree to the coercer's proposal and pay the high emotional price for the visa. She is then successfully exploited. Here the key feature of the situation is that the coercer violates the victim's moral rights, such as fair play and personal integrity. Without this idea, we cannot describe the situation as exploitative. Moreover, notice that only if the governor prevents the victim from leaving without the visa and having performed the sex act does he coerce her, in addition to exploiting her.

We may now compare some theories of exploitation. Deidre Golash writes about exploitation: "A exploits B if and only if A uses factors that give her more bargaining power but do not affect the value of the commodity exchanged to obtain a bargain more favorable to her than would otherwise be possible."[3] In our exotic-country example, the governor knew that the value of the visa was very high, but what are those factors that are supposed to give him more bargaining power? Were his legal rights relevant as to exploitation? This cannot be so! Golash has not much to say about these issues.

Hillel Steiner's trilateral theory of exploitation is more promising. He says roughly this: it is the governor's "forcible exclusion" of all other agents from the interaction with a victim that makes it possible for him to ask an unfair price for the visa.[4] If some other persons could deal with the traveler or even control the governor, his demands in the situation could not possibly succeed. I do not think that either Golash's or Steiner's theories of exploitation are convincing, even though they illustrate the key features of some relevant right violations.

The notion of a moral right indeed enters the analyses and explanations of repressive social exchanges. Yet it is not at all clear that we could not do without right in some cases of essential coercion and deterrence. Perhaps only utility distributions are important to the victim. Nevertheless, at least the coercer might try to justify his own policies as offers by saying that he has a right to act as he does. The victim, however, will then disagree. Rights are especially important when we deal with alleged economic coercion. Wage offers may indeed be coercive, because they violate the worker's rights. The key issue is whether the worker has a recourse to a normal life in case he turns down the "offer." Coercion seems to imply that the victim does not have a feasible choice, and if such choice is his right, then and only then does coercion entail violated rights. It does not seem to follow that this implication is uniformly embedded in all examples.

There are also cases in which a normal life is not a right: consider a criminal in prison. He is under coercion because he cannot return to normal life, but he has no legal or even moral right to it, anyway. Workers and criminals under forced labor are coerced and threatened by punishment, although only the former's rights are violated (presupposing a general theory of punitive justice). Normal life is not our basic and inalienable right; instead, it is a thing uniformly desired. Threats go typically against desires and not rights, although in some cases rights are what we rationally desire. Rights that are not wanted are void.

My tentative explanation of why we are tempted to explain coercion in terms of rights is that the idea of exploitation contaminates the examples. Exploitation must always be described in terms of violated entitlements and rights. We tend to think in terms of our basic moral tradition and make it a part of an agent's liberty that he may realize his wants and desires as far as possible. No one should prevent that without good reasons. Another's own competing desire to make an extra profit or to satisfy his private dreams is not such a good reason. This idea enters all our examples concerning economic life; but we have, as a counterdose, the theory of free competition, supply and demand, fair price, and the bargaining process. In this way, we are able to handle some of our moral qualms. But once we get an example, like the anthropologist versus the governor, where the deal cannot in principle be fair, we have an illustration of the basic idea of exploitation.

It is also noteworthy that noncoercive exploitation does not restrict the victim's freedom at all. Such exploitation resembles an offer. The governor had the right to refuse the visa, and the victim could go home and continue her normal life. In principle, she had no unconditional right to travel in that foreign country. The only rights violation that took place was the governor's proposal, which quite evidently did not limit her freedom in any way. She is able to get the visa or, if she prefers, go home. It is like any price with respect to its effect on her freedom, except for the fact that it is immoral. Compare this with the robbery case: it is merely ironic to maintain that the victim could have kept his money. This is not freedom.

Threats restrict freedom, but they are largely independent of moral rights. Exploitation, on the contrary, cannot be justified in any conditions, simply because it is defined as a violation of rights in such a manner that no excuses have room to enter. Threats involve a violation of rights only as far as their effects are at the same time exploitative. If they are not, they can well be justifiable in the moral perspective. Anyway, many coercive exchanges are truly exploitative, and the coercer has no right to do what he is doing against the victim.

In sum, coercive threats are sometimes exploitative. If they are, their characterization logically demands the use of moral terms. But nonexploitative threats can be identified without a reference to moral elements. Also, in certain cases circumstances are coercive by being unfair or otherwise undesirable.

Rights and welcome threats: a critical review

This section focuses on some additional details, namely, those that have received systematic attention in the literature. My treatment is mainly critical. I hope it provides some evidence in favor of the strength of the analysis presented in the previous chapters.

The first issue is the scope of coercion. A relevant problem emerges, because any definition of coercion like ours can be said to open the floodgates and to make all kinds of trivial interactions coercive. The intuition behind such an idea is that coercion is something practically significant, disturbing, and demanding. How can one satisfy this intuition? It must be satisfied, especially as I already criticized the theorists of sociological power by saying that their object of interest is so broad in its scope that it simply vanishes into thin air. The standard solution is to say that coercion is an essentially normative notion to be defined, say, not in terms of preferences but in terms of rights and practical reasoning. Mark Fowler writes as follows: "A coerced agent must be faced with the choice of yielding to a threat or acting contrary to practical reason. He is forced to perform his deed because he literally has no reasonable alternative. . . . Persons have standing practical imperatives to avoid what are serious harms given their life goals."[5]

Fowler's account is not quite convincing. The main difficulty is that if a robber threatens his victim so that, in order to resist, he should act against practical reason, and he is the sole victim in this interaction, then it is typically the case that he is required to act against his preferences. In fact, to act against practical reason logically entails acting against preferences. What else is required? Fowler does not succeed in his answer to this crucial question, as he merely refers to "immorally reduced options" as being characteristic of coercive threats.

It seems to me that Fowler's distinction between actions against a victim's preferences and actions against practical reason is simply the same idea as that behind serious threats. Some threats are dramatic infringements of rights and welfare interests. And if the user of this construction is not allowed to utilize it as an escape road from the coercive flooding, neither should Fowler be allowed to utilize his construction. He writes: "coercion is intrinsically prima facie immoral for it always involves forcing an individual to perform an action in such a way that there occurs a prima facie infringement of his right to shape his own life."[6] Now, whenever a victim is made to act against his will so that his liberty is thereby restricted, Fowler's prima facie condition is satisfied. And freedom may be limited with respect to small things, too. If I could not chew gum during my classes, I could possibly claim that my rights are violated. Right violations need not be spectacular. Small things may also have much symbolic value. What is important and what is not is an empirical question.

The main victim of the floodgate argument is supposed to be H. J. McCloskey, who launches a "motivational conception" of coercion; it is quite like mine. He is not worried about the wide scope of coercion.[7] Some limitations are needed, but they can be found in the preference and utility structure associated with coercive threats. It is one thing to recognize this structure and another to feel that some real-life coercive phenomena are so alarming that one should fight against them, and for this reason keep their picture unstained before our eyes.

The following considerations tend to show where our ideas lead us if we deny that coercion may exist without right violations. We commonly think that coercion reduces the victim's culpability and moral responsibility for his actions. Intuitively this is so. However, McCloskey writes as follows: "Clearly, many coercive threats do not excuse at all . . . the ambitious woman who is threatened with loss of a senior appointment if she does not enter into an adulterous relationship with her employer, cannot successfully morally plead . . . that she acted under coercion."[8] This is an interesting example but it need not imply coercion. It may refer to exploitation without coercion: the lady can retreat and go home to her "normal life," assuming that she is just too ambitious and the position did not belong to her. The point is that if she is overambitious, she should not refer to this psychological characteristic in order to justify her mishaps. It seems that to deal with moral matters in the present context is to confuse coercion and exploitation. If the job rightfully belongs to her, the interpretation may change, too. Morality matters in this case.

Without exploitation, coercion is only prudently harmful. It need not be a serious thing, not even in the sense exploitation is. My conclusion is that the floodgates issue does not lead us anywhere. Philosophical analysis cannot judge whether some issues are practically and subjectively important or not. And just as prudent considerations may be minor problems, some prima facie right violations are not so important, especially if social conditions are otherwise dramatic enough. The notions of *normal life* and *equilibrium* come as close to providing the analysis of an important issue as possible.

The next topic is that of coercive offers and welcome threats. We have already wrestled with it, but let us now see how our former analysis works as a critical tool. David Zimmerman takes up the issue of a factory owner who offers a worker a low salary but does so in such a manner that the worker cannot refuse.[9] I sympathize with Zimmerman's uncompromising argument to the effect that coercion is to be defined always without normative concepts. We have seen, however, that this is not quite true. In some fuzzy limit cases, say, rights must enter the picture. Yet, Zimmerman's starting point is correct. The problem with Zimmerman's argument is his reluctance to see the relevance of such cases as the cliff-hanger, where the victim's distress is not causally produced by the coercer.

Zimmerman writes: "I would claim that for P's offer to be genuinely coercive it must be the case that he actively prevents Q from being in the alternative pre-proposal situation Q strongly prefers.[10] Each offer is to be counted as coercive (in part) because P prevents Q from having, indeed literally removes Q from, his highly preferred alternative pre-proposal situation."[11] It is indeed ironic to consider how these quotations should apply to our cliff-hanger case. Indeed, the really interesting coercive offers are just those made to a person who cannot return to his preproposal state, and this fact in no way depends on the coercer. He was not there when the mountain climber first slipped. Zimmerman's examples are too narrow.

Daniel Lyons has written two very interesting and sophisticated papers on these issues.[12] He reviews a number of tricky examples, following the style of Nozick's path-breaking paper "Coercion." Lyons concludes that no definitive analysis of coercive offers can be given in the light of the variety of possible examples and counterexamples but that his own suggestion, given in terms of rights, comes as close as it is possible to come.

Let us first reject a suggestion that, though it is a nice rhetorical invention, cannot be correct: Lyons says in reference to Nozick's whipped slave that to this victim the threat was actually welcome. (Of course, also the mugger's victim welcomes the possibility of saving his own life, if the threat was fully convincing, and if the threat was presented first and as if independently of the demand of the booty.) These are "should without would" cases. Lyons suggests the following new case: "Suppose powerful P has owed Q money for months and has no intention of repaying Q. Helpless Q has practically given up hope, but he begs one last time for the money which he needs so badly. Suddenly P thinks about a nasty job Q could do for him; he proposes to give the money to Q for the job."[13] Is this an offer or a threat? P should give the money to Q, but he will not do so. It is also a presumably welcome threat, if it is a threat. It is really questionable whether Q can gain anything by working in his present situation. All the available money is already his own.

I think that the following is true of the example. At least three subcases must be distinguished—namely, (1) the stolen money is vitally important to Q, in the sense that Q cannot live without it; (2) the money is not vital but just useful (no moral rights need be mentioned here); and (3) in their culture, Q's rights are violated so seriously that his position does not qualify as normal.

Now, suppose the first case obtains. Q realizes that there is one and only one way to survive and that is to do as P demands. Q is coerced to act. The fact that the money is his own anyway does not change the essential structure of the situation; on the contrary, it just modifies its emotive description by making the case more moving. The only things that really count are (1) that Q is supposed to have no recourse to normal life (in the descriptive sense of the term) without P; and (2) that Q does not want to work. The case resembles Nozick's story of the slave.

The second case is different: Q can leave the interactive context that is dominated by P's powers. However, if the positive value of the money to Q is subjectively more than the disvalue of the demanded act, Q may well perform the action. He will not like it, so we intuitively suppose, but whether he does it or not is up to him. Here, we should recall our analysis of the structure of constraint in coercive cases. Threats deprive one of the real possibility of performing a certain combined action, like keeping both one's money and bodily health. In the present version of our example, such combined action is possible: first Q could not get the money, which he can now do. What happens here is that Q is able to leave without any novel harm. This means that no coercion occurs. P of course makes an exploitative offer to Q, which Q may or may not accept.

To state the main alternatives. In case (1), Q cannot leave the situation and keep (in the long run) his life; thus he is coerced. But in case (2) he can do just this and he is deprived of nothing just because he refuses to interact with P. But (3), if the position of Q, after his retreat, is considered too unjust, it is a real loss to assume it; thus Q is coerced to work for P.

I cannot quite see what his own opinion is, but Lyons tries to back up his analyses of the role of rights by saying that "it is somehow odd to say that Q has something to gain from facing a new threat, from being coerced."[14] But is it so strange after all? And is it so strange that some threats are welcome to the victim? Lyons does not recognize that some offers can be not so welcome! Let us see what this means.

Suppose that a person gets a lottery prize of ten gallons of milk. Being allergic to milk and having no refrigerator, he refuses the offer. He did not like it, but it was an offer. In the case of a normal robbery, there are circumstances where the victim might be afraid of meeting a worse threat than the one finally presented. In many cases, a less than maximal threat, or such a "sentence," is indeed welcome. Thus it seems to me that a threat that is presented to the Nozickian slave

or to our cliff-hanger may well be welcome — and not at all paradoxical as a threat. This fact leads us to the familiar topic of exploitation:
it is a historical fact that many exploited people have been happy
about the treatment they get from their superiors.

Now, Lyons says about his master example: "some admitted
threats would be welcome even to a continent man. Therefore I see
no gain in stipulating that P's proposal to pay his debt to Q, if Q com-
plies, is not a welcome threat."[15] This is true, but then Lyons goes
astray when he gives his ultimate definition of coercion in terms of
a "rationally reluctant" victim: "1. P knows that Q is rationally reluctant to give y to P for x; and 2. either Q knows that he has a right
to x from P on easier terms, or Q knows that P would have given
x to Q, on easier terms, if the chance had not arisen to trade x for
y."[16] One might wonder whether this attempt, which is inspired by
Lyons's tricky master example, can hold water. It cannot because,
first, clause 1 is now clearly irrelevant and, second, clause 2 applies
to exploitation better than to coercion.

The first clause need not occupy us any longer. The second one
is a different matter, however. It is merely exploitative because it does
not imply any limits to the victim's freedom to escape the interaction situation. Lyons's definition may be only partial, in the sense
that it mentions a necessary condition of coercion. But certainly it
is not sufficient, as it makes some merely exploitative situations coercive. What I mean is that I may have your cigarettes, which I offer
to give back to you if you lick my shoes. You do not want to do that.
I have no right to suggest such an exchange. It is also clear that without the shoes being dirty I would have given your cigarettes back
without any extra demands. Because you are rational, you will now
consider the two alternatives of letting me keep your cigarettes or
licking my shoes. It is up to you to do what you like. If you let me
keep your cigarettes, I have not deprived you of anything that you
unconditionally had before my "offer." I had the possession of your
cigarettes already at the beginning of our sick exchange. Lyons's formula makes some exploitative offers look coercive. He writes, "I ask
the reader to consider whether there are clearly non-coercive offers
this formula would label as threats." I have done just that. The conclusion is that the formula fails to convince us of its own sufficiency.

It seems indeed true that rights, or any other moral terms, need not be always utilized in the analysis of coercion. They will come in through the back door, though. Exploitation has an essentially normative dimension, and many a coercive case is also exploitative. And our idea of normal life is basically normative, just like the idea of a normal person. Nevertheless, the crucial factor in the definition of coercion is its cruel structure: the victim is facing two bad alternatives, among which he cannot refuse to choose. And the process deprives him of something he already had. Still, it is quite possible that the victim is himself a criminal, or that coercion is justified, or that the threat does good in the long run, and so on. Coercion is a morally negative notion, but its undesirability is a substantial moral question and not just an analytic truth based on the definition of the terms *threat* and *coercion*. One should not be deceived into thinking that the fact that a coercer takes something away from his victim makes this action prima facie wrong in any interesting sense. Suppose a robber has some booty that the police try to get back. It could be argued that if the robber is coerced to give away this booty the situation is at least analogous to a rights violation, and thus the normative definition of coercion applies to it. This is a bad idea simply because the robber has no right to keep the booty freely; and yet he may be genuinely coerced to give it away. Coercion is cruel, even when it is justified.

4 | Coercive Institutions

The motivation of institutional coercive agents

Institutions: a blueprint

One agent is unable to coerce another one, his intended victim, as we have already seen, if his threat is not believable and convincing. This means, roughly, that he must be visibly motivated to coerce and the victim must have no chance to escape, either because of the coercer's power advantage or due to coercive circumstances. The crucial question concerns whether the coercer will be willing to realize his personally intrinsically disadvantageous threat. In other words, the coercer must be taken to be rigid in his behavior— he must be supposed to follow a plan without a modification.

My argument is the following: the coercer's rigidity outside its rare personally motivating contexts can be understood only if the coercer is backed by a formal or informal coercive institution. A social contract makes power exercise possible. The rules and the roles of coercive institutions provide the coercer with such a distribution of social utilities that, if he subscribes to them, he is able to motivate his action in a suitable manner. Much conceptual clarification and normative argument is needed before we can judge this thesis. However, this much is clear: the institutional coercer must be able to forget his own strictly personal and prudent good.

It is impossible to understand the wholesale requirement of the rigidity of coercive policies if they are not based on an explicit and even a formal institution. We miss the rule, which the victim should know and which makes the coercer's threats convincing. All this seems plain enough: an agent participates in an institution only if he has a sufficient reason to do so. It is always possible to ask exactly why one promises something, or presents a threat. And in the case of threats, we have already failed to locate any systematic intersubjective rules for selecting the kind of strategy that makes sense of the coercer's decision to realize the threat should the victim resist.

When we face the idea that the coercer's utilization of the threat institution remains incomprehensible in some fairly normal, everyday situations, we must then conclude that threatening is not sensible as a relatively isolated social practice but is sensible as an integral part of an institution. If the institution's organizational and legitimate role does not provide a rational function for threats and coercion, we shall simply fail to understand that area of social life.

To repeat the main point: an institution is utilized by a coercer because of some sufficient reasons. Now, threat is itself a social institution whose utilization does not seem to be justified by good reasons in a large number of cases. This is the problem to be solved in terms of the more advanced institutions. The police and army are the paradigm coercers. Their practices show us what threats really mean. Amateurs only imitate them. As an empirical hypothesis, we may suggest that private coercion emerges only after its formally institutionalized counterpart.

Examples of such explicitly organized institutions that are neither formal nor legitimate are the Mafia and the more recent Italian Red Brigades, an extreme left-wing terrorist group. Their objectives are different; one coerces for private profit, the other for a utopian social order. Their justification is also different, but it is almost impossible to say what it is, as their rule of silence is strict, and if broken, leads to dishonesty anyway under the pressure of old and new commitments. Secrecy both constitutes and contributes to their group identity.[1]

Even if the norms are insufficiently known to their own members, both examples illustrate institutions that are not formal but are still explicit and structured. They are also generally recognized as illegitimate; actually, they are illegal. This means that their norms, practices, rules, methods, and values cannot be written down, made official, and be openly enforced, in the normal senses of these terms. Illegal institutions cannot be fully consolidated. Although this is even trivially true, it must not be forgotten that many efficient factors prevent such institutions as the Mafia and the Red Brigades from suffering from an internal dispersion should the members become rebellious.

The basic factor in the game theoretical perspective is the applicability of a multiagent prisoner's dilemma to the situation. Suppose the institution starts deteriorating and becomes a trap to its own members. If all agents quit, practically everybody will be best off, but no one would like to be the first one to go; and yet somebody must be first. The internal persecution agency is working, however, simply because the members are still participating in the life of the institution. Therefore, the first one to leave will suffer terribly. No one can either leave first or even communicate such an idea, and thus all must stay, even if they would all profit by escaping cooperatively. Now, they must be content with a less than maximum personal expected utility.

However, if there is a widespread motivation to escape and it happens that the internal violent control mechanism is temporarily made inefficient enough, an ensuing mass escape will make the institution collapse. The Mafia and the Red Brigades can be supposed to suffer from this basic weakness. Their structure cannot be enforced in such a way that its effectiveness would be independent of the present strength of the institution itself. Mere self-control is like a house of cards.

My basic questions concerning explicit but not formal institutions are the following. What makes the life of a coercive agent different within an explicit coercive institution, such as the Mafia, from that of the paradigmatic private robber? And, more specifically, what makes the Mafia so eminently convincing to their victims? Anyway, we know how efficient and deeply ingrained in our social life such violent institutions have always been and how inefficient the battle against crime has been, as waged by the coercive agencies of the legitimate political states.

To start with, we assume now that a coercive agent within an explicit coercive institution accepts his institution as subjectively desirable or valid, in the present, rather special sense of the term *valid*. In other words, the coercer commits himself to an institution I shall call an explicit coercive institution. His reasons for his commitment form an empirical sociological problem, which cannot be solved in a philosophical study. The coercer may think that the institution provides a social revenge, fulfills a historical and traditional purpose, is a valuable element of popular justice, is a religious absolute norm, is useful to all its members, or is profitable to him personally. The possible reasons are many and varied and seem to range from religious fanaticism and belief in destiny to petty self-interest and camouflaged egoism.

Nevertheless, no individualistic prudent motivation can suffice to make coercion convincing to its victims in the cases in which it must be used as a consistent policy. Therefore, the purely egoistic motivation of the coercer in the institution may be left out immediately; it just confuses the main issues. The basic thesis is that an explicit institution has an effect on the coercer's motivation such that his threats become convincing to the victim in even those cases that are not convincing within the personally motivated, prudent cases of motivation. An informal social contract is made and recognized.

Can the distribution of the coercer's subjective utilities within the institution differ from the noninstitutional case in such a way that the coercer's prudent motivation will become convincing as a policy to the victim? The answer will be given along the following lines. We know that personal coercion is very seldom prudentially rational. Therefore, when the coercer, an individual agent, starts coercing the victim within the institution, he cannot presume that its rules apply only to those cases that, by chance, happen to be also the prudentially rational instances of coercion. The coercer must show evidence for the fact that within the institution he sometimes crosses the limits of prudent rationality. If he thinks of himself as a rational agent within the institution, he should also be able to solve this conflict between the emerging irrationality of individual action and the independently accepted rationality of social action—that is, action according to the rules of the coercive institution. The effect on the distribution of the coercer's own subjective utilities may be only secondary. The ultimately effective factor in establishing the convincingness of the coercer's threat is his visible commitment to the goals and principles of the institution.

Formal coercive institutions

Merely explicit coercive institutions are typically illegitimate. In a political state, these institutions are secret in the sense that implies restrictions even on their internal information flow. Only legitimation makes a coercive institution fully knowable, but such a status also risks its functions and even existence. Recall that the term *legitimation* need not imply moral acceptability in any objectivist sense but merely the simpler idea that the institution in question is open to all. It may also be arranged in a certain way within the system we call the state, that is, the institution may be part of the state. Let's take a simple example: the Mafia is an explicit but illegitimate institution (it is not and it cannot be public and open); a private security agency is a legitimate institution (it is public and open); the police force is a state institution (its principles and purposes are specified in the law).

The main problem concerns institutions like state intelligence agencies. They are legalized and secret at the same time. Perhaps we can say that they are legitimate, because (or if) their code of conduct is written down, their decisions are at least indirectly under the public control, and their vacancies are open to talent. Citizens are often afraid that this is not the case. It is indeed quite possible that an unjust state may have institutions that are illegitimate and live their own camouflaged life, like the South American death squads organized perhaps by the local militia.

What, then, are coercive formal institutions, in the strong sense of the term? As I am not constructing a political theory, I shall not try to provide a full account of these matters, important as they are. Instead, I shall give a minimalist account of coercive formal institutions in terms of some necessary conditions of their existence. In other words, such features are mentioned that will allow us to identify a formal coercive institution among a set of its merely explicit variants. The ideas I shall present now will exclude the private security business, as discussed by Robert Nozick. I shall return to it.

Now, a *formal* institution must satisfy the following conditions:

(1) it is an element of the state, when the state is understood in its normal political sense in an international comparative perspective; (2) it is constituted through rules and norms that are systematic, public, controlled, and enforced, and, moreover, can be changed through some special, partly bureaucratic methods; and, finally (3) it has a positive normative status for its individual agents, so that they are under the typical obligations created by the very existence of the formal institution. These various and not quite mutually independent conditions give us a picture of what is meant when one calls the formal institution a legitimate institution: the institution is arranged in such a way and is embedded in such a context that any individual agent will both know the institution and be under an obligation to act in full recognition of its existence and goals.

Examples of formal coercive institutions are easy to give, and they can be classified immediately in terms of their relations to state power. First of all, we have a court system, which is an overarching control mechanism with a double function: courts both utilize and control the actions of coercive agents. This is to say that some formal coercive agents realize the orders of law courts and are responsible before the law. This is the key official idea. Nevertheless, as we know, sometimes the maximal efficiency of some specialized branches of the formal institution may require the relaxation of the idea of responsibility in the legal sense.

Second, we have such examples of the formal institution as the police, penal institutions, the intelligence service, and the army. These institutions have a primary right to present threats in the sense that no coercive institution of the state can exercise coercive power against them. All actual coercive power is located here, so that these institutions are responsible for presenting the ultimate threats against victims who might escape any situation that does not entail, say, police action. Their threats extend to killing.

Third, customs and internal revenue services are examples of formal coercive institutions that may not have their own resources to realize any serious threats. Still, they are at least partly genuine coercive institutions in so far as they present threats against the welfare of some individuals who act in unacceptable ways. For instance, a person may believe he is taxed unfairly. If he does not pay, he is threatened by the internal revenue service by extra taxation. He may take his case to the law court, but if he loses the case he will be faced with police action against him. In this way, the threats of customs and the internal revenue service and the like are not immediately serious as to their consequences, mainly because those institutions cannot use violence. Yet, ultimately they are able to utilize the power of the institutions that do present violent threats.

This reveals how and why legitimate coercion has a hierarchic structure. Many threats are indeed serious, and their use is restricted to some special agencies, even if other agencies can present threats which in the end presuppose violence. And there is no doubt that the police and the army are able to maim and kill people more or less on a routine basis.

Fourth and finally, any social structure contains coercive institutions that are not really parts of the state organization but that are entitled to coerce, even moderately violently, because they have special permission from the state. Examples are private security firms and the organizers of various types of public events. These bodies can use violence, and as such they are in line with the police and the army, but their rights are more limited in this respect. Ultimately, they are supposed to borrow the power of the state institutions. The state can grant coercive rights to institutions outside the state, if this is seen as desirable.

In sum, there are both serious and nonserious coercive positions. The state coercive institutions form a hierarchy with respect to their access to serious—that is, violent—threats. Moreover, there are two types of coercive institutions, those that are part of the state and those that get their right from the state. Such institutions are controlled by the state.

The main results of the discussion are as follows. First, because a rational motivation to coerce or a perceived rigidity must be explained, special attention must be paid to how different institutions solve the problem of motivating its agents. If the motivation problem is taken care of, and if the solution applies to a specific coercive game, the victim can be coerced, granting that the victim knows where he is and against what kind of coercer he acts. Second, it seems natural to suppose that the coercer's deep commitment to his own institution helps and, indeed, solves the motivation problem. However, in the case of merely explicit coercive institutions, there is no guarantee that this solution via conscience will succeed regularly enough. Certain precautions against lapsing should probably be taken. In the case of formal coercive institutions, the same problem returns in a different form: if an agent is not the ideal coercer nor a completely socially oriented agent, he normally should not be trusted, especially if the value of social justice is set very high. The individual's own life and limb are, quite naturally, closer to him than considerations of abstract justice; not perhaps when he thinks of the principles of life in some more solemn settings, but when he actually faces the possibility of getting badly hurt. If the ideal coercer is postulated, the discrepancy that is bound to exist between the prudent and the ideal coercer becomes clear.

Private coercive institutions

At this point we turn to a consideration of private protective associations, to use Robert Nozick's term.[2] He gives an interesting account of the emergence of a dominant private protective association in the state of nature. His main point is, simply, that the protection business is something we need both in the state of nature and also later on in more civilized social conditions. According to his natural rights theory, we are entitled to this type of service and, therefore, if we purchase it, it can be sold to us quite legitimately. Competitive life has its hazards, which lead to the emergence of a new type of business, namely, protection. And of course, this is no protection racket arranged in the mobster style, so that we would need protection from our eager protectors. We are dealing with an honest private deterrent institution whose object is to protect the customers from both unjust and immoral attacks and from the exploitation of the controversial interpretations of the rules of social competition. Finally, we see that a dominant protective institution is prone to emerge simply because social resources and efficiency are crucially important, and they tend to become monopolized. If there is neither a state nor a second-level coercive institution to enforce antitrust laws, it is quite natural to suggest, as Nozick does, that a coalition will take over the whole business within the borders of some geographical area. We need not go any deeper into the details here.

Nozick finds this monopoly institution lacking in effectiveness and certain properties demanded by natural justice. He thinks that no such "ultraminimal state" that is constituted simply by a dominant protective institution can be morally justifiable as a state. It seems to be the case, however, that he misses the real criticism against such institutions as possible states because the criticism entails a much more complex social life than he is willing to recognize. His libertarianism is conceptually too poor to give an account of how problems concerning protective agents can be overcome.

Nozick's own tentative reasons against a private protective institution are, first, that it provides protection only to those who can pay for it. Not everyone can pay and, therefore, anyone who cannot will be left on his own. This state of affairs is certainly unacceptable from the point of view of justice. Basic safety belongs to all; it is one's basic natural right. Second, a deeper reason emerges: the state-resembling institution may be expected to make an announcement to the effect that it claims the monopoly of power for itself, so that it will punish all other wielders of violence-based power. As Nozick says, no private institution can morally do that. If you don't pay, the institution allows people to use force against you. But the institution, however dominant in its own time and sphere, should not announce that no other enterprise may now or later compete against it. Private business is indeed a free market. Any monopoly claim without the corresponding competitive edge is without foundation.

Both of these problems are real, but neither of them hits the mark. I shall argue next that a private protection institution cannot recruit reliable workers from the population of rational libertarians. The job is too demanding. Nozick's workers may join the protection institution even if they will not work reliably. Some requirements will be too demanding, although it may be tempting to take the job — especially if one knows that it is permissible to refuse to act.

Let us suppose that a person wants protection and gets it from the dominant protective institution. What is he supposed to get? What must the private institution offer in order to convince the customer that the services are in principle adequate? The institution should make it fully evident that (1) the agents will really help even in extremely demanding and dangerous cases; and that (2) such action is fair. Notice that even if you suppose that the customer is a rugged frontier man who can take care of his own business in all conceivable circumstances, he may still need the insurance given by the private institution. He is afraid of the inconceivable.

Whatever the personal characteristics of the customer, he still needs the insurance policy to cover the inconceivable cases. Even the strongest cannot rely merely on their own power. Luck may be against them. If insurance is available, why not buy it, just in case? Notice that modern fire insurance is unsatisfactory just in this respect. They do not cover the rare, strange, and suspicious cases.

So, let us suppose that a strong, enterprising, but careful person hires an agent to take care of those dangerous cases that he cannot handle himself. The agent has made a very bad deal. He has now promised to get involved in those cases that are difficult or even impossible to handle. And if the customer is tough-minded enough, he need not care very much in what kind of conflicts the agent (hired coercer) will become involved. He is just a hired hand, who should have known better before he signed the contract. Business deals are matter-of-fact things, which should be exploited in full in order to minimize their costs. Our strong customer can now start things he earlier never dreamt of. Correspondingly, the coercive agent will find his life expectancy shortened.

All this is perfectly consonant with the natural rights theory. Another example of a bad business contract is that made by some African blacks who actually sold themselves to slavery for some colorful cloth and a handful of beads. The contract was supposed to be valid and not unilaterally breakable, however disastrous later results were for the blacks. Prudential and utilitarian arguments are supposed to be void before the natural law of respecting a freely made contract. The fact that the slave did not quite understand what he was doing when agreeing to sell his own right to his future master is simply irrelevant, at least according to this strict interpretation of the natural rights and law. As Richard Tuck has put it: "According to Molina the 'Aethiopians,' that is the blacks, were in that position: there was no reason to suppose that they were not voluntary slaves, and they could have made themselves such for any sort of return, ranging from their lives to a string of beads. . . . It was a theory which involved a picture of man as a free and independent being, making his own decisions and being held to them."[3]

Nozick's private protective associations have employees who, as libertarian free men, are so severely constrained by the demands of natural rights and laws that they sooner or later find out that they are in equally deep trouble as that in which the slaves used to be. Moreover, their ideological situation is similar, as no salary and no remunerative efforts can ultimately compensate for what their jobs involve. The hired coercer may be worked to death or may be put through a probabilistic survival machine again and again, until his luck runs out.

My conclusion is that no prudent and well-informed individual will sign an unconditional employment contract with a coercive institution, except for a limited period of time in such special conditions where catastrophes are known to be very rare. Normally, he would want to include a clause that makes the change of employer easy.

As to the second demand on the coercion business, that is, that it should be fair, we notice that a hired coercer may face two of his client's enemies, enemy #1 and enemy #2. Suppose enemy #1 is stronger and meaner than enemy #2. What should the hired coercer do? The standard idea of fairness dictates that he should not distinguish between the two enemies on the basis of their power differences. On the contrary, he should deal with both in a similar way. If he cannot take on both at once, or sequentially, he should use a fair lottery, or toss a coin to choose his opponent. Suppose, moreover, that the threats presented by the two enemies against the client (the victim) are similar in terms of their expected harm, so that it is immaterial to the victim in what order the hired coercer deals with them. The two enemies may in this case insist that the coercer not distinguish between them, especially if each feels he is entitled to attack the victim's interests.

Compare the situation again with that of police action: police cannot suppose at the outset that their targets are guilty. They are not punishing people, and even if the worst crimes should be punished first, suspects should to be treated equally. The idea of being a suspect can be compared to the two enemies having the same expected negative effect on the victim's interests. Therefore, the hired coercer should treat them equally. Nevertheless, no private institution works in this way. In the free market, every agency must minimize its costs, and then we may expect, ceteris paribus, that the coercer will deal with the weaker opponent first. Notice that the duty to deal equally with both enemies has nothing to do either with formal contracts or with bargaining. Each enemy will insist on equal treatment on the basis of his natural right.

Moreover, if the threats presented by the two enemies are not similar, the victim will naturally insist that the worst case, say enemy #1, is taken care of first. But a prudent coercer tries once again to handle the weaker opponent first. Such a bias must be settled already in the business contract between the victim and his hired coercer. But the effects work again against the hired coercer, who tends to become formally committed to dealing with the worst cast first: he will suffer because of his weaknesses. He has again taken a step toward a hopelessly demanding job.

To conclude, let us return to the position of the hired coercer. He has signed a contract that allows the victim and the institution to demand supererogatory decisions from him as his duty. This is an inconsistent idea, of course, because supererogatory acts are not duties, according to the definition. It is, nevertheless, true that supererogatory deeds can be expected from a commercial power-wielding agent on a routine basis. No one is bound to go into a flaming house or stop a bullet, except the poor agent whose contract says so. It is indeed the case that there are jobs like fireman and bodyguard where exactly these heroic performances are required. If they fail, they did not do their job. They may be called heroic, but this is only lip service. They were duty bound to do it anyway.

A soldier's career is a still better example. When the state starts losing a war, individual soldiers are quite normally used like cannon fodder, in the name of national survival. They are subject to mutilation and death without heroic overtones, as a matter of strictly enforced duty. And if luck in warfare changes, then the winner's sacrifices in terms of the large number of deaths may remain unquestioned. Thus there are jobs, like those of a police officer and a professional soldier, which effectively demand supererogatory acts on a routine basis; but there are also natural positions, like that of a nonprofessional, drafted army private, whose duties cross the limits of genuine heroism in crises situations.

I do not think that this cruel aspect of duty within coercive institutions has been seen clearly enough in the recent debate on ethics and social philosophy. We all expect that we are adequately protected. Even if we are the ones from whom someone is protected, we still insist that the protection business be absolutely fair. Most of all, we reject exceptions because of variable circumstances. But you cannot buy that kind of ideal service. You may buy ideology and promises from the owner of the safety business. You cannot expect that someone would really fulfill those dreamy promises. Like Machiavelli's mercenary soldiers, the protection institution will ultimately leave the loser on his own and stay with the winner in order to share the booty.

The problem we must focus on is the following. How is it possible that a well-informed and prudentially rational individual may come to believe that a protective agent really resembles the ideal coercer to such a degree that it is conceivable that he will not back out from the situation where he faces uncompensated, prudentially unjustifiable risks? It also is interesting that the problems that we found hidden within Hegel's state and its power machinery reappear in the case of Nozick's libertarian politics. But the roots of the problem are identical: there is no road from private business and prudential subjectivity to the acceptance of social duty. I mean of course that duty according to which individuals adopt others' goals and demands as their own. As I argued, exactly this is required in the case of coercive policies. But why should anyone accept such a coercive role? The answer I suggest is that the role is internal to the coercive institution. I also suggest that this internality logically entails the concept of authority. If the relevant social authority is broad enough, an agent may have no choice as to whether to accept it or not. He is originally under its control, and thus the demands of a coercive role need not appear as new and shocking even to a beginner. He does not join a society but is originally within its bounds. No choice apart this exists. This is to say that every citizen is, in this present perspective, tied to the authoritative demands of the state. I think this is close to what Hegel is aiming at, although his idea that one may make a prudently motivated career choice looks so misleading.

Models for moral motivation

The limits of coercion arise in at least five ways. First, a rational coercer is supposed to present believable and convincing threats and, depending on his less than maximal degree of rigidity, his victim may negotiate a deal or present a counterthreat, so that the coercer's grip relaxes. As I explained above, the rigidity of the coercer determines the limits of his power against the victim across possible situations. However, the descriptive aspects of these limits do not interest us any longer.

Second, a well-informed victim is bound to realize that a merely prudent agent will not be able to stage a serious threat. The limits we are discussing here concern the kind of convincing threats that are supposed to be communicated to the victim. If the coercer is an institutional agent, is he really going to risk personal loss in order to fulfill the demands of his institutional role? To answer this question affirmatively, all parties involved in the exchange must believe that the coercer has justified the idea that his social commitments overcome his personal good in such cases where he presents a threat. A rational agent needs reasons for all his decisions.

This leads us to the third point: an institutional coercive agent can justify his actions only as far as he sees the institution he is part of as morally justifiable, fully motivating, and worth supporting. Moreover, the coercer's personal relation to the institution is such that it is fit for him to support it through the required coercive measures against the victim. These two aspects, justification and motivation, are indeed mutually independent: a person may well see the reasons for, say, strong police action, but it does not follow that he should try to participate, or even admit that someone should participate. And it is not clear why the coercer, as a police officer, should accept as just the requirements of his role in all relevant circumstances. The missing link in the argument is the premise that the coercer's personal position within the institution is such that he can ground his decision to present a threat on the alleged fact that his institution is embedded in an acceptable, good, and just social order. However, morality does not motivate us quite that easily. The moral limits of institutional coercion are drawn, thus, on the basis of the victim's perception of the coercer's motivation to accept his own institutional role, when the acceptance presupposes the coercer's reasoned belief in the morality, or justice, of this part of the global social order.

These ideal limits of successful coercion are too narrow. As I shall argue in due course, coercive institutions typically need a number of coercive agents working in the most variable circumstances. And once the victim realizes that the given coercer might have already crossed his own personal limits of acting in his role, the victim need not find the threats convincing. The coercive institution itself must take precautions against certain demanding situations where the coercer's loyalty to his institution may collapse.

In a rather surprising manner, the institutional motivation of the coercer is not only a necessary, but also a sufficient, condition of the successful threat. Therefore, the fourth limit can now be identified: the coercive institution must check that its power does not depend only on each coercer's personally accepted moral ideas concerning his own actions and the justice of the institution. This last limit is drawn by the institution's ability to motivate the coercer to present threats even in those cases in which he himself fails to see what his own positive reasons are. In other words, the coercive agent's power to convince depends on the power the institution exercises over him—presumably on coercion and authority. This fourth limit is the crucial one. It is at the same time both an important and a vulnerable factor: coercion is typically the organization's answer to some extreme and surprising situations. Even for this reason alone, the coercer's personal ideas about it cannot be granted any decisive status; but, on the other hand, if his personal ideas do not count, it is not rational for him to go on. The dilemma is soluble only within some rather narrow limits, namely, in those cases where the coercer has good reasons to accept the idea that it is part of his role to coerce even without seeing why he does it. He may recognize a global justification for his role, without being able to derive any local—moral or prudent—justification for his case-specific decisions.

From the point of view of the coercive institutions, no merely agent-relative justification may suffice. In some crucial survival situations, it may well be necessary to coerce the coercer to coerce. This fifth and last functional limit—which determines when the coercer will become a victim—is certainly problematic in a normative perspective, because we suppose now that, even if a rational coercer does not accept coercive policies, the other members of the institution might demand it from him. It seems that this fifth limit is usually built into our central coercive agencies, like armies in combat. Survival is one of the basic motives for the exercise of power, and in crucial crises moral considerations tend to become irrelevant, distorted, and reinterpreted, so that the coercer's original justification will be lost, too. Moral considerations then give room to our more elementary needs and goals, as David Hume for instance was prepared to argue.[4] The coercer himself faces something like coercive threats, should he fail to act.

Accordingly, it is important to any coercive institution to construct its basic structure in such a manner that these five limits can be incorporated into it and their constitution explained in an intelligible way. Otherwise, social power collapses into naked violence, which cannot do the work we expect from power.

Next I shall explain what simple elements of a social structure are needed, how they should be arranged, and what moral ideas and ideals must be invoked if the coercive institutions are going to be fully convincing to the victim and effective in general.

Perhaps the most interesting aspect of this whole topic is revealed when we ask whether there is one uniform set of moral notions, or a single moral theory that makes the success of coercion look rationally understandable both from the point of view of the coercer and his victim. I shall argue that no such theory exists. On the contrary, the coercer and the victim should follow different moral guidelines. The coercer's case is especially complex, as he should be able to replace his prudent and generally utilitarian conceptions by some strictly deontological ideas of social duty.[5]

I shall argue that when a coercive agent justifies his own role within an institutional coercive organization, he must at some point employ deontological theses; otherwise personal justification is not functionally acceptable. The social structure needs and demands such guarantees. The basic fact is that his personal justification must show how the ultimate limits of institutional coercion can be reached in real life. Thus, my question is, How does he construct a moral justification that is both personally motivating and socially functional? A rational coercive agent cannot let function and mere efficiency override morality. But no social structure needs protective institutions whose members fail to act in the all-important hard cases. It is time to question how far a social system can push the limits of efficiency of its coercive institutions and still retain their basic justification.

The six structural elements that determine the limits we are seeking are as follows.

1. First, we have the coercer and the victim.

2. Each of these agents needs arguments that subjectively justify his actions and decisions and make sense of his situation. The idea of coercion itself implies certain normative requirements of the coercer and the victim, in the sense that if coercion is to be a successful mode of social interaction they must be inclined to reason in certain normatively binding ways. But because of a conflict situation, it cannot be automatically supposed that both parties take notice of such normative arguments: the victim may be especially unwilling to consider the coercer's reasons. Therefore, successful coercion may require also that the victim is under normative pressure to act in a certain suitable way.

3. Now, the victim's normative ideology is subject to strong influences from his reference group. His surrender will bring about causal consequences to the members of, say, his family, his political party, or his nation. Thus, the victim's justificatory and motivating counterarguments will depend not only on his own prudent ideas about the consequences but also on the social demands of his reference group. All the social considerations of honor, virtue, duty, solidarity, and rights will make his decision more difficult.

4. If the victim's reference group is his source of motivational tension, the coercer's reference group has, on the contrary, a facilitating effect. If he is weak in his commitment to his role or if he uses the wrong motivational arguments, he will make the members of his reference group (his fellow agents and their institution) look less credible. A formal coercive institution has its typically hierarchic structure, so that the coercer is bound to recognize the presence of the superior coercive agent, or someone who occupies a higher level position within the institution. A necessary condition of coercive institutional motivation is therefore the superior coercive agent, with his (or their) combined authority, coercion, and manipulation-based methods. The coercer cannot be expected — by the superior coercive agent — to accept personal losses in a systematic and predictable fashion if no sources of control exist. The superior coercive agent advises, surveys, punishes, commands, and manipulates the agent with a view to guaranteeing his success. It is important that the coercer's personal

justificatory arguments take explicit notice of the existence of this superior agent; the superior agent's presence makes it easier for a rational coercer to accept that he should be the ideal coercer, or an ideally responsible social agent.

5. However, it is not just the fact of the superior coercive agent's being there that is important in the present normative context, but the idea that he or his institution can offer a justificatory argument of his own. What is needed is an explicit statement of why the superior coercive agent is functionally needed, why and how the coercive institution is supposed to work, who its members are, and what its relation is to the rest of the social order. My conjecture is that this second-level normative argument is essentially related to the basic survival rights of society and its members. The whole structure of a formal coercive institution is, typically, based on the idea that any social order has the right to protect its members and to guarantee its own continued existence as a necessary condition of the well being of the citizens. This idea may be simple, but considerable complications will arise in the course of the exploration of its details.

6. The last element in the complex structure we are sketching is the global justification, given in terms of ascriptions of justice, to the whole social order—and consequently to its elements. In general, we presuppose that the whole society in question is just and its political order is legitimate. Then the coercive institution is also automatically acceptable. The normative characteristics of society and the social order are the most necessary general elements of the argument a rational coercive agent needs. We want to stipulate that the society is just and fair.

In sum, we recognize in these six elements problems in three general areas. (1) Why does a society need to coerce? (2) How can a coercive institution guarantee its own efficiency and at the same time grant a rational status to its own agents? What is the social motivation of the coercer? What is the nature of the authority of the superior coercive agent over the coercer, given the legitimate social order? Should this authority be complemented with a second-level coercive relation, against the coercer? (3) What are the individual coercers' subjectively correct answers to the questions in (1) and (2)? Why would a rational person stay in the business of legitimized coercion? These are the questions we shall address in what follows.

We cannot understand institutional coercion without a theory of authority. We can, however, proceed quite far by using the common-sense notion of authority, so we need not worry about it as yet. The crucial difficulty will be our attempt to explain the interplay between coercion and authority in the case of attempts to guarantee the rigidity and convincingness of threats against a relatively powerful and determined victim, supported by his right claims.

Now, every single interaction between the coercer and the victim is embedded in a nested set of social structures, from decision making at the global level all the way to, say, a pistol shot—a realized threat. The actual combat zone is located, necessarily, between two individual agents. A threat implies a relationship between two actual individuals. It is strange that this simple fact is so often dismissed. Institutions cannot fight; only individuals can. The key point is that action takes place at the level of individuals.

Justice, perversity, and survival: demand of coercion

The argumentative strategy I am going to use is to start from the most abstract personal motivational considerations we may entertain and proceed toward situational prudence. When we start from the abstract levels of social legitimization and general rights, we find these conditions to be necessary but not sufficient to overcome the paradoxical nature of individual coercion. We must construct some duties, too.

I am not saying that this is the only possibility of establishing a sufficient condition for the motivation to coerce; it is only one alternative, whose validity and suggestiveness must be judged separately. Another way to proceed would be by referring to a saintly or heroic agent who internalizes the requirements of his social morality so deeply that he forgets his prudent self altogether. This strategy, which is used at least implicitly in many traditional moral treatises in order to explain what one should ideally do, is clearly not feasible in the present context. We want to explain—not assume—heroism.

So, what is the most general ideology the coercer can find to support his decision to accept his role? Of course, it is the double thesis that his society is both legitimate and just. The first element is, as we may stipulate, a descriptive one; but the second is, on the contrary, fully normative. The former fixes the area within which the justice-related considerations apply. If we are clear about its context, we may speak about justice alone. Nevertheless, we shall be using the term *legitimized social order* every now and then, because we need its descriptive message, namely, the idea that coercive institutions are embedded within a historical state and its power hierarchy.

I cannot present anything like a theory of social justice. Luckily, it is not really needed. The present topic does not concern what R. M. Hare calls the "fully critical level" of morality but rather its practical roots.[6] Therefore, any comprehensive idea of justice is useful for our present purposes, but in fact we should have in mind John Rawls' full-scale conception.[7]

As an individual agent, the coercer is supposed to reflect on moral principles. Those considerations will provide him with a motive to act, however weak. The only important constraint is that these principles should not categorically deny the use of, say, punitive action and all violent threats against other human beings. But this is a weak constraint indeed; we can say that no theory of justice is even minimally complete without an account of punitive and corrective justice.

No account of punitive justice is accepted if it denies society's right to punish. But it cannot punish without force. It is evident that punishment can be understood as a realized deterrent threat, as in cases in which the victim breaks the law knowing the likelihood of being captured and subjected to personal suffering. And at least in some cases, justice requires coercion, too. Another way of thinking of these matters is to posit that any social order that permits punishment must also permit violence against those to be punished. Absolutely nonviolent punishment is optional for its victims to accept. However, if violence is used, presumably coercion must also be accepted. Coercion uses threats, which embody violence only contingently and occasionally, and without being morally more dubious than the methods of direct violence. On these grounds, it seems safe to conclude that any complete, realistic, or nonanarchistic theory of justice allows in principle for coercion by institutional agents. Thus, given a just social structure, we need to ask in what situations coercive power can be used. To make the following discussion more realistic and to avoid unnecessary complications, let us stipulate that the society we are referring to is ideally just, but its members are only relatively moral, to a degree short of final perfection. And we presuppose that they cannot profit from psychiatric treatment. They may be wicked, but they are sane.[8]

My basic point is this: given a just social order, it is not demanded that its members always act according to their social obligations. Let us now look briefly at ways in which even a perfectly just Rawlsian social order may get involved in serious punitive business and be required to deter and actively coerce its members. Rawls makes a distinction between morality and justice, so that the latter concerns the primary institutions of the social order and the former, individual persons and their virtues. Yet Rawls writes: "Among individuals with disparate aims and purposes a shared conception of justice establishes the bonds of civic friendship; the general desire for justice limits the pursuit of other ends. One may think of a public conception of justice as constituting the fundamental charter of a well-ordered human association."[9]

It is certain that Rawls is not doing moral theory. But he constantly mixes morality and justice and creates the impression that his principles of justice, which apply to any broad social order, can also work as principles of individual moral virtue. In this passage, he simply supposes that justice motivates individuals to act justly. But to act justly is a moral demand, and if justice is independent of morality, it cannot provide an efficient motivating moral principle. Justice says merely what the representative social agents are supposed to do. It does not explain why they would do so.

Rawls of course postulates that his agents are both rational and moral. If they are "moral representative individuals," they certainly follow the prescriptions created by the original contract made behind the veil of ignorance. But if they are only prudently rational, or if their pet moral views are somewhat weird, there cannot be any guarantee that everything will go smoothly after they have emerged from behind the veil.

The problem is that the state of ignorance is completely different from the situation in real social life. I agree while behind the veil to obey the rules of justice simply because of some precautionary minimax measures. I cannot but support liberty and grant the validity of the difference principle as a lifesaver, should I happen to reemerge as an unfortunately situated social agent. But once I am back to social life, if I am rich and strong, I need not recognize any motive for following the difference principle independently of its consequences to my own present welfare. At least in some exceptional cases, I shall feel tempted to go back to the less demanding Pareto principle, or merely effective distributive measures; in actual social life, if I profit and no one loses, it may be difficult to persuade me that I should not utilize the opportunity. According to Rawls, I should not do so. Behind the veil of ignorance, I may be easy to persuade, but only because I happen not to know that I shall be on the winning side in the course of the future transactions.

It seems indeed to follow that no existing social order should assume that, once a just social order has been created, the state can relax the deterrent and punitive grip and let the citizens do what they please. Prudent nonrepresentative agents will be prone to forget their part in the social contract. If they are fully moral, they will certainly not forget; but it is implausible to stipulate that they indeed are moral. Moral motivation is fragile and cannot be made the independent foundation of social life.

In Rawls' *A Theory of Justice*, the postulation of the existence of moral agents allows us to avoid the question of punitive and corrective justice and the dilemmas of social conflict. The success of this avoidance is merely stipulative, though. Anthony Flew puts this idea well: "Rawls is thus talking as if people always and everywhere are or ought to be the passive creatures of active social institutions, with all goods of whatever kind doled out as unearned benefits to inert recipients."[10] But what else one would expect from the people who must decide about their most important social arrangements without any information about themselves? Originally, they could not want anything special. Later, they are supposed to be happy with their impoverished lives.

It is indeed strange that Rawls does not work consistently at the level of the basic structure of the social order and its representative individuals but insists both that these agents be moral, real, individuals and, furthermore, that they find the shared principles of justice as motivational ideas: "the sense of justice is a settled disposition to adopt and to want to act from the moral point of view insofar at least as the principles of justice define it."[11]

Of course, if our "sense of justice" is only a necessary but not a sufficient condition for the realization of justice, it does not diminish the need for coercion. We must, however, recognize that the state should in some cases restrict the liberties of its virtuous citizens because of the imperfect conduct of less virtuous agents. This could not happen if we all retired behind the veil of ignorance and emerged as moral persons. Where are those disturbed persons supposed to come from? If they are real, the motivating effect of the original contract must be merely fictional. And it certainly is so; the basic structure should embody those principles established behind the veil, but they must also be made legitimate and enforced social norms and institutions. Individual morality cannot replace law and order, especially if the citizens are merely prudently motivated. But if complete morality is presupposed so that the original contract guides agents' joint social deliberations, no institutionalized social structure is needed at all.

As Rawls himself writes: "Liberty of conscience is to be limited only when there is a reasonable expectation that not doing so will damage the public order which the government should maintain. This expectation must be based on evidence and ways of reasoning acceptable to all."[12] This quotation shows why we may need coercive measures and therefore also a state structure. It hints at rather deep social conflicts.

I do not criticize Rawls. He leaves the problems open. However, we should keep in mind that justice-oriented motivational principles cannot be so complete as to counter the need for punitive measures against real individuals. And no distinct necessary conditions for the realizability of the Rawlsian social order are interesting, because we know from history that an incredible variety of different social orders, just and unjust, have been both stable and able to survive for long periods of time.

Justice must be taken to be logically independent of citizens' actual decisions and actions. This latter point is almost trivial: criminal acts may exist even in a just society; and the further away this society is located from the nexus of an absolutely ideal order the larger is the degree of prudent rationality that must be granted to some crimes. It might be possible to argue that within an ideal order and in good natural conditions all crime is simply irrational and even insane. Perhaps this is so. And in the same vein, the more our society deviates from the just ideal, the more alleged crimes there will be whose status and evaluation as irrational is unclear. Political terrorism is an example. Social changes and their associated problems bring about social unrest. A person may act against the customs and practices of a social order to such an extent that his action is criminal, but at the same time not immoral. Perhaps this agent is a competing moral theorist, for example, an anarchist; perhaps his religious values and empirical background beliefs are really widely different from those of the majority.

It must also be realized that society is an entity in real historical time, in the sense that its political, economic, and technical situation in the world changes constantly and thus the details of its normative constitution possibly change at a similar rate. All changes open up new problems, and no modification of, say, laws can be so fast and flexible that the possibility of justified disputes against them never arises. There is no natural, unequivocally clear, idea of justice, acceptable to everyone. On this basis, it seems clear that even in a just society there will be a definite need to use protective coercive measures against those agents who criminally or for ideological, theoretical, or personal reasons act against its established principles.

We have seen that both crime and "deviant" moral and religious theorizing constitute sources of disobedience and unlawful conduct even within a practically just social order. There is, however, a sort of independent explanation of these phenomena of unrest. This explanation does not cover all the relevant motives and subjectively posited goals in this area, but it does offer an interesting perspective on the problem of socially defined evil. The point is that some aspects of what we called social unrest incorporate elements of cruelty and exemplify the perversity of human motivation.

Philip P. Hallie gives quite an impressive analysis of the motivational grounds of human violent action, especially in his accounts of the "philosophies" of the Marquis de Sade, Edgar Allan Poe, and Friedrich Nietzsche.[13]

Let me quote Poe: "Induction, *a posteriori*, would have brought phrenology to admit, as an innate and primitive principle of human action, a paradoxical something, which we may call *perverseness*, . . . through its promptings we act, for the reason that we should *not*."[14]

Poe offers illustrations of what he means in two short stories, "The Imp of the Perverse" and "The Black Cat." In both stories, the narrator commits murder due to his malignancy, in one case in rage and in another because of ruthless financial speculation. They try to avoid the law in a perfectly prudent way by covering their tracks. And they are successful. Nevertheless, they are perverse and reveal themselves to the police by behaving in a self-destructive way. In the first story, the narrator simply confesses everything. In the second, he does the same in a symbolic way: he boasts that he is safe in his house, which is actually his murdered wife's burial chamber. But the devil hits back by making the hidden black cat lead the police to the corpse. In this way, Poe's idea of perversity is both clear and interesting; in some special cases, the stimulation we get from acting as we should not is so primitive that it cannot be successfully resisted. We know that we should not act. We are indeed prudent agents.

From our point of view, it is important to see two separate points. First, a person's perverse motivation works only against the background of his prudent rationality. It is because he sees that what he shall do is personally harmful and unreasonable that he is so strongly tempted to do it. Second, no moral edification or preaching can work against perversity. Only if moral education involves simple and strong indoctrination and conditioning can it be effective. Any acceptable moral education will probably have just the opposite effect: a perverse person acquires his motivation through a clear idea that he will do something wrong. That is why his moral norms are already presupposed by his motivation. Furthermore, the stronger the norms, the stronger the perverse motivation will be. In a paradoxical manner, the more a person is committed to morality, the stronger the perverse motivation will be. Perversity, Poe says, it is an "innate and primitive principle."

All this tends to show that state coercion is needed. Moral training and propaganda cannot be substituted for it. Whatever moral obligations, legal duties, and prescriptions of prudence there might be, they are open at least to perverse violations. Morality is motivationally self-defeating in a nontrivial sense.

Hallie also shows why Sade is an interesting moral philosopher, at least if we are ready to depart from the tradition of enlightenment and proceed toward the deeper and murkier waters of romanticism.[15]

The implicit point is that Sade is a non-Epicurean hedonist. Most hedonists are Epicurean, emphasizing the continuity of their pleasure and its future prospects. But Sade is different; passion and its delirium justify everything, especially the further reaches of pleasure based on pain and cruelty.

I mention Sade because he sheds light on Poe's views; Sade requires and deserves a more thorough treatment elsewhere. Anyway, cruelty is a strong stimulus to the sadist, simply because it is both forbidden and creative of wholly new vistas. It is a motive, too. Thus Sade adds pleasure to the set of elements of perverse behavior. Poe, on the contrary, sees the idea of wrong as intrinsically motivating, without any emotions like pleasure. He simply postulates a rule that specifies that wrong intrinsically motivates a perverse personality. For Sade, perversity motivates us only through its consequences, as it makes our blood boil. Regardless of any technical details and theories, it should be clear that wrongdoing and irrationality may have their own motivating properties. Therefore, no degree of justice or general morality will make state coercive institutions redundant. The truth may be just the opposite.

Hallie identifies the "paradox of cruelty": "In general it may be said that the paradox of cruelty is this: the destruction of men . . . is both readily justifiable (in terms of stimulation, economic, or social need, etc.), and totally unjustifiable."[16] His point is that although cruelty is self-evidently wrong, people often do not regret acting cruelly. On the contrary, they may find it useful and fascinating. This is in the core of perversity.

In my view, we may admit that perversity, among other things, necessitates a coercive institutional machinery, working through its agents. And then the above-mentioned paradox comes in the following form: the coercer's action against the victim is often cruel, and as such it is impossible to justify; yet, cruelty is needed and made desirable in existing societies. Countercruelty—against a perverse opponent—may be justified, although cruelty is unjustifiable. This is indeed a paradox.

My suggestion is that countercruelty is a social necessity without an alternative—a necessary evil. And "ought" implies "can," so that one ought to avoid all cruelty, only if one can. From this it follows that because some cruelty is impossible to avoid it is not uniformly wrong. This idea works if and only if cruelty and violence are actually impossible to avoid. I shall try to explain in due course how this crucial sense of unavoidability is created within a social institution.

More important than the mere recognition that any state needs an army to protect its real or imaginary international interests is the following fact. Any state needs its internal coercive agencies, like the police, for the reason that it is possible that in the course of time internal rebellion and crime will emerge and increase. Power is typically a precautionary measure. Even if the social order is just and the members of the society are moral and uniformly support their social order, it does not follow that coercive institutions are not needed. As I already remarked, politics is an activity tied to ever-changing material and psychological conditions. With these changes, new situations emerge that create conflicts; but if the coercive capacity is not ready to be used, the formerly consensus-supported, just social order will collapse. When the consensus disappears, if there are no institutions embodying social power, it is open to anyone who desires to seize power. Then private individuals will rebel, finally organize themselves, and even establish private protective agencies— or armies.

The precautionary nature of coercive social power should be clear indeed. Power is not something a person grabs and uses every time he needs it. On the contrary, any social power base, or resource advantage, must be typically established well ahead of its actual use, whether this aims at some new positive achievement or merely at basic survival. Deterrent and latent power may become insufficient. A low crime rate is no argument in favor of dismantling all police organizations. Police are needed in case crime reemerges. Still, if we are able to predict scientifically that crime will never again reach any real magnitude, we may be willing to minimize our spending on the police. But no sociological knowledge may possibly convince political decision makers that all the relevant aspects of coercive institutions are absolutely redundant. People change their minds, and historical conditions turn around. Solid and persisting power bases are typically directed against such changes; their deterrent effects are thus utilized. Real societies, which do not approximate to any ideal conditions of justice, also guarantee the continued existence of their own unjust aspects by means of coercive institutions. Power can be used against all kinds of change. Coercive and especially deterrent forms of power are conservative; their repressive effects tend to be more permanent than their creative uses.

Let us then formulate the basic motivating principle for acquiring coercive and deterrent power: the basic motivation behind power and its exercise is the protection of power bases. This is a necessary condition, characterizing certain rational exercises of power. It does not seem to be a sufficient condition, though. That would be an exaggeration, like the otherwise interesting view of J. Rudnianski, who writes: "To the justified question: 'why?,' the answer is 'in order to stay in power,' for this is what the individuals wielding power desire."[17]

Now, many instances of the exercise of power imply goals that surpass the basic one. Let me discuss this interesting question briefly. It is indeed possible to give away power. There is nothing irrational in the story of a king who marries a divorced woman against the laws of the land that govern the behavior of the king. The king is then no more a king, and it is a matter of his personal preferences whether this suits him or not. But, compare this to the case of the Prince of Troy, who takes Helen by force and as a consequence finally loses his power base. If a person uses power to secure an asset and consequently loses power, the result is that he will not be able to keep his booty. Of course, he may be willing to exchange some of his resource advantages for the pleasures of female beauty; but, nevertheless, the basic ingredients of irrationality now become visible. He weakens his ability to get what he may want in the future and to retain what he already possesses. If he will actually lose what he has got by force because of the weakening of his resources, we have a clear-cut case of irrationality. But even in a case where the balance between power differentials remains in favor of the original winner, even after the partial loss of his power, it still may be said that he acted somewhat irrationally: he exchanged the possibility of acquiring further goods for one fixed good. In other words, by keeping maximum power a person might acquire more than the amount of goods he actually would receive in exchange for part of his power, or coercive potential. There is a close parallel in the case of money: consumption at the cost of capital is a paradigm of bad policy.

The result of the discussion above is, simply, that coercive potential is a necessary precautionary measure, whose possession is motivated by a constant need to guarantee the control over and survival of social institutions. One of the most basic considerations is our well-entrenched idea of the basic Hobbesian right to bodily survival. This extends easily to cultural and institutional survival. In the case of such a basic need and right as survival, precautionary measures cannot be too easily relaxed, and there need be little hesitation about the justification of violent methods conducive to that end. The demand of coercion is real.

Obligations and the supply of coercion

A subjective justification for coercion is available to a coercive agent of an institution. However, it is of such a general nature that nothing can yet be said in any particular case about whether his action is an example of the justified type of coercion. He is not rational if he surrenders his judgment so completely that we cannot ask any longer whether what he is doing by means of his threats is still within the subjective limits of the justified activities of the state.

Any coercer needs a supplementary criterion by means of which he can judge whether or not his actions are morally acceptable. There are two possibilities here: (1) the coercer is a part of a hierarchic social order; or (2) he is not. In relation to (2), the key problem is that a legitimate but noninstitutional coercive agent must always compare two ideas, namely, that his action is in general justified and that it could be avoided in this given case. Its possible avoidability itself has two sources: coercion is either outside the limits of legitimate action or outside the limits of prudent action. It may happen that the coercer does not see that his coercive efforts are justified at the level of state-related survival needs. The coercer may alternatively see that, by coercing, he will hurt his own interests in such a permanent manner that he really should back out now. Both types of decisional hesitation make systematic coercion impossible. The coercer may fail in some crucial cases, and we already saw that this is intolerable.

It is because of this hesitation that we need a hierarchic institution supported by authority; the superior coercive agent both determines when the coercer should present a threat and provides some guarantees that he will stay on course. To achieve his goals, the superior coercive agent uses both authority and coercion (see below).

I have already explained both (1) how and why the coercer's decisional rigidity is all-important if his threat is to be convincing to the victim; and (2) why the coercer may be expected to have a tendency to back out: his threats may backfire and they are risky. Therefore, a superior coercive agent is needed. He is located at an upper level of the institutional hierarchy and is authorized to supervise the coercer. He may also present threats and issue commands. The superior agent in his turn needs both a prudently motivating and a justifying argument for himself in order to make decisions to control the coercer in controversial situations. Let us deal with these one by one. Once we have clarified the superior agent's role, status, and methods we shall also have an account of the coercer's persistent motivation.

First, we must understand that the superior coercive agent makes his decisions because he accepts the general justificatory argument for institutional coercion (this is the survival case above). The superior agent also needs his personal, prudent motives. But, of course, these are drastically different from those of the coercer. This is important indeed; the problems of the subordinate coercive agent are related to violence and dramatic losses, like loss of life or limb. The superior agent is not a direct coercive agent, and his self-related considerations need not focus on any irreplaceable things (although this might happen in such cases where a judge is threatened by a terrorist group). Typically, the superior agent considers whether the subordinate agent's action will create blame against him and hinder, say, his career advancement. The superior agent indeed may be expected to have his own prudent motive for abstaining from supporting coercive policies in extreme cases. But as the superior agent is not directly involved, we need not always pay attention to this fact. In this way, the superior agent's influence is impersonal.

It seems that from the coercer's personal point of view the superior agent's verifiable rigidity is now especially important. If the coercer sees the superior coercive agent wavering, he need not see any reason for staying rigid regardless of the consequences. If the coercer is expected to accept the ultimate risks in connection with his threats in some demanding situations, the coercer should not anticipate the superior agent's indeterminate reactions in those situations. The coercer must be certain of the superior agent's support. Therefore, although the superior agent's rigidity may not be much of a problem to himself, he must be able to show a rigid face because of the difficulties the coercer must be expected to meet in severe cases.

The superior agent's rigidity requirement is an easy one. As he is never directly involved, it is more or less a stylistic feature of his authority over the coercer. But something can still be said about it: he, of course, is not a proximally effective agent in relation to the victim. Therefore, his moral responsibility for the suffering and the losses experienced by both the coercer and the victim is rather different from that of the coercer's. For example, if the victim is killed, the superior agent is not unproblematically counted as the killer. He just lets killing happen. Even if he would have licensed it, he could not have prevented it within the limits of the actual context of the killing. He accepts the killing, but he could not have prevented it, had he wanted to. He was not present. In this important way, the responsibility for the consequences of threats is more abstract and "thinner" than that of the coercer's. He deals with sets of licensed but still merely possible acts. He is not unconnected with these policies, but they are not his particular acts.

Our popular morality tends to put a great deal of weight on this simple point: the ultimate responsibility rests on the proximal agent. Distal agents have a much hazier role. If an occasion arises where their contributions are made the object of explicit moral and legal judgment, the case proves difficult to handle. Such situations are judged post hoc (as the war crimes of Vietnam show, compared to those of World War II).

Now, when the superior agent makes decisions, which all have unpredictable effects, he need not be too worried about their individual characterizations and ex post facto evaluations. He should keep in mind only the legitimate character of the state institution. He does not know what exactly the coercer will do or what the situation will prove to be like. He deals with sets of possible actions. Because such possibilities contain mutually incompatible alternatives, no unique moral judgment may emerge. If something wrong is actually done, something good and right might have been done in its place. The superior agent was not responsible for the actual decision.

The superior agent works in an open situation, where he need to take into account only the general justification of coercion. He works at the policy level. The higher the status, the thinner the responsibility: the agent at the highest levels need not worry about the proximal effects of the threats by the subordinate coercive agents. Nevertheless, sometimes this line of argument breaks down, as Adolf Eichmann saw in Jerusalem. Anyway, my conclusion is that the superior agent has a much thinner moral responsibility than the coercer has. He need focus mainly on the legitimacy and justice of the social order of which he is a part. His prudent considerations hinge on problems quite different from the coercer's worries.

Let me mention two examples involving such a distant attitude toward human life. First, millions of people starve to death every year, even though the Western world has surplus food. Normally, we are not willing to provide help that might have a negative influence on our own economic situation. But we are still shocked to see pictures of starving children, and we are ready to absorb great losses to save even one clearly identified person. To us, a person is an actually recognized, and not only an abstractly recognizable, human being. Psychologically, we find it difficult to care about what we do not see, as we cannot get emotionally involved with it.

Second, in war, it is a crime to murder children with whom you are face to face. Yet it is not a crime to drop a bomb on a hospital full of children from thirty thousand feet above it. Suppose that a person drops napalm bombs on a city knowing that they will kill only civilians—but not how many and who they are. He explains that his purpose is to terrorize the survivors and their leaders, but not to kill. Killing is only a means (in executions, it is the goal). It is ironic that the explanation of why this bombing is not a war crime is that the bombardier does not know who he kills, or that he does not intend to kill them, or that every individual has a random chance to survive. In direct shooting, this would not be the case; here, the agent directly intends to kill. The relevant fact is apparently that distal killing is different from face-to-face killing, because then the agent intends to shoot specific persons. The death of merely numerically identified stochastic human beings may be lamentable, but it is not unacceptable. The basic presupposition is that we tend to think of persons in terms of their perceived individuality and not in terms of their numerical identifiability as a member of the human species. Ultimately, only such identified persons matter.

If we really think in this way, it is easy to see why the superior agent's problems are different from the coercer's. Because he is not directly involved, it is not necessary for him to care either about the coercer or the victim. And the higher he is in the authoritative hierarchy, the lesser the motivational problems he faces as to the fate of the coercer. His motivational problems hardly exist.

Let me conclude this discussion by noticing how the moral responsibility for coercion and its violent threats tends to disappear into thin air when we seek for the roots of responsibility within the uppermost levels of the legitimate institutions. The coercer is directly responsible for what he did. The superior coercive agent deals with a number of similar cases and merely provides the guidelines for the coercer. Suppose then the third-level agent, who controls and observes the superior agent; this agent has lost all his connections to the coercer's violent tactics, as he merely takes care that the superior agent takes care that the coercer acts within certain predetermined limits. Our third-level agent deals with statistics, and his fate is identical with that of the whole system.

The logic of the hierarchy of institutions is just this: if the third-level agent is not directly responsible for threats and their material consequences, which may be quite serious, he becomes capable of exercising his authority and controlling his area of influence. It is even required that he must not become directly involved in proximal threats, even if he so wanted. The judge is never a hangman. Abstract principles and general guidelines of control become more and more concrete as they (in the form of commands and authoritative obligations) flow toward the proximal agent (the coercer), who finally finds himself in a situation where backing out is the only prudent alternative. He is, nevertheless, expected to stay there.

The superior coercive agent is in an authoritative position with respect to the coercer. His position is just. Moreover, it is an essential part of the social ideology that the coercer is responsible to the superior agent. We can now explicate some aspects of the limits of coercion. A responsible subordinate coercive agent can be expected to be willing to suffer personal losses from his own particular action. He realizes, however, that his institution is part of a just social order and that the survival rights of both the members and the institutions must be protected. These rights create obligations for him.

It is then arguable that the coercer's motivation does not extend very far; he is also protecting himself. He could not be trusted in any situation where the victim is stubborn and presents a solid counter-threat. Thus a superior agent needs to take precautions against a subordinate agent. Now, coercion can be used by a superior agent along with authority and manipulation. For example, in war, an army uses ruthless coercive measures against soldiers, who cannot be trusted as they are trusted in the less demanding conditions of peace. Cowardice is punishable by death.

However, before we deal with the case of the partial breakdown of authority, we must make it clear what authority is. Authority has a double nature. It is at the same time a moral and a power notion. It assumes two forms as "in authority" and "an authority." And it has a double function as a source of commands and authorizations.

Varieties of authority

Definition of authority

We cannot avoid the concept of authority. The limits of coercive activity are impossible to determine without knowledge of the factors that make the superior coercive agent's moral position personally acceptable. Authority is one of those factors. Certainly, legitimate coercive institutions are authority oriented, often to such a degree that we call them "authoritarian" and accuse their agents of being morally blind and immature. It is not my purpose to emphasize either the more perverse versions of or the abuse of authority. On the contrary, I presume that some aspects of authority have a rational core that makes them socially unavoidable and even morally viable forms of human cooperation.[18]

Coercion may be said to rest on authority. However, coercion and authority are two categorically different forms of social power, understood as types of interpersonal influence relations. Therefore, our previous analyses of coercion cannot shed light on authority. We need a fresh start. I shall first present a fragment of a general theory of authority, trying mainly to drive wedges between some forms of social power. I shall analyze authority independently, too. One of my main conclusions will be that only if we can find a median between the extremes of "hard" coercion and "soft" authority can we find a solution to our earlier motivational problems. Elements of each are needed in order to make the superior agent a proper part of a formal coercive institution. It is unnecessary to anticipate too much.

Let us turn to the analysis of authority. We shall start from the case where an individual person exercises his authority over another person. Other cases are a person's authorization to do something, and general authority, like that of laws and religious codes. Authority is ultimately a consensus-based idea, in the sense that a subordinate agent obeys a superior agent because he thinks, and agrees with other people—the superior agent included—that the latter agent knows best, is entitled to command, has a right to be a leader, has a higher relevant status, and so on. It may happen that the superior agent makes the subordinate agent act against his own preferences, but in the case of authority-derived power, the subordinate agent still thinks that his own present values and preferences must be overcome. This is a matter of his second-order preferences. The subordinate agent's second-order preferences, which are in favor of the priority of the superior agent's judgments, determine his decision to suppress or suspend his own first-order desires.

We have a generalized Ulysses and the Sirens case applied to social life: a person believes that a coercive agency, say, the police, has a legitimate right to arrest him when he is suspected of having acted against the law of the state, because all citizens, among them the person himself, have founded the police institution to protect them and subsequent generations against their own impulses, needs, and desires. In this case, no real coercion is needed and no threats are presented. The person may have a hard time trying to accommodate the idea that he really should let himself be arrested and interrogated. He may try to escape. He may even resist arrest. But if he finally agrees that the arrest is justified, he is under the authority of the police. Certainly coercive methods can supplement authority, but authority still implies a consensus. Consensus will, moreover, have a definite motivating effect on a person's decisions and actions. In addition to its legitimate and moral face, authority has an effective and motivating face. It claims to answer both questions of why one should do so-and-so and why one in fact did so; de jure and de facto cases must be carefully distinguished.

We need a simple but sufficiently comprehensive typology of the types of authority and their definitions. I suggest that we start from the simplest form and then proceed toward more complex cases. This constructive approach will give us a chance to deal with the more difficult cases with maximal clarity. Authority is certainly one of those social notions that have their simple uses but that soon tend to become so complex in any real-life contexts that their user just cannot explain them. The analysis given, say, in terms of rights and social structures is so problematic that it cannot help us understand the analysandum. Let us try to avoid that problem.

My typology of the forms of authority has three main parts: (1) effective de facto authority; (2) specialist or theoretical authority; (3) normative de jure authority. Let us start from the first form in order to show how it is nested within the second, just as the second is nested within the third, which, accordingly, represents the full variety of authority. The main problem will in the end be the location of commands.

We have de facto authority within a social institution when the subordinate agent simply accepts and supports the superior agent's preferences, opinions, judgments, behavior, and so on, as something to be followed and obeyed. This is certainly a very weak form of authority, and it is questionable whether it is authority at all, especially if we make the idea apply to some forms of rational interaction. The point is that one agent may respect another one as his authority without the latter knowing anything about it or presenting a claim to authority or any other kind of social superiority. The subordinate agent may also be the only individual who respects the superior agent in this way. Let us take an example before we evaluate the superior and subordinate agents' simple relationship and proceed toward more interesting cases.

Imagine a very distinctive-looking and well-dressed young woman. Another woman admires her immensely and tries to imitate her in every conceivable way. Certainly, the first woman is the second's fashion authority, in the de facto sense. However, we may say that her authority is of some degenerate form and that the second woman is irrational. But why should we say this? It seems that if a person takes on the role of subordinate agent, following the practices of someone she sees as a superior agent without any social context — that is, without other people doing so and perhaps without the superior agent even knowing that this is the case—the subordinate agent behaves irrationally. And if the superior agent's mode of influence is only de facto, her conscious intentions may well be taken as irrelevant. They need not make any difference to other agents. There is no purely personal authority. An authority is social function.

I know of no special term to describe this type of idiosyncratic authority formation. *Emulation, hero worship,* and *groupieism* come to mind. We can mention familiar cases of it: some immature persons who, like children, are attached to certain adults; or in politics, a self-made leader who is sometimes followed by a fanatic. This type of behavior may have hysterical and even pathological overtones, although it is a mode of reaction familiar to all people. Part of our own personality may be transferred onto someone else. We follow his or her example as if that person were ourselves. I suggest that we locate at least part of the alleged irrationality of this case to its absence of social context, namely, to the fact that the irrational woman consents to following the other's example without either her own reference group or her heroine knowing anything about it or influencing it in any way. This is an important fact: her consent to suppress her own judgment and to take the other woman's judgment as authoritative is not really enough to constitute a rational form of authority between the two. (I shall deal with the superior agent's claims below.)

What we need here is first the idea of the subordinate agent agreeing to the fact that a superior agent should be followed and, second, the idea of the subordinate agent consenting to be influenced in these matters partly because of a consensus. Rational de facto authority is a consensus notion more than a consent one. For example, suppose a woman follows a recognized fashion leader. She realizes that if she dresses like this leader no one will ridicule her, as used to happen before. In this case, the woman has made quite a normal decision on the basis of her expected utilities. Certainly, such an authority-based decision is different from that based on utility calculations. All or many subordinate agents believe in the superior agent because she is an authority to them. They may have various reasons why that person should be an authority; but once they are clear about her status, they follow her without further questions. Nevertheless, this consensus does yet not imply any idea of a justification for her authority. Such things as traditional codes of behavior and inherited social status need no justification, even when they create stable authority relations.

The problem of why a subordinate agent accepts an authority leads us to specialist authority. The subordinate agent's idea of the authority may be based on sheer admiration, without any cognitive reasons at all. But to take the next step away from de facto authority is to recognize that a person may have qualities that make him a well-founded authority but still not demand the status of a normative authority—that is, a person who should be followed by anyone else. A paradigm example is scientific authority. Other examples are people with a wide experience of things and places, or old people. In all these cases, such people are authorities to anyone interested in just those things about which these authorities have special expertise.

A scientific authority can certainly insist that, if his area of science is studied and taken as an object of interest in general, his opinions should also be considered and an appropriate epistemic weight put on his judgments. But he cannot plausibly demand it. Actually, he may have no reason to suppose that anyone would recognize his authority or to demand that anyone show interest in his scientific field. His expertise has its limits. He may have revolutionary and perfectly valid theories, but if a potential follower does not want to become interested in them, it is nonsensical for him to insist that he do so. On the other hand, if he is a scientific authority who is working in the subordinate agent's field, the latter is either epistemically or practically irrational if he will not recognize the other's ideas. It is, as we shall see, counterfactually true that were the subordinate agent interested in science, this person would be an authority to him.

Here we have a case where the social consensus aspect is present in full, but, nevertheless, the superior agent has no valid claim to authority, except in a limited way—when someone wants to enter the realm of his competence. The superior agent has power over the subordinate agent only if this person approaches him first. Otherwise it does not make sense to say that he should assent to the superior agent's judgments. The same idea applies to the world of fashion: if a woman wants to be fashionable, she had better dress like the superior agents from Paris, as everyone agrees they are the authorities. Moreover, the superior agents may insist they are authorities, so that if a woman does not follow their example she shows lack of good taste. However, if she does not want to be fashionable, she need not care at all. The superior agents have no claim to saying that she should be so. All such claims already presuppose her special standpoint of aesthetic and commercial values.

Our third type of authority is a normative authority, whose judgments constitute a general practical norm. Here we can take up cases like moral, political, religious, and legal authority. Their common feature is simply the fact that the superior agent may now validly demand that the subordinate agent be interested in his authority claims and his corresponding judgments. He may say that all moral and political beings, or all adult persons, should recognize that his judgments require their attention, and his position entails that they suspend their own judgments and act according to his directives. He is in authority over others. This is full-blown authority, which entails both the superior agent's specialist status and social consensus among the subordinate agent's reference group. An authority in this sense should also be supported by good reasons why he is such: his special relation to God, his political status based on a contract in which the subordinate agent participates, or his superior moral sense. His social position confers him power. Yet, position alone cannot be sufficient. Being social in authority presupposes minimally that one is an authority. Positions are only partial power bases. Authority in its full sense requires that the superior agent has consensual support and that his status rests on some good normative reasons for his claim to power and to be respected and obeyed.

I present the following five-point rough definition of an authority. The five conditions can be dubbed conflict, consent, consensus, utility, and power. Definition AU: *The superior agent A is a normative authority to the subordinate agent B if and only if (1) it is realistically possible that there emerge such an initially controversial issue x that (2) agent B believes that at least in ordinary circumstances there are good reasons for giving his consent to A's passing his judgment on x; (3) B agrees with his own reference group that he should suspend his own judgment concerning x if A expresses his opinion; (4) x is an issue relevant to expected utilities and to practical reasoning on their basis; and (5) A claims a right to express his opinion on x and wants to express it.* A exercises his authority if x actually occurs. In this case, the relevant reason he presents is used as a premise in practical reasoning.

The first condition tells us why an authority is needed and why it is also a prima facie conflict notion: there is some controversy in the air. The second condition specifies the role of pure consent: B does not try to prevent A from saying what should be done to or thought about x. This condition is needed, because being an authority certainly presupposes consent in some form. But at the same time, it seems as if a separate consent condition is needed, if only to prevent the perverse possibility that B would not allow A to say what he thinks. B either actively prevents A from doing this or totally avoids A's presence. It may indeed happen that x is so controversial an issue that B does not want to hear what A says. (No authority is absolute, either effectively or normatively: if a person does not want to join the army, he tries not to read the draft notices, for instance.)

Our third condition is essential, though: consensus is the basis of all rationality of authority. It is indeed a social notion. B is also supposed to suspend his own judgment concerning x for some relevant normative reasons. It must be noticed, however, that no suspension of judgment can, or should, be absolute. Only fanaticism requires absolute obedience to commands with or without reasons. It may be best to say that fanaticism does not need or imply reasons, because no set of real reasons can prescribe absolute obedience. All authority has limits, beyond which a rational B cannot and should not follow A's prescriptive ideas about x. In all normal cases, we presuppose that both A and B know the location of the fuzzy limits of the authority claims. For instance, an economist cannot insist that his theories of development are to be followed in cases where the state is on the verge of an internal revolution because of some unlucky economic adventures. He should admit that a politically safe compromise is needed more than another risky scientific experiment. When circumstances are nonstandard, requirements are strange, and risks are deadly, A should not suppose that his usual authority extends to those cases, too.

Now, none of our first three conditions says why A's authority brings about a modification of B's reactions. Authority is supposed to be an efficient social factor, and even an ingredient of power. This intuition is taken care of by our fourth condition: if x is important to B, and if A's judgments are to be observed by B, a sort of practical inference entails that B will act according to A's judgment concerning x. B needs to make a decision about controversial x, and because x is important to him, he is prepared to act. Now, when A offers B a solution to his problem, B is committed to acting along the lines that A specifies, given that the external conditions are close to normal. The point to recognize is that A may successfully convince B about the importance of x. The issue need not be independently important. Authority may be also creative and not only advice related.

The fifth and last condition states that there cannot be intentional influence or power without somebody who wants to exercise it. The point should be understood broadly: an authority must be interested in x and in other people's reactions to it. Some remarks can be made concerning this issue. Look at the following example: in a democratic society, the citizens offer the role of political authority to someone who may be less than eager to assume it; but in an autocratic society, the prospective rulers demand their positions from the citizens. Some mediating alternatives exist as well: a person may *offer* his services as a political authority to the citizens. Now, the first example, a power position that is offered, is a maximally weak type of power. However, it may well be real power. And the same is true of a power position that is demanded. The main point is that an authority must in the end have the right to exercise the power and must want to do so. This situation need not be an original one but rather a result of some definite authority-formation processes.

Our AU definition is logically rather weak because, as is easy to see, if agent A does not express any opinion concerning x, agent B is thereby left free to form his own opinion. It may be difficult to see how he could do this, because it involves the question of why he should accept an authority in the first place. Perhaps we should say that, if (3) is not satisfied, B wavers and seeks another authority to make the decision for him. Nevertheless, he is still free. Also (3) and (5) make sense together, as A may claim the right to express an opinion on x, may want to express one, but still fail to do so. B may not know what to think and may, therefore, be ready to accept almost any opinion as authoritative. This, of course, would be an irrational strategy.

Furthermore, as to (4), notice that authority is a latent power base, which can be used in relation to all those whose interests are shared by A. When we move to normative cases, we see that moral issues also satisfy the utility condition (4) of definition AU. Moral problems make a difference to us. Political and legal areas are defined in more limited ways; yet, their avoidance is practically impossible to any citizen of the state. Apparently, this unavoidability is closely connected to the normative force of some types of authority. There are interests that cannot fail to be shared ones.

Authority is certainly an enigmatic combination of controversies concerning x and social trust in A's judgment about x. Yet, authority is a paradigm explanation of the fact that social agents are not just atomistically independent utility maximizers, self-responsible individuals, and carriers of their rights. We join together into groups in order to give away our own decision-making power. In rather too many cases, we apparently do not know how and what to decide. Moreover, our social life does not admit of the norm that we all decide always on important things independently. We must streamline our decisional machinery as well as limit its scope and internal variety; and then it will be easy enough to trust some authority. Many decisions are made under both informational and valuational uncertainty. We do not know what to expect will follow causally from our actions. We do not even know how to evaluate those results when they emerge. In a sense, we are weak agents because the social pressure toward conformity, cooperation, and cultural continuity is often more important than our own basic and much-cherished right to full independence. Only a thin line runs between our reason-based social acceptance of authoritative positions and our merely idiosyncratic willingness to obey, regardless of good reasons, social or individual.

Three sources of authority

If there are agents who possess authority, there must be sources of their power. The main question concerns the proper reasons for agreeing that a person is an authority. I shall analyze the birth of authority within human interaction. I do not think there is anything like a natural or objective basis for authority.

Within an interactionist perspective, we can distinguish three models for the sources of personal authority: (1) a maximizing bargaining model; (2) a conventionalist model; and (3) a contract model.

By *model*, I mean a way of conceptualizing the underdog's (the subordinate agent's) reasons for assuming an affirmative consensus position regarding the alleged right to decide about x. We already recognized such authority as de facto, specialist, and normative. Now we ask why exactly anyone would like to live with and under someone else's authority. Our familiar structural placeholders are the superior agent and the subordinate agent. Their relationship is definitely interactive. I call the power wielder a superior agent, since he is not yet a real authority: the point is that we try to understand the formation of its grounds. Let us check what the first model is like.

Now, suppose that a rational subordinate agent accepts an authority—or that he in some sense surrenders his judgment. What are his possible reasons? And what are the effects of his decisions? We can now interpret these questions in relation to examples of each of the three models mentioned above.

I shall start with the maximizing bargaining model. An authority tends to satisfy his social interests in the optimal way so that this utility aspect grounds his claims to authority. He can point to a record of earlier success; a shared agreement concerning his talent arises. We have historical evidence that he possesses knowledge. Examples are easy to give. Suppose a person (the subordinate agent) is a heavy smoker and a physician (the superior agent) insists that he stop smoking because cigarette smoke causes cancer, according to medical science. Moreover, suppose that the subordinate agent is not competent enough to judge the evidence for this proposition, but he knows what the general epistemic status of science is and that the superior agent is an established member of the scientific community. Because of this knowledge, he may rationally surrender his judgment concerning the apparent effects of smoking. He accepts the superior agent's status as a medical (specialist) authority. Specialist authority presupposes an acknowledged imbalance of the relevant epistemic resources.

The maximizing model entails other requirements, too. Suppose now that one has a good reason to believe that the superior agent alone has access to a utility matrix in which the utilities are fixed, given his preferences, values, and causal influence. The subordinate agent stays behind a cognitive barrier. For example, the plausibility value of the scientific hypothesis that smoking causes lung cancer is high, and cancer is against the interests of any person. The subordinate agent should also realize that the superior agent is a nonegoistic and objectively oriented player in this interaction. He has no reason to mislead his subordinate. Of course, if such a condition is not uniformly satisfied in the case of medical doctors, this diminishes their authority according to the maximizing model. In general, the superior agent is able to provide the expected values of some action alternatives. His primary source of authority is knowledge, and the secondary source his position in the world of science.

We see that there is nothing irrational in a subordinate agent's surrendering his incompetent judgments concerning the effects of the available action alternatives in favor of more complete judgments: an authority is able to fill the empty slots in the utility matrix, and he supposes that some definite values obtain. An authority may be systematically wrong, that is true, as doctors often have been in the history of medical practice. The source of their rational authority is then just the fact that they have socially recognized methods to fill the empty places in a subordinate agent's utility matrix. He must do something anyway and therefore turns toward an authority. Thereby, he becomes able to make some decisions. He simply takes the action with the largest expected utility number, according to the estimate provided by superior agent.

Our conventionalist model represents a slightly different situation: a person is now supposed to believe or do something, but in addition to the fact that he has no way of fixing any of the values in the utility matrix independently of the superior agent; he does not even know whether all the slots have a value attached to them. Example: the superior agent relates to the subordinate agent the acceptable dress code for a particular social occasion. The main difference from the maximizing model is, therefore, that the subordinate agent cannot evaluate the validity of these claims so that he can tell whether the utility numbers displayed are approximations of something that really exists or not. There are no independently right solutions. But he is required to act and thus needs some guidance. The best thing he can do is to accept an authority. In this type of nonrealist case, the status of the superior agent may be more or less well founded, in the sense that he presents claims to authority, or may have a historically based right to be one, or may have some evidence showing that his value ascriptions are at least intelligible and coherent.

A fashion leader is so influential that her prescriptions become fashionable. Such an opinion is self-fulfilling as to its success. Her authority is thus well founded independently of her knowledge of any causal connections in the real world. This authority is simply worth following.

Certainly in typical cases, no counterevidence against the superior agent's action can be presented; the subordinate agent need have no grounds for making his own judgments. In this way, rather unexpectedly perhaps, the conventionalist model need not contain the phenomenon of surrender of judgment, simply because the subordinate agent may have no judgment in the beginning.

Our model explicates a conventionalist way of creating new judgments about the issues that are felt to be practically important. Is this model at all rational? Certainly it is in some rather peculiar sense. Although we do not find proper decision theoretical rationality, nevertheless, there are realms of human life in which something must be done, even under the conditions of final ignorance. The best overall strategy is to nominate someone as an authority, let him judge, and then adopt his views. This guarantees cooperation. The idea of social rationality should be able to accommodate this phenomenon. At least the total chaos of too many opinions and the resulting mental paralysis is avoided.

Certain areas of social life can indeed be arranged according to the principles of the conventionalist model: he who dares to make a judgment is taken as a candidate for authority. He will fix the values of situations that we do not even know have values. An authority is, in the more extreme situations, constitutive of value and utilities. Religious risks come close to what I mean here: epistemically rational subjects really do not know whether God exists and what he wants us to do. But if he exists and wants something, his subjects are doomed if they do not entertain the correct judgments about him. In such a Pascalian wagering situation, the best strategy is to believe something. Being totally ignorant about our own real situation, it is best for us all to believe one and the same thing, namely, that he exists. We want to simulate the truth. Such an authority may be assigned to positions as well as to individuals.

The superior agent who actually delivers the accepted belief constitutes a conventionalist authority. We may say that human nature abhors a cognitive void: as we must make decisions, we simply cannot afford to admit our ignorance. To avoid paralysis, we stipulate how to fill the gaps. The history of science is also full of examples, like alchemy. Some aspects of moral authority belongs here, too. Many aspects of folk norms and customs are felt to be very important, although no solid reasons for their acceptance is provided. The guardians of such norms work like authorities.

Next, we turn to the contract model of authority. The subordinate and the superior agents must both make strategy choices that determine their payoffs. The results are norms. The players know some features of the structure of an objective utility matrix; for example, it displays a prisoner's dilemma situation (where c = confession and $-c$ = no confession):

$$
\begin{array}{cc}
 & B \\
 & \begin{array}{c|c} c & -c \end{array}
\end{array}
$$

		c	$-c$
A	c	3, 3	1, 4
	$-c$	4, 1	2, 2

Certainly, successful cooperation is needed here if the agents are going to get their best joint possibility, or $<2,2>$. The equilibrium point is only $<3,3>$, which is not too attractive. According to the present idea, the contract model allows them to reach $<2,2>$ by making the superior agent an authority who in advance guarantees that he will not confess, come what may. If the subordinate agent believes him and trusts his promises, or if the superior agent is indeed an authority, he need not confess. That the superior agent will take the risk is known beforehand. In other words, he assumes the crucial social position that creates the normative "in authority." The question is, of course, why anyone should accept such burdensome leadership? We return to our earlier motivational problems.

Both agents are now supposed either to make or endorse a contract to the effect that both will cooperate in order to get their best outcome $<2,2,>$ instead of the suboptimal equilibrium outcome pair $<3,3.>$ Both parties agree that cooperation is necessary, and the superior agent is made an authority in the special sense that he chooses the strategies for both agents and takes the risk of ending up with the worst possible outcome, allowing the other agent to profit unduly from $<1,4.>$ This is the risk he takes, but the present meaning of authority is just that the subordinate agent subscribes to the idea of following the superior agent's strategy choices. Accordingly, the latter agent is in authority, and his decisions provide the norms.

This position is made believable partly because authority is an iterative as well as a social condition: the superior agent must have a past history of cooperative choices, otherwise he could not be an authority. In this way, we have one agent whose suitable choices are risky to himself, and thus predictable and nonexploitative. The other agent can choose a better individual prospect, as otherwise would be the case. He also has his chance to double-cross the authority, but this means, as we shall see, that the superior agent is not really in authority any longer. This is to say that, if a person knows that he is in authority over others, he need not hesitate in regard to his own cooperative risky strategy choices in, say, prisoner's dilemma cases. All this entails that authority may be a genuinely normative notion; otherwise, the agents could not explicate the basis of their mutually risky trust.

Authority is based on consensus and trust, and the breakdown of consensus implies the end of authority, as we shall see. Any authority relation is, however, a very weak guarantee of cooperative success. The subordinate agent may indeed double-cross the superior agent if he feels that he no longer needs the cooperative possibilities that were granted to him earlier. But then he is not supposed to know so much about the further developments of their joint long-term utility matrix that he could tell what other kind of game situations it will contain and what will face them in the future. This cognitive uncertainty makes the denial of an authority definitely less attractive than if he were just playing one isolated prisoner's dilemma game against the superior agent. The contract that makes the superior agent an authority was supposed to be a kind of long-term insurance against many future uncertainties. The result is an authoritative position and a set of norms. Being in authority entails being an authority, too.

Many aspects of social morality follow this pattern in their genesis. Morality guarantees some cooperative successes in the world of uncertainties. We need norms. We simply make a contract to the effect that we behave honestly and respect the rules of the games we play. And if morality is a source of authority, we need someone to exercise the relevant power. Social morality is not just an empty and fashionable convention. It is a contract.

We are now ready to see what lessons we have learned. One of the basic points is the following: cognitive and decisional authorities need not be identical, as the differences between the maximizing and contract models show; decisions need not be cognitively or epistemically grounded at all, and still they may be quite reasonable. Authority is a way of overcoming some typical limitations of human decisions. However, a subordinate agent must be careful not to extend the scope of authority so far that all decisions under uncertainty can fall under it. If he could have known a proposition or reached certain outcome independently, then the superior agent is not an authority to him; there is simply no reason why the superior agent should be an authority. The latter implies a basic (actual or anticipated) incapacity, which must be overcome. One method of overcoming it is to accept a second person's authority. No guarantee of an ultimate and objective cooperative success is needed, however. What the subordinate agent wants is simply to step out of the stalemate brought about by his cognitive, personal, or social situation. Many forms of authority get their prima facie rational justification in the present perspective, even if the agents under authority should try to get out of their personal subordinate situation.

We constantly encounter social problems that are insoluble by our own given means; then the resort to authority provides new possibilities of making at least one step forward. The core of the rational acceptance of authority is that it offers a shortcut to social cooperation in some difficult decisional cases.

Let us next examine the motivational effects of our three models of authority.

Certainly the maximizing model is strongly motivating: it represents the subordinate agent's best possible chance of increasing the payoffs in situations whose relevant characteristics he cannot individually expect to scan. However, this model cannot be analyzed in moral terms: the subordinate agent takes care of his own good, and if he fails to do so, or accepts unreasonable authorities, that is his own business. No generalized, interpersonal, motivational commitments, norms, or obligations can be derived. The fact that others still believe in an authority does not tie his hands.

The conventionalist model is a novel case. The subordinate agent's motivation to accept an authority is not based on his own personal reasons. The authority creates social ideas and positions. There exists no motivation to accept a superior agent's views independently of his claim to authority, or before its explication. A subordinate agent may entertain no independent judgments concerning the subject matter. In this sense, any motive to assent is a weak one, and he may waver as to the status of the superior agent without reaching a long-lasting conviction during a given period of time. However, as to the normative part of the superior agent's conventionalist authority, the situation tends to turn around. In the social and moral perspective, such an authority is strong and difficult to reject. The conventionalist model belongs to an authoritative social category, as examples of religious and political ideals show.

Since the subordinate agent has only general value-based reasons for the acceptance of the authority of the superior agent, this status must be strictly social, that is, based on general social acceptance in a historical perspective. The idea is that if he had neither cognitive nor utilitarian reasons for accepting an authority, he must do so on the basis of pure social consensus-related considerations. Accordingly, an individual refutation of an authority implies intentional deviation and even self-exclusion from the subordinate agent's group membership. The belief in an authority partially constitutes the group. And no rewards may follow. This type of move has its own negative consequences, since the reference group has valid reasons for fighting against the loss of its members. Within the conventionalist model, authority constitutes a group-forming principle; but as its individual motivational value is not great outside the value of the group membership, it is important that the value of membership is made as high as possible. Only in this way can the relevant authority survive.

The contract model combines both the features mentioned above in connection with the other two models; the acceptance of an authority is now highly motivating. A subordinate agent knows enough about his own expected utilities to be able to calculate and compare alternative payoffs. An authority also has some definite social and procedural normative components. The members of the subordinate agent's reference group want to use the cooperative possibilities granted to them through the authority's presence, too. They need him in their own prudent perspective; and all need him similarly. Thus they must try to guarantee loyalty to him by means of social pressure in that direction. This case appears to be strong enough. The contract ties the hands of all parties, so that no one-sided retreat from it is advisable or permissible. Such a case has its strong moral overtones. Authority in this sense is a moral category. Authority provides norms.

Let us, however, note a difference between two different aspects of a subordinate agent's rejection of a superior agent's claims to authority: first, he may reject them by refusing to deal with the superior agent at all. This is irrational. Or he may reject them by selecting, in the prisoner's dilemma case, the best individual alternative, thus reducing the superior agent's expected cooperative profits to a disaster. This violates procedural justice, or the idea of fair play. We see that both the motivational and moral aspects are quite clear-cut here.

I shall suggest briefly how personal authority is transformed into impersonal respect for the authority of laws, conscience, or public opinion. The main idea is this: the subject of authority, the subordinate agent, sees a real or fictional person as representative of an authority-conferring position. Thus the difference between personal and nonpersonal authority is simply that the agent is either an individual or a structural placeholder. We may consider how well the models of authority apply to such roles in social life. A judge is a representative of the law; therefore his is impersonal authority. His personality neither fixes his decisions nor creates his social position. But there is no authority without a personal focus. A superior agent cannot work in an authoritative position without being a personal authority. The types of authority are never pure, however desirable that might be.

I have now concluded the basic survey of some relevant types of authority. The next topic is the difference between authority and coercion.

Authority as a special type of power

Joseph Raz has presented an interesting analysis of the structure of reason in authority, understood as a form of social power. He maintains that effective authority presupposes legitimate authority, which alone can provide the reasons for the subordinate agent's assent to the superior agent's power claims. Legitimate authority is a form of social power. Raz first defines negative second-order reasons that are exclusionary reasons by saying that they are reasons that make some other reasons void. An example given by Raz is a father who tells his son to ignore his mother's requests. The son has a second-order reason not to recognize the mother's statements as reasons for action.

Next, protected reasons are defined thus: "sometimes the same fact is both a reason for an action and an (exclusionary) reason for disregarding reasons against it. I shall call such facts protected reasons for an action." The next step in Raz's argument is the following: "An act is the exercise of a normative power if there is sufficient reason for regarding it either as a protected reason or as cancelling protected reasons and if the reason for so regarding it is that it is desirable to enable people to change protected reasons by such acts, if they wish to do so."[19]

Finally, Raz draws the important distinction between power and authority by noting simply that one may have power over both oneself and others but authority invariably and necessarily concerns others. Therefore "power over others is authority over them."[20] It seems to me that something goes wrong here. I cannot see, for instance, how one could present a coercive threat against oneself.

The point is that Raz makes the connection between power and authority so close that it becomes impossible to find room for coercion. And as I shall try to show, it is quite intuitive to claim that authority and coercion should not be conflated. Raz does not make their relation clear.

Now, suppose that a superior agent has normative authority over a subordinate agent. It makes good sense to say along with Raz that this means that if the authoritative agent, say, commands the subordinate agent to go home, the fact of saying so provides a special second-order reason, which suppresses all his first-order reasons, such as his desire not to go home. The superior agent is able to mobilize some of the subordinate agent's commitments, which are categorically stronger than his desire-related first-order reasons. We also recall that in his definition of normative power, Raz stated that it should be *desirable* to change the protected reasons. This seems to assert roughly the same thing as my consensus and consent conditions in definition AU: the desirability condition implies a social and impersonal valuation of the superior agent's status as well as the subordinate agent's consent to what the authoritative person is doing or will do in the future. As plausible as this is, Raz cannot possibly find room for coercion in his scheme of power.

If authority is the same as other-regarding, or as social power, then a coercive threat may at least in some instances be at the same time a fact that (1) changes or mobilizes protected reasons but (2) is not desirable in the relevant sense. This would make the concept of a threat that of power independent of authority.

Let me illustrate this idea by means of an example. A person (coercer; superior agent) threatens another person (victim; subordinate agent) by pointing a gun and saying he should leave the room. This provides the victim with a first-order reason for leaving. The same utterance provides him also a second-order reason to leave, which can be seen as the mobilization of his commitment to personal safety; any motive that is independent of the threat is unreasonably costly and therefore ineffective. The victim is now prepared to ignore other people's advice and requests as well as his own basic desire to stay. The coercer's action constitutes the protected reason. But this fact is not part of the exercise of authority, simply because the situation does not exemplify any desirable elements; nevertheless, the case certainly implies an exercise of power. It also implies some normative elements: the victim should be reasonable and not allow the coercer to harm him. Raz's definition of normative power is logically too strong, because it leaves some relevant cases outside of its scope.

The source of trouble seems to be that some acts of power are actually undesirable. They are repressive. But it seems to be a rather shady proposition to suggest that a mere distinction between the desirable and undesirable uses of power could constitute the definitive difference between coercion and authority. For example, the abuse of authority is not desirable, but it is not coercion just because of that. Undesirable pseudoauthority is not coercion; it is authoritarianism, blind obedience, or the manifestation of some kind of personality disorder. Coercion, on the contrary, is an understandable form of social interaction.

It is also possible to argue that when a police officer, who is a legitimate authority, presents a threat against a criminal and then also against a law-abiding citizen, he indeed provides protected reasons whose existence is socially desirable (or at least indifferent). We need the police. Nevertheless, the criminal is genuinely threatened — the superior agent cannot be efficient against him without this threat. In the case of the innocent citizen, on the contrary, the superior agent's threat is redundant, as this person would obey even without the threat.

As I see it, this means that authoritative protected reasons constitute a mere subclass of all the possible protected ones. Some protected reasons are based on threats and, consequently, they are not accepted personally by their object persons. This seems to be the crucial fact: authoritative acts of using the reasons are accepted by the subordinate agent but coercive acts are not. Authority leads to the mobilization of personally accepted commitments. Coercion leads to the mobilization of personally unacceptable commitments. Authority does not entail subjective harm, like coercion does. The overall desirability of authority, as mentioned by Raz, is not the whole story. We need to mention the subordinate agent's subjective reactions and their use as well.

Coercive reasons are genuinely protected. They are in many cases socially desirable, but they are never subjectively acceptable in the context of their presentation. Yet, a rational victim should follow them, unlike in the case of force, where no "should" applies. Let us try to see in a more detailed manner what the difference between coercion and authority is really like.

Raz has the following escape route available to him. He writes: "Orders are made with the intention that they should prevail in certain circumstances even if they do not tip the balance [of subjective utilities]. They are intended to be taken as reasons for excluding certain others that may tip the balance against performing that action."[21] Should we not say that coercive threats are simply such reasons that do tip the subordinate agent's balance of utilities in favor of obedience to the superior agent in a given specific situation? If this is so, Raz's definition of normative power would simply exclude coercive power without involving any conceptual confusion.

There is confusion, however. Raz defines authority in terms of some norms of action and deliberately excludes all considerations of expected utility. This makes authority a nonutilitarian concept, in the sense that it cannot be understood or justified in the utilitarian or economic rational decision-making perspective. But it should be possible to understand coercion in terms of nonconsequentialist rules, too. If the language of authority is nonconsequentialist in nature, we may be able to use the same language at least in some cases of coercion. I mean that, when the superior agent threatens the subordinate agent, the latter may have already accepted the normative principle that a person must never deliberately risk his own life in social interaction in conflict situations. This might be based on his social commitments and responsibilities. The superior agent then threatens the subordinate agent's life, and although the probability of getting hurt may be so small that it cannot alone tip the balance toward yielding to him, the subordinate agent obeys.

This happens because the subordinate agent subscribes to his second-order exclusionary reason, which the superior agent now successfully exploits. Certainly, this repressive interaction is coercive in spite of the fact that it fits the original definition of normative power, which was supposed to provide the basis for the definition of authority. The mobilized commitments of the victim lead him to an intrinsically coercive and not to an authoritative situation. Its description mentions a genuinely violent threat against his life.

Only some deontic considerations convey authority, so that authoritative speech acts can be based on them. Compare, for instance "I should not resist anyone with a gun" and "I love and respect my father." The first one gives rise to coercive exchanges and the latter to authoritative ones. The first allows the superior agent to formulate a coercive protected reason. It is a sort of anticipated response to severe threats.

Of course, this criticism of Raz modifies my own original position as well: we should admit that a threat is sometimes efficient only under certain nonutilitarian rules, norms, and reasons. However, I have already hinted at this idea, and we'll deal with it below.

Richard Flathman states, quite surprisingly, that perhaps authority is not power. He defines power explicitly in terms of threats.[22] Of course, such a conceptual move more or less evades the real question. His narrow concept of power is tailor-made to exclude all authority, manipulation, and other subtler forms of interpersonal influence. He tries to draw the line between power and authority thus: "Acceptance of power as a feature of one's practices does not yield an obligation, indeed does not *itself* give the subordinate agent any kind of reason whatever, for doing any specific *X*. . . . Authority, as we might put it, has a deontological quality that power altogether lacks."[23] He also says — strangely enough — that an act of power exercise is a reason for *not* doing what the power wielder wants. But all this sounds strange. First, the maximizing and conventionalist models of authority are not unproblematically deontological. Second, if an authority logically presupposes a norm requiring a subordinate agent to follow the superior agent's judgments and commands, it would be equally true that the superior agent's coercive power is a good and sometimes sufficient reason for the subordinate agent to do what he wants (compare deterrent threats and stable situations).

Let us consider Flathman's main point. Certainly if the superior agent has (coercive) power against the subordinate agent, and the subordinate agent for this specific reason refuses to do what the superior agent wants, he is irrational. And we may well argue that he should avoid plain irrationality. Therefore, the type of power provides a norm for the subordinate agent. It is quite sensible to say that the subordinate agent should yield to genuinely coercive threats and power, ceteris paribus, because the subordinate agent wants to avoid personal harm. He is supposed to be a prudent rational agent, and therefore he accepts the norm that everyone should avoid needless losses. When the superior agent enters the picture and through a threat changes the subordinate agent's distribution of expected utilities, he at the same time changes his behavior through that prudent norm. Many aspects of institutionalized coercion depend on this fact. Moreover, personal coercive attempts tend to be unsuccessful because of the lack of suitable norms, which the victim would be willing to observe. Coercive power is exercised through intentional interaction. This may imply the mobilization of social norms. The real difference between coercion and authority is, of course, that the former implies the weaker party's more or less efficient dissent from the prospects of interaction.

Flathman also maintains that "whatever the authoritative agent's resources . . . his power over the subordinate agent can only be so great as the subordinate agent allows."[24] It is amusing to recall that Hegel says exactly the same in his *Philosophy of Right*. However, one may equally well refuse to follow an authority (see below). Intuitively speaking, it is certainly easier to dismiss authoritative orders than orders backed by threats.

It is, however, perfectly true that authority in one sense provides rather unique norms; we might call them internal norms. A subordinate agent always accepts the superior agent's authority in a situation in which he has a choice. Authority is like an offer and unlike a threat. And this implies that he lets the superior agent influence his opinions and actions. He thinks that he should do what the superior agent says, as this represents the best possible new alternative to him. (Compare coercion: unharmed escape used to be his best possible choice, but that is now excluded from the set of action alternatives.) The case of authority is not really that much different from the prudent case of offers.

According to definition AU, authority is based on social consensus. It is a social offer. This fact also goes a long way toward explaining the moral obligations that make authority so effective. To act against an authority is often to act against social consensus and the common good. The superior agent's power therefore crosses the limits of mere individual prudence. When a subordinate agent accepts a superior agent's authority, he does it in a larger social perspective than when a victim accepts a coercer's power. Yet, no threat may be believable and convincing if the relevant exchange does not rest on some rules, norms, and behavioral regularities. An oversimplified account of threats suggests the opposite. Convincing threats depend on mobilized commitments.

However, not even authority as such creates obligations, simply because a person must first accept the authority claim; for instance, it must not be made in such extraordinary circumstances that the superior agent's status description will not apply. Only consensually accepted authority mobilizes norms and obligations, for instance, through the idea of loyalty to the group. This indicates that authority may or may not be an effective way of influencing a subordinate agent's actions and decisions; group pressure and individual acceptance interact in complex ways. Authority has its double face, because it is both a claim to a right to power and an effective power.

Authorizations and commands

Let us see next how an effective power face can be explicated. It is not easy to see how the necessarily quite strong deontological quality of authority is supposed to emerge in its social setting. Certainly, I do not want to postulate any naturally binding deontological authority. Power is somehow built out of simpler elements. Ultimately, we want to understand commands, but we must start from some milder uses of authority. Otherwise, we cannot really appreciate how difficult it is to explain the rational use and acceptance of commands.

Authority, in its weaker forms, is used to grant permission and also the corresponding type of right. The superior agent authorizes the subordinate agent to do something. This is authority-to. Authority is not only "the right to command."[25] Notice that we are here dealing with acts and not with any other type of object—say, beliefs or norms. The following three propositions show what I mean. (1) The superior agent authorizes the subordinate agent to do x by doing or saying y. This is a strong permission, which implies that the subordinate agent is free to do x without anybody's rightful intervention; y may be the superior agent's example, expressed opinion, and even a command to other agents, excluding the subordinate agent.

However, the following proposition sounds strange. (2) The superior agent authorizes the subordinate agent to do x by stating his intention that the subordinate do x. The point is, simply, that (2) confuses a strong permission and a weak command: if the superior agent authorizes the subordinate agent to do x, this means that he has a right to do x. Yet, by stating his intention in the form of a command, the superior agent does something more than to give a right. Indeed, a valid command logically entails the right, and that is why (2) sounds strange. If the superior agent's command really entails the fact that the subordinate agent is authorized, permission through obligation may sound strange, but it is unproblematic. Yet, it may also happen that the superior agent commands a subordinate agent to do an x that he has no right to do. In this case, he should first be provided an independent authorization with respect to x and only then commanded. If the subordinate agent acts beyond his rights, he cannot defend himself by saying just that the superior agent commanded him to do so. The subordinate agent should also show that the superior agent has indeed authorized him to do x. When this is clear, the command is an excuse to which one may refer in any future controversies about the case. If we do admit both that the authorization is logically presupposed by a command and that the command does not follow simply from an authorization itself, we must then explain what authorizations are and how they are brought about.

One interesting feature of the validity of authoritative permissions can be taken up now. If the subordinate agent is permitted to do x by the superior agent, on what conditions can he refuse to accept the fact of having the right, or permission, to do x? I said earlier that when he refuses to follow an authority, this tends to breach the norms of the reference group.

Now, permissions are such weak consequences of the exercise of authority that their denials have different moral results. A group may be interested in an individual subordinate agent's weak rights. Sexual practices are an example. No moral pressure need be directed against these practices, although this may happen in some cases. Normally, the subordinate agent's refusal of authoritative permission is impossible for logical reasons. According to the social rules of authority, the subordinate agent actually has this right if it is granted to him by the authority and is something he cannot turn down. To refuse to recognize the right is to make an idiosyncratic and socially incomprehensible decision, in the following sense. Some rights may be inalienable. A man may be granted the right to have two wives. He may not like it, but it is his right. One-sidedly refused permission is an anomaly. In this case, the authorizing authority is as binding as anything can be. But permission may not change the subordinate agent's behavior.

Let us consider next the following proposition. (3) The superior agent commands the subordinate agent to do x by presenting his authoritative opinion (or intention) to the effect that the subordinate agent do x. This is hardly informative. What is this opinion or intention supposed to be like, and why should the subordinate agent consider it as binding? In reference to definition AU above, we can now say that the superior agent has expressed his intention to the effect that the subordinate agent do x. The subordinate agent suspends his judgment about the issue. Therefore, he will presumably do x. He is also automatically authorized to do x.

Is this right? It is, but we must very carefully notice that AU requires that x be interesting to the subordinate agent and that his reference group entertains a consensus concerning the superior agent's authority. In this type of situation, the superior agent can present an effective command to the subordinate agent. He will feel like doing it, because he sees that if he does not want to breach some social norms it is within the range of his interests to consider the issue and also to obey. It is his own decision.

It is easy to guess that such commands cannot be reliable in the case of such demanding issues where the subordinate agent must expect a large subjective disutility. Anyway, an authority wields commands through the opinion that he should decide about the issue that is the content of the command. But this also presupposes that the members of the subordinate agent's reference group agree on the fact that the superior agent's message is indeed an actual command. This judgment may make them act, as we see, but as such it does not constitute a valid command.

Contrary to what Flathman seems to say, authority has no intrinsic and unconditional deontological characteristics. Authority either grants liberties or fixes judgments. Nevertheless, it may also, rather miraculously, be able to present valid commands.

Joseph Raz seems to hit the truth when he writes as follows:

> It was never intended, one could claim, that one should obey even if it turn out that there was a strong moral reason for not doing so or if obeying would severely damage the recipient's interests or be unlawful. When such considerations amount to a justification and lead the agent not to follow the order, he cannot be said to have obeyed it but neither did he disobey it. It was not intended that he should follow it in such circumstances.[26]

This is a marvelous statement, as it shows exactly why authority is not a source of valid commands. Commands belong rather to the sphere of the abuse of authority. Let us see why this is so.

Commands, as based on authority claims, presuppose some norms accepted by the object of command, the subordinate agent. But no norms or obligations can override the moral obligations Raz mentions above. Therefore, the subordinate agent cannot know whether he is validly commanded to do x before he knows that it is not immoral (Raz's qualification of "strong" is certainly superfluous). Thus the subordinate agent should check the (im)morality of the command and, according to Raz, even its utilitarian effects on his own interests and the superior agent should make it clear to the subordinate agent that his command is morally and prudently justifiable. But in any situation that is morally problematic, existentially critical, or allowing for no waste of time, this requirement is simply impractical and even impossible.

Such requirements make most commands void. Commands are designed to sidestep moral and prudent considerations. It seems to me that commands are needed exactly in those cases where decision-making power, for practical reasons, cannot be distributed along the normal social hierarchy. People cannot always be made to know exactly what the real point of a command is, because either it would destroy the prospects for a successful mission or it is technically impossible (like lack of time). One might even suggest that moral indifference should be required for justified commands. If the subordinate agent does not consider it wrong, he may obey. But even this requirement is so strong that it destroys the point of commanding. A command that is open to subjective acceptance is no command. In other words, commands entail their bindingness within the situation where they are issued. We shall return to the problems of authoritative commands.

It does not sound right even to say that a rigid obligation or a command is based on a consensus within the subordinate agent's reference group to the effect that he do x, given again that the superior agent expresses this opinion. To surrender judgment and to obey a command are necessarily two different things. If the subordinate agent does not know who should perform, in the sense that he agrees that it should be done but does not know who the actor will be, and the superior agent tells him that he will be the agent, no command has yet been issued.

It may happen that the subordinate agent knows perfectly well both that the action should be done for some prudent reasons and that he is the only person present who can do it—and still the superior agent's command is needed to start his activity. Therefore, the subordinate agent's judgments concerning the institution and concerning his own action toward the object are two mutually independent things. It is possible that the subordinate agent knows who will do it but, all the same, needs a command in order to start acting.

Our concensus view of authority does not lead us far in our attempts to understand authority as a form of social power, that is, as a source of valid and binding commands. And we could not accept such a simple noncognitive theory of authority that says merely that the subordinate agent is supposed to follow the superior agent's commands, if he is an authority with regard to the relevant issues. From the perspective we adopted above, this proposal leads to simple irrationality and exemplifies an abuse of authority. One cannot be supposed to obey without any qualifying reasons and independently of the specific social context of the decisions.

Therefore, we have simply failed to explain how the authoritative power to issue commands is constituted and why it would be accepted by rational subordinate agents. We shall return to this crucial problem after we have dealt with the issue of how to make a clear-cut difference between coercion and authority, supposing that the latter really is a form of social power. I shall suggest that someone may be authorized to command, yet, his efficient commands are not based on any authority understandable along the lines of definition AU. Actually, commands work in a context where their effect does not result from the authorization to issue commands. The context of commands exemplify what I shall call their closed nature. We cannot escape from it; the circumstances are threatening. Commands resemble a coercive threat.

In sum, the main point is that, according to definition AU, an authority may say who should do x and why; but even if the subordinate agent then knows that he should do x, he need not accept any practically effective commitment. He may refuse to recognize a command.

Authority and coercion once again

Suppose a person wants to smoke but also knows that an authority condemns the medical effects of cigarette smoking and happens to trust that opinion. This superior agent is then his personal de facto authority. No coercive power exists. It is, accordingly, natural to argue that even if we called authority a form of social power, as I want to do, it is certainly radically different from coercive power. The typical threat position that creates a short-term apparent but false consensus is always present in coercive cases. This is not true of authority.

We can illustrate this aspect of social power by means of two rather weak counterfactuals, of which the first, a power counterfactual, is usually reported in the literature: PCF: *If the superior agent had not exercised his alleged power, the subordinate agent would have acted differently.*

The second, lesser known, but actually more interesting counterfactual is a coercive counterfactual. It can be formulated thus: CCF: *If the subordinate agent had resisted, the superior agent could have used his power resources to overcome this resistance.*

It seems that both PCF and CCF are necessary conditions of power, the difference being only that CCF is somewhat the stronger of the two. Yet, it is not the case that CCF merely specifies the message of PCF; there is a rather deep difference between the two counterfactual propositions, as we shall see. PCF deals only with the exercise of power, or provides a necessary condition of the existence of power; that is, power can be exercised, otherwise it does not exist. PCF is also coercively neutral (see the explanation of this below). But CCF says something essential about the specifically coercive aspect of power, which is not true of PCF, namely, that even if the superior agent did not exercise his power just now, he still can do so. In other words, resistance to power attracts a threat-related counteraction, or a coercive measure, which will be more or less successful. Coercion is a method and coercive power is a capacity to overcome resistance.

Now, the key idea is that the wielders of coercive power can plausibly try to force their own will on their subordinate victims. If this possibility is lacking, I cannot see how we could ascribe coercive power to superior agents. However, in the case of authority, the position is radically different: PCF characterizes authority, but CCF does not. Take the case of a purely cognitive authority under our maximizing model, or religious charismatic power under the conventionalist model: the rejection of the authority involves two types of problems, that is to say, motivational and moral ones. Once the subordinate agent rejects, say, the superior agent's charismatic status, what can the superior agent do to counter this decision? It seems that he can do nothing but repeat his claim to an authority status or emphasize its beneficial consequences for the subordinate agents' welfare as well as its social and moral effects on his goals. Moreover, his commands are not feasible as speech acts, as the subordinate agent does not listen to them. However, no cognitive argument or group pressure can have any but contingent relevance on a subordinate agent's decision to dissent.

What the superior agent really should do in case of the rebellious subordinate agent is to use his authority to convince him of his mistake. But we already supposed that the subordinate agent does not admit of the superior agent's authority claims in his own present case. Therefore, should he reject the authority claims, the superior agent has in principle no way of making the subordinate agent accept his self-alleged and socially confirmed status. A superior agent's authority extends only as far as the social consensus concerning it extends. The case here is drastically different from that of coercion: threats presuppose the lack of consensus about what one is doing. Coercion is a conflict notion, unlike authority, whose structure resembles that of offers.

Some counterarguments against my position can be repeated. It may be said that, in the case of such a legitimate authority as, say, the police, one cannot escape their authority just by denying its validity in one's own special case. The police may coerce, and they have the right to do so. Therefore, as it seems, the existence of authority is, at least in legitimate cases, independent of the consensus concerning it.

The answer is simply as follows: Authority can be taken in two different senses. We have already distinguished between its effective and morally evaluative senses. Thus when a subordinate agent ultimately loses his trust in an authority, or when the motivational aspect of the denial becomes prominent, the superior agent's alleged status as an authority is no longer efficient. The subordinate agent will deny that the superior agent's authority motivates him. Granting this premise, we must admit that no reference to the superior agent's authority may explain the subordinate agent's subsequent actions. Such disobedience may be irrational, but it may also be perfectly prudent.

Nevertheless, it may still be true that the moral aspect of the denial of the superior agent's authority remains intact, and in its morally evaluative sense it is still true that the superior agent in fact is an authority, despite the subordinate agent's personal rejection of the idea. So, the superior agent's relevant power does not extend to that subordinate agent, but it still extends to his reference group, whose members subscribe to the authority. In this sense, the consensus-supported authority remains intact. It can be said that the subordinate agent should follow the superior agent's directions: the superior agent is an authority to all members of the group and hence is *in* authority even for the dissenting subordinate agent.

A subordinate agent's status as a group member is naturally unclear, as in some cases he can leave a group just by saying so; in some other cases, group membership is largely independent of his personal will—for instance, in the case of national identity. Anyway, my conclusion is that an individual makes an authority inefficient by removing his trust in that superior agent's powers. The moral aspect is independent of the efficiency problem. It may happen that a good claim to authority exists. Furthermore, if the whole subordinate group reaches a negative consensus concerning the superior agent's authority, in its evaluative sense, that aspect of authority will dissolve, granting the subjective nature of moral principles. Against such an opposition, the wielder of authority power does not have a chance.

The difference between coercion and authority can also be presented in another way. Two applications of PCF are necessarily valid. PCF1: *If the superior agent had not exercised his efficient authority, the subordinate agent would have thought or acted differently.* PCF2: *If the superior agent had not exercised his coercive power, the subordinate agent would have acted differently.* This is what I mean by saying that PCF is coercively neutral: definition AU shows that authority must change its object person's behavior. His motive to accept an authority is exactly that he can thereby think and act in ways not open to him otherwise. Authority effects a change in its object, although not necessarily against his will.

In the case of PCF2, the subordinate agent is tied to the coercive situation, from which he would escape if he had the chance. Because of a threat against him, his actions and decisions now depend on the superior agent's will, whose coercive effort may well be unsuccessful in the end. But we already granted the superior agent the initial success of staging the threat, as a matter of the logic of coercion, and this means that the subordinate agent "would have acted differently" without the threat. Both instances of PCF are accordingly true, and no difference between coercion and authority can be found here.

Yet, the same is not true of CCF. It is not coercively neutral. Look at the following two instances. CCF1: *If the subordinate agent had resisted, the superior agent could have used his efficient authority to overcome this resistance.* CCF2: *If the subordinate agent had resisted, the superior agent could have used his coercive power to overcome this resistance.* Only CCF2 has now some contingently true instances, as CCF1 is self-contradictory. Coercion that is never successful is a dubious candidate for the role of real coercion, but patently unsuccessful authority is nonsense. And resistance indicates the lack of success. Accordingly, we believe on empirical grounds that people really are able to coerce each other, at least in some suitable conditions, but we should not believe that the rejection of authority could be overcome by means of just the same source of power that was earlier rejected. Something like persuasion or manipulation is needed.

It is paradoxical that a form of social power—authority—exists only if the agent exercises it successfully. Ordinarily, we think that power leads to success, and really does not presuppose the success of its own exercise. Coercion becomes all the more central a notion when we see this. In the case of coercion, it is not the success itself that matters but rather the presentation of threats. The resulting obedience is a contingent fact. *Authority*, on the contrary, is a name for certain successful agents. It is a fully finalistic term, while *coercion* is more a causal term. The former presupposes the power wielder's success in order to be satisfied at all. The latter presupposes a process leading toward success or increasing the probability of success, if threats work well.

In sum, authority and coercion are two different types of power because efficient authority, unlike coercion, presupposes that the subject will not resist. If he resists, authority does not in that case signify power but degenerates into a more or less well-founded "should." The moral aspects of authority may prevail even in those cases where no power exists. When it comes to authoritative commands, we have seen that they also presuppose the object person's acceptance, both morally and personally.

Coercive constraints and commands

Abuse of authority

Stanley Milgram's psychological experiments, reported in full in his book *Obedience to Authority*, focus on commands.[27] I presume that the general idea of these experiments is familiar. Milgram's assistants asked the experimental subjects to administer electric shocks to invisible but audible mock victims. The upshot of the experiment was that the subjects were ready to hurt their victims quite seriously because they were commanded to do so. Milgram asks why this is so. He thinks that the observed obedience reflects some important properties of normative authority, as the source of the commands and the resulting action against the subjects' own judgments and prudent reason.

Now, Milgram explicitly compares his experimental subjects' decisions under pressure to those of war criminals, like certain Americans in Vietnam who were ordered to kill civilians, and who obeyed. Nevertheless, the analogy to institutionalized and well-defined command structures is not really present. His studies concern something like "pure obedience to incomprehensible commands." This is because the experimental subjects were tied to a strange laboratory environment involving equally strange instructors, without knowing what to do. If they wanted to participate at all, they had simply to observe what the instructors told them to do and then act accordingly. Otherwise, they could not play the game; the situation looks indefinable without the instructors' role.

The conventionalist model of authority is what we should apply here. It seems to constitute a weak and indifferent type of motive compared to the full-blown contract model, like the army. In this latter case, the subject has a clear-cut reason to obey. In Milgram's experiments, on the contrary, the subject just wants to participate, for the simple reason that he happens to be there — out of curiosity, the need for money, or for no reason at all. And if we reject the conventionalist model, the next alternative may entail that the instructors are specialist authorities in the sense that they create the impression that they really know what to do and that they are acting on some kind of scientific plan, unknown to the experimental subjects.

In this kind of situation, an authority is based on cognitive specialization; yet the final interactionist perspective is certainly conventionalist. Nevertheless, from the subject's own point of view, these characteristics do not fit together well. A scientific specialist is hardly in a position to give commands. Also, the conventionalist model does not make commands really binding and efficient. The subject obeys only because he does not know what else to do in a situation in which he has, say, promised to participate but which now reveals nasty new features that seem to make the earlier promises void. He may argue that he did not promise to participate in such madness. What may also happen is that he started to participate under a maximizing idea. He thought he might profit by letting the experimenters tell him what to do; but of course, this did not happen. The experiment was therefore a highly confusing trap, as it seems.

Commands should ideally break the resistance from the side of the object person's own choices according to the initially preferred action alternatives. It seems, therefore, as if Milgram's experimental subjects displayed surprising obedience to commands. This, however, cannot be based on authority. It is based on the abuse of authority. The experiments dealt with obedience but had not much to do with authority as the main explanation of this obedience. The experimenters were in no position to issue binding commands. They could ask the subjects to deliver shocks, but the resulting obedience may not have shown any effects of authoritative commands. Milgram writes:

> Many subjects will obey the experimenter no matter how vehement the pleading of the person being shocked, no matter how painful the shocks seem to be, and no matter how much the victim pleads to be out. . . . It is the extreme willingness of adults to go to almost any lengths on the command of an authority that constitutes the chief finding of the study and the fact most urgently demanding explanation.[28]

Milgram quickly identifies obedience and recognition of authority. Moreover, he supposes that all authority is effective power, or a motivational factor. This is hardly so. Some subjects suffered even if they obeyed, and thus it is really enigmatic why they did not quit. Others quit. Perhaps somebody behaved irrationally—meaning that no reference to authority can explain the results. Blind obedience implies mere abuse of authority.

In what follows I shall follow a hint from above, namely, that one important factor explaining the binding force of some commands is the subject's inability to see a way out of his interactive situation with the person issuing problematic commands. Such a context can be constructed in a rational manner, too—unlike that used by Milgram.

The main constructive idea is that, even if authority does not restrict a subject's freedom like coercion does, the interaction may occur in a situation that lacks open alternatives for action. Commands are efficient when they mobilize commitments with no alternatives. Otherwise, commands are just speech acts. The problem is how to understand commands issued by a superior agent to a subordinate agent within a coercive institution. How does one guarantee the subordinate agent's motivation by using commands?

The enemy is a variant of the mistaken application of the effective versus the normative concepts of authority, connected to a sloppy notion of a rational agency—that is, the idea that the superior agent's authority would entail the subordinate agent's actions according to commands. On the contrary, if the subordinate agent is rational, and not merely psychologically conditioned to respond favorably to certain characteristic command contexts, he will judge all novel situations as they arise. He wants to check that the second-order advisory or authorizing reason actually applies (recall that normative conflicts may make it void). Then, the superior agent's authority must fail to guarantee just that which it was expected to guarantee. This happens if we do not have a person whose socialization processes and moral education have been so strict and effective that he has lost his psychological ability to judge action plans from his own point of view. None of the citizens of a modern state is totally free in this psychological and positive sense. Nevertheless, it is reasonable to suppose that all of us should be fully free.

A large part of socially responsible living presupposes that we do not accept too much on the basis of authority claims alone but are able to accept or reject social regulations on the basis of how we individually judge them. These judgments imply assent to authority together with dissent from its abuse. In this sense, authoritarian demands conflict with the general moral atmosphere of a democratic society. No person can be supposed to be a robot programed through authority ascriptions and their related commands.

In the present perspective, we see that if the superior agent is expected to command he must either himself or via some other agent be prepared to observe and punish the reluctant subordinate agent. If the superior agent wants to do it himself, he will find both that his original authoritative status will change toward a more coercive one and that his work load will increase considerably. Otherwise, an increase in the number of subordinate agents will follow, which in fact is true of the coercive bureaucracy. However, this condition is the more important of the two: as we explain the superior agent's role and its moral characteristics, we imply that he is not involved in direct coercion himself. It was just by this feature that we gave an account of the ideas of how he can justify to himself his own role and its demands and why he is a suitable authority within the coercive institution. The discharge of responsibility demands that he not make threats. And without the superior agent, the institution cannot work.

Once a subordinate coercive agent rebels and rejects the institution's legitimacy, his role from his own point of view is not substantially different from that of the victim of coercion. Certainly there will also be some differences: the victim may have been educated in a totally different culture, so that he need not understand the idea of the legitimization of the institution. He need not know any members of the institution personally. The coercer's rebellion, on the contrary, arises within the state and its institutions. This can be supposed to create a special form of reaction, which will differ from a victim's corresponding action. But then we may also suppose that the victim's life history is that of an average citizen of the same society of which the institution is a part. In this way, our theory might well minimize the differences between the two targets of power exercise. Yet, no great weight can be put on this fact.

Again, we are talking about principles: if systematic institutional power cannot be built on the idea that a subordinate agent remains loyal to the authority of the superior agent, no correction of this situation can be expected in terms of other coercive agents. They will have to experience the same problems as the original superior agent did. A network of coercive relations within an institution cannot work. What can be done in order to certify obedience to the superior agent's commands is to use some of the subtler forms of coercion we reviewed above, such as deterrence and the exploitation of coercive circumstances. Two cases are relevant here.

First, we have a situation in which the superior agent's deterrent means are known to be smooth and effective. This happens where the status quo has already been established between the superior and the subordinate agents, after a period of initial struggle based on the fact that the duties are dangerous or unmanageable. After this stage is over, even if the superior agent may have needed some coercive threats in order to establish the balance, he needs now only an implicit deterrent threat to keep the situation as it is. The subordinate agent may be so well accommodated to the status quo that he does not even form the intention to rebel and will not consider the threats. Yet, it is still true that, should the implicit threat disappear, he would find the prospect of escape from his difficult tasks very attractive indeed. But as it is now, he obeys the superior agent's commands without visible resistance. I think this type of implicit, deterrent warning is an important factor in a coercive institution.

The acceptance of internal deterrence need not be irrational. We find an illuminating explication of this fact among our examples of coercive conditions that are not causally created by a coercer, cases like the cliff-hanger and the exploited factory worker. In these, no explicit threatening action could be identified, and yet they both exemplify strict coercion. The crucial point about both was that no return to the normal state of life was possible for these victims of coercion. In the cliff-hanger's situation, no one was causally responsible for the desperate conditions, or in other words, the coercer himself created no threat. He just found someone hanging there and "offered" his help. The victim had no hope of returning to anything like a normal situation. He could choose between the two alternatives of (1) falling to his death or (2) paying a high price for his escape. His utility distribution is analogous to that created by a highwayman's coercive threat.

Something similar happens also within a formal coercive institution: the subordinate agent is inside, and his escape from its bounds would lead to a situation in no way normal. He might escape and, say, emigrate illegally from his country. This is no normal state of affairs. Or, alternatively, he might stay and obey the commands even when he feels that the task is far too demanding, repulsive, and dangerous. It is important to see that the superior agent need not present any threats. He may leave the subordinate agent free and alone. However, in case of disobedience, the situation within the institution may be expected to become somehow nonnormal. The subordinate agent is supposed to want to be disobedient as little as he wants the abnormal life outside the institution, which is all that is open to him after he has escaped.

If the subordinate agent's starting position is such that no return to normal life is possible, the superior agent may make him obey his commands without ever creating an explicit threat position. Under such conditions, the subordinate agent may fail to obey and not receive punishment if his situation within the institution becomes drastically nonstandard—say, because of strong peer pressure. The subordinate agent may also suffer a permanent psychological loss by acting against his deep emotional commitments. Obedience is in those cases like the lifesaving rope thrown to the cliff-hanger by his old enemy: it saves, but the price is high.

I think that this picture is a realistic one. In most cases perhaps, obedience is secured by the subordinate agent's realization that an escape to "civilian" life cannot lead to any normal social conditions, even if his disobedience within the institution would have equally sad effects. If the institutional structure is optimal, only in the most demanding cases are direct internal coercion and threats needed. This motivating structure is usually rounded off by the subordinate agent's experiences of the superior agent's proper deterrent measures in the earlier stages of professional training. The three factors—hidden coercion, deterrence, and education/training—provide that background without which the effective commands would not be possible within the bounds of a formal coercive institution. Although its agents follow commands that are not backed by explicit threats, the circumstances themselves are implicitly coercive.

Closed social situations

We have found a possibly plausible solution to one of our remaining problems concerning the justification of institutional coercion. I shall suggest next that we combine the notions of authority and implicit coercion at the conceptual level. We have seen how some forms of effective authority and its commands come sufficiently close to outright coercion so that no separate threats are needed to support authority. I shall then try to show that the idea of coercive authority makes sense. The term is certainly somewhat misleading. It is only because coercive authority has some effects similar to coercion that it deserves its name.

If authority is like an offer and coercion entails a threat, then we should apparently explicate some coercive offers in the present context in order to make sense of institutional commands. My basic idea is simple. Authority gets coercionlike characteristics in those special cases in which the subordinate agent is (1) within an institution and (2) under the authority of the superior agent but (3) has no realistic chance of escaping from the interaction with him or his representatives. The closed situations employ coercive circumstances and work like virtual threats.

Now, these respective situations are not that different, except perhaps psychologically, when the subordinate agent, under the authority of the superior agent, must coerce a victim. Suppose the subordinate agent is alone against the victim, who seems to be armed and fully determined to fight and who should be arrested. The subordinate agent (now in the role of a coercer for his institution) does not know much about either the victim's utility function or his moral commitments. The victim may be in a very strong starting position. What coercer does know is (1) he is expected to take action because he is under a relevant authoritative commitment; and (2) he may back out of the situation only on condition that a plan is available that specifies what he would do when he retreats. He is supposed to be prudent, which implies that, if he can figure out neither how to avoid the action against the victim nor how to estimate its consequences, he cannot change his previously prescribed course of action.

A merely impulsive escape reaction is clearly out of the question now, even if it certainly occurs often enough in the irrational real world. In order to escape and minimize his expected losses, the coercer needs a feasible plan. It may be just one action alternative or a whole plan for the rest of his lifetime. Does he have such a plan available? This is an important question, which requires careful consideration. It seems natural to maintain that he indeed has escape roads open to him; but all things considered, those action alterna-

tives may not look attractive. He may go back to his car and drive
away, or he may apologize to the victim by saying that he was wrongly
identified. If he is alone, he may well think that he can get away with
this type of risk-minimizing move. In such a case, he is under no
authoritative commands. The escape move is not convincing. The
authoritative coercive institution will require the coercer to continue
his search, so that the present interaction will probably be repeated
again. He will have to explain what he did on that mission. He will
have to file an official report. And thus he will become committed
to personal and formal lies. He also knows that if the victim is captured, he will probably tell about the coercer's escape. We may even
suppose that the victim will consider the affair as a personal show
of power and as a victory over coercive state machinery, which provides him with a good motive to publicize the case. Thus the duties
of a subordinate coercive agent are typically difficult to evade.

Two examples from literature illuminate the extreme nature of such
a social trap, constituted by a formal institution through its code of
duty, virtue, and honor. Any sea captain has an important authoritative position among his men and everybody else on board his ship.
He has the right to use coercive means, too.
    Joseph Conrad's classic *Lord Jim* tells the story of Jim as an offi-
cer on a small steamship carrying a load of pilgrims in the Far East.
His sailors are an untrustworthy bunch of men, the pilgrims are like
cattle, and the ship is a rust pot. Then a storm rises, and everybody
knows the name of the game: if panic strikes, no one can escape, since
there are only a couple of life boats. In the mad rush, everybody will
be doomed. Jim's captain and men occupy the boats in secrecy; and
Jim shows unforgivable weakness of will by joining the sailors and
leaving the ship before it sinks. This is already bad enough, but the
ship does not sink, since the storm subsides. The case becomes public, and Jim's pangs of conscience become overwhelming. He has broken the most important single authority-constituting rule of the code
of sea officers. Instead of escaping, he should have gone down with
the ship, had it sunk. Jim is driven to seek his lost honor at the conclusion of the novel, where a suicidal death is the only fitting end.
He is happy to die. A return to any form of normal life for a man of
his status and character is impossible. No prudent utility calculations

can be applied to his life plans after the basic catastrophe. The breakdown of his internalized moral commitments have deep effects on his personality.

The Finnish author Volter Kilpi tells a similar story of Captain Lundstroem. He is sailing in Swedish waters, staying in his cabin and drinking, when his ship in a storm hits some rocks and sinks. Lundstroem and his cook are the only men who manage to save themselves. This is his end both psychologically and socially. He teaches navigation to the local youngsters for thirty years. He gets his salary in the form of hard liquor. There is nothing else he can do. He knows only how to sail, and he is psychologically and socially unfit to try anything else; so he drinks and teaches.

Both examples convey the same message. From a formal institution, there is no open escape route after a person has broken the rules central to its functioning. Individualist social philosophy too easily forgets this basic existential truth. People do not change their status, role, and explicit goals, as they change their clothes. Institutions are formed on the grounds of people's mutual expectations, beliefs, norms, and explicit promises. When they leave the institution in the wrong way, they are bound to break all those social conventions that now handicap them in relation to their future expectations. If they break a promise, they will be unable to issue promises. And if they do not have alternative skills, social connections, and a possible status, they have no place to go. Also, their self-image is built on the foundations of institutional commitments.

As Conrad and Kilpi are keen to emphasize, people do not have any purely external perspective on institutional life and its commitments. There is no Rawlsian veil of ignorance. On the contrary, those commitments are part of each person's own character, in its internalized sense. When they violate them, they are bound to hurt themselves, as well. Even if they are capable of self-deception for awhile, once they are outside the institution, it is very difficult for them to know where to go.

However, this is no all-or-nothing affair: people, places, and institutions are different. Each institution and social system has its own degree of bindingness. Each utilizes the methods of moral internalization and lack of open alternatives in different ways. Some escapes may be relatively easy; some are practically impossible. Once the alternatives to staying within an institution are practically nonexistent, or poorly defined or explored, it becomes difficult to know on what basis people could make a decision to leave it. We could suggest that, according to the minimax rule, a police officer should throw away his badge before he meets Jack Dillinger eye to eye, so that he avoids the worst possible personal alternative, or death, and can reach an alternate possibility. But what is this alternative? Certainly he can save his life by escaping. But what is he doing when he escapes? Where is he going? He may construct an elaborate lie and avoid all punishment. But once outside the institution, what are his short-term and long-term future alternatives? He does not know. It seems that the apparent choice between meeting and not meeting Jack is not always a real one, simply because "not meeting Jack" is not a well-defined action. It has no content, as our officer does not see what it entails. It has no subjective consequence structure. It is a mere expression of his weakness of will, or an impulse that cannot be explained in any rational manner. The goal is missing.

The main feature of this type of case is that if one believes, like Lord Jim, that he is going to die, he also seems to know what the worst alternative is and, accordingly, what he should avoid. In Conrad's novel, Jim of course ended up seeking his own death. But in a less romantic perspective, we can only say that death is not everything. During a war, a certain percentage of soldiers are supposed to die. Yet, no one supposes that mass escapes will take place simply because young men are going to die in colorful ways. Soldiers try escaping only when the war seems to lose its inherent purpose and, because of this, they suddenly see how and where to escape. This is what the enemy propaganda often tries to achieve, by giving "information" about alternative motives and goals as well as about methods of reaching them.

I do not think that social philosophy has always seen clearly enough the restricted nature of our institutionalized lives and the purposes served by our specialist positions. Our commitments, if broken, may leave us without a place to go; at least this is true of a number of the most important and demanding cases. An example is that of a former convict who tries to return to a normal law-abiding life. Recovering mental patients can also be mentioned. Often there is no return, as they are stigmatized by prison or mental institutions. They have no plan of life open to them; they cannot estimate the value of their future social expectations. It is a well-established criminological fact that many ex-criminals head straight toward a social void.

Military law may specify that anyone who first suggests a cowardly or rebellious action to others is, as the leader of the conspiracy, automatically responsible for all the consequences. Here we are again in the middle of the familiar multiperson prisoner's dilemma: the first who suggests the escape will be the worst off, even if all will profit from a simultaneous and spontaneous agreement. However, someone must take the initiative. Actually, such demanding coercive institutions as armies have taken this type of case into account in their legal codes, reflecting the valid idea that, after one person has taken the initiative against authority, all others profit from simultaneous assent. The possibility of the first step is due to the leader. Cooperation is profitable, but the one who starts it makes himself worst off, even to a catastrophic degree. The crucial point about this example is, then, that no one knows how the others will feel about the details of the novel situation or what the suggestion to act against the authority will reveal. I think this explanation extends quite far in the direction of Raz's thesis about the nonutilitarian characteristics of the protected second-order preferences on which authority is normally grounded.

We can now see how the agent's rights fare in a case where he would like to escape from the institution, if he could. We already compared the impossibility of escape, when it is against the rules and conventions of the institution, to a coercive situation without a specially created explicit threat. This may imply exploitation and a prima facie violation of the agent's rights. Nevertheless, in the present case the problems with rights are not evident. If social life is historically arranged in the form of institutional patterns so that those patterns are functionally well founded and in normal life not too demanding or cruel, it is difficult to argue that this social form of life would be as such right violating and exploitative.

All systems have their crisis situations, when an extra effort can be demanded. If the agent is involved in such crisis situations as a responsible member of the institution, and he cannot see any well-defined escape method, he can hardly maintain that his rights are violated. This fact presupposes that he is not exploited. Before the crisis, the agent should fully understand that the functioning of the institution is also for his own good. The prospect that in novel circumstances he may lose more than can ever be compensated is irrelevant. The agent then simply has bad luck. He has joined the institution freely and has taken the risk of getting trapped; or, in a case of a national army in war, he was born as a member of the society and thus "joined" it through his birth. This is not a freely chosen membership but a natural one. In the cases of both free and natural unexploitative memberships, it would be too strong a conclusion to say that the agent's institutional situation includes the violation of his rights, because it is not always the case that he has an actual right either to return to normal life or to choose a new and more comfortable life.

Once the norm of nonescape is made clear in the beginning of the agent's career, by saying that he may leave the institution only via some established procedures that are applied in noncrisis conditions, the agent cannot claim to have the right to escape at any moment he likes. And if the agent feels that he has a basic human right to escape from a too hot situation, he may even be granted that. But no alternative plan of life need be specified. Even if the agent is allowed to escape, that his rights include a ready-made alternative plan of life cannot be demanded.

I need not deal further with this problem. It seems clear, however, that any nonanarchistic theory of justice must both allow and specify the optimal limits to an agent's right to escape from the authority of an institution and to quit for some self-protective reasons. Some escape routes must be left open; but their existence should not make the institution impotent to take care of those demanding tasks for which it was originally created. (Unlike some Nozickian private protective associations.) Justice and the completeness of action programs should be fitted together. The main principle could perhaps focus on the reasons the agent might use to defend his own failure to act, namely, when his activity would have been essential to the success of the institution's goals. We cannot deny, however, that power institutions have a cruel structure, with respect to both their own agents and their victims. Coercion may be necessary and even fair, but it is never desirable.

In sum, because the institution and the superior agent are elements of a legitimate social order, the context of authority is necessarily a structured one. It is held together by authority relations. One of the purposes of this structuring is to make it partially closed to the subordinate agent. If he wants to avoid a task, he must do it in a predetermined and accepted way. In many cases, the agent must admit that he is trapped in his present situation. This idea is relatively independent of his calculations of expected utility, which can always and in principle be performed. Yet problems may be rare so that in many institutionally defined situations the calculations are too open-ended to give any real direction to the agent's desired decision to escape. All alternate goals are left undefined. Commands are efficient in relation to the agent's inability to plan his countermoves. Without escape routes, he cannot avoid personal harm and losses. The actual availability of such escape routes is an empirical issue.

5 | The Requirement of the Diversity of Morals

The victim's morality and its functions

Institutional coercive action ideally takes place only in those conflict situations in which the consensus of values is missing or breaks down, or the conflict is deep and serious, or at least one party resists all reasonable compromises. In such situations, any application of the utilitarian-style calculus of preferences and values is difficult. We may say that the method is impossible to apply, as its implementation presupposes some cooperation. This can be said to be true of prudent as well as more generalized utilitarian ideas of reasons for action. In crises, we need the kind of emergency measures that establish at least a minimal short-term social peace: any social reform takes time, and sensible institutional coercion and deterrence give us time, though the costs may sometimes be prohibitively high.

This is part of one of the more acceptable-sounding general justifications for coercive institutions. It is also a realistic view. People are still required to amalgamate their mutually incompatible preferences, desires, and needs.[1] Moreover, their values normally have an internal priority order, so that even if they are ready to compromise about certain lower-level elements, such high-priority elements like moral values (think of the abortion debate) are outside the democratic means of decision making. Now, once the issue is subjectively important enough and when voting paradoxes emerge in the relevant group decisions, an insoluble conflict emerges. Makeshift compromises do not work, and no rationally grounded democratic recommendations for mutual respect of each other's views can be observed.

All this may sound tough-minded. Yet I think it allows us to understand the social fact that in institutional coercion it is important to emphasize commands, norms, and duties, and to duly dismiss the problematic subjective consequences of an agent's action. Think of traditional military virtues, for example: here a subordinate coercive agent faces rigid social exchanges in the sense that he fulfills his duty thinking that the evaluation of consequences, as to its generalized social aspects and value, will be made independently of him in a different place and time. Certainly, this sometimes happens. No individual is supposed to know what the master plan he is helping to realize really is like. Ignorance is acceptable and even desirable. Thus the superior coercive agent's role approaches an authoritarian one, and the subordinate coercive agent is supposed to accept commands blindly. A libertarian may say that such institutional coercion is a morally dubious practice, regardless of its alleged status as a social necessity.

Any coercive social role demands basic rigidity in its bearers. Look, therefore, at the other side of the coin, namely, at the victim of coercion. He is, ideally, a consistent and prudent consequentialist, in the sense that he calculates his personal losses in terms of those expected utilities that the coercer's action will bring about. He may also be willing to take notice of certain effects on his reference group, which may vary in its size, constitution, comprehensiveness, and personal importance. Or he may be committed to more general values. Here we apparently return to the topics discussed in chapter two: there I argued that the victim, when he faces the coercer in a noninstitutional context, may be supposed to act in a prudently rational way or to follow his own revealed preferences and values when he reacts toward the coercer's initial efforts. However, if the victim is sufficiently confused or irrational, he cannot be coerced. The same conclusion follows if his preference structures and background culture are sufficiently strange so that the coercer cannot possibly understand them well enough. In this sense, if coercive institutions are taken to be socially necessary, it is quite natural to stress the normative features and the desirability of a consequentialist conscience.

The upshot of these general ideas is simply that prudent conse-
quentialists are the ideal victims of coercive institutional agents when
a deep enough practical conflict prevails. Persons who take no notice
of their own good cannot be coerced. Also, generalized utilitarianism
is desirable, from the coercer's point of view, in the victim's moral
attitude; he would then try to minimize the losses to all those people
whose values he at least partially shares. The coercer may use this
feature of the victim's personal moral code to direct an efficient threat
against the victim's welfare. The coercer is, however, required to mobilize more effort than that required to coerce the victim alone. Is
it typically costlier to deal with a group of people than with only one
direct counterplayer? Let us not oversimplify; the victim may well
be markedly less determined to let others suffer than to suffer personally, and those others' welfare might be already fully dependent
on the coercer.

We are really dealing with abstract problems of moral education
now. We ask, What kind of normative principles and ideals should
be taught to prospective social agents? This area can be approached
from two opposite directions, namely, from the point of view of those
who under the conditions of the uneven distribution of power identify themselves with the coercive institution and that of those who
identify themselves with the potential victims. The former group
naturally emphasizes the duties of the coercer and the prudence of
the victim. The latter group cannot say anything about the coercer,
except perhaps that he should not exist at all. We know that prudent
coercers are neither believable nor convincing.

The victim's attitude is interesting. If he emphasizes the coercer's
prudence or consequentialist orientation in general, he is in fact saying that (1) coercion can be reduced to personal egoistic immorality,
in those rare cases where it is understandable in the first place; or
(2) coercion should not be a socially institutionalized conflict resolution strategy. This latter attitude does not really concern the coercer
but rather his social status and its evaluation. The victim cannot say
much about his coercer in any constructive and sympathetic manner.

Concerning moral education, it is quite predictable that a state institution that uses threat-based security measures will contribute
toward its own suitable ideological background. Obedience to au-

thority in its many symbolic forms is a recurrent theme in schools. Without an ideological background, coercive threats can be expected to lead to violence, terrorism, and civil war. Yet, as we have seen, in many cases coercion is needed, at least in its minimal sense, when the state has reached a suitable degree of complexity and while it is still at the mercy of unpredictable changes. The state needs to protect itself and to guarantee its own survival. Coercion is then at least prima facie justified. As a precautionary measure, a state must try to create the ideological and moral conditions that allow its members to engage in coercion. One of the main functions of the educational system is to reproduce the culture. Hence, it should also reproduce a climate of values where coercion makes sense. I shall argue that a clear-cut diversity of morality is thus presupposed. No uniform ideal moral system can fulfill all those requirements necessary for social survival. My argument runs as follows: social conflicts are always at least a real possibility, and if the coercer's and the victim's interests and values do not differ too much, the one with the most resources can utilize its power. Conflicts are dissolved in this way.

However, we cannot accept as fair a system where a coercer threatens the victim only in those cases in which an individual prudent calculus of values shows an expected shared profit. We want systematic and just coercion and so give the monopoly of power to the state. The social function of institutional coercer can be satisfied only through their code of duty, and this rests on legitimate authority. But because the coercer works in a conflict situation, he cannot suppose that the victim accepts his reasons for action in all possible cases. On the contrary, the victim will instead not do so, and therefore he must realize that he needs countermeasures against the coercer's potential power exercise. For instance, a citizen facing state power is in a situation wherein he cannot win a resource race against the state, and so may instead adopt softer methods. The result may well be the development of a moral ideology that leads his reference group toward a rights orientation. Such a move prevents smooth coercion, because the victim now becomes relatively immune to his own private good and prefers instead to focus on liberties, personal integrity, and social honor.

It is interesting to see why the liberalism grounded on philosophical utilitarianism not only recommends but actually presupposes and requires a very weak "night watchman" state in order to be feasible at all. A liberalist cannot fight back. Therefore, given a strong state and turbulent social circumstances, any purely prudent citizen will be in difficulties in trying to face and deflect the state power. And modern social conditions are in fact turbulent. Moreover, we have strong state machineries throughout the world. Not even the much-cherished Western democracies are free of superefficient state power. A partial explanation for their strength is the constant danger of international large-scale war. Anyway, states are strong, and the liberalism of their citizens, who want to retain their relative independence and decision-making potential, needs something other than utilitarianism to support it. They simply cannot think that the basis of liberty is that everyone can maximize his own preference satisfaction and take care of his own welfare. Those who behave narrowly prudently are the ideal victims of coercion and are ultimately incapable of taking care of their own liberties should a conflict occur with the dominant powers represented by the state apparatus of institutionalized violence.

Therefore, it seems quite natural that the victim should have revitalized ideas of rights, like freedom, self-realization, and private property. *Right* should be understood here mainly in the sense of liberty, although sometimes it means the ability to present claims against the state. Virtues like courage, temperance, and solidarity also work well in the present context. As Rawls makes clear, no financial compensation may be accepted to counter the effects of the loss of freedom of speech, the denial of religious beliefs, and the forced change of geographical location. Liberty is prior to welfare in terms of compensation. This is a radical move away from the liberalist ideology of utilitarianism, as it makes the victim largely immune to institutional coercive power.

If a victim does not pay primary attention to his own welfare and if he is not expected to accept compensations, it is easy to see why he is difficult to coerce. But this attitude does not lessen the seriousness of the conflict, either. If he sticks to his idea of rights and insists on the bindingness of a coercer's corresponding duties when the coercer does not see the point of this claim, the conflict will collapse into violence. That is a type of degenerated coercion. Both its emergence and results will be predictable.

In international affairs, even the victim's attitudes may be so rigid that the coercer cannot expect to change them by means of mere threats. The result is war. In this way the rights view, especially in its Rawlsian priority sense, is a socially explosive idea, especially if it is applied during turbulent times to, say, an antiegalitarian society. Nevertheless, the rights view is a natural social reaction to institutional pressure and conflict. Of course, everything can be softened if the parties think in terms of their own prudent good in some special cases that are not socially predictable in advance. Rights must be no straitjacket.

Coercion is bad enough without the extra requirement that it should always be resisted regardless of personal consequences: a prudent victim cannot be uniformly blamed. But if the victim thinks in terms of rights, it cannot benefit the coercive institution. Actually, the institution's relevant moral framework is more limited than that of the victim's simply because it has one means to its goal. The victim's main interest, avoidance of harm, can be obtained through several avenues.

Next, a counterargument against this schema can be repeated: the typical "soft" behavior of the victim, as desired by the coercer, can also be achieved by explaining the victim's fully internalized, deontological ethics. Therefore, the victim definitely need not be a consequentialist. It is certainly true that if the victim is a deontic agent, the coercer can get him to do what is wanted by designing a situation so that, if the victim does not comply with the commands, he will necessarily act against his own cherished duties. For example, say the victim has explicitly promised to take care of his family's welfare in some especially troubled social conditions. Now, if a coercer threatens to make this impossible to do, such a prospect might be an even more efficient factor than threats against the victim's welfare, simply because the victim sees it as his moral duty to keep his promise. In other words, the coercer may be able to mobilize the victim's internalized duties quite effectively.

Yet, it does not follow that the coercer need not emphasize, at the level of educational policies, that it would be better if the victim did not consider duties to override his consequentialist considerations. In general, it would be better if the victim acted according to expected utilities. This can be seen as follows. If the victim is a serious deontologist he can, of course, be supposed to be willing to make rather large personal sacrifices in terms of expected utility if he can thereby avoid right and norm violation. This much I am ready to admit to be unquestionable. But then it does not follow that a consequentialist victim would not be easier to coerce than a deontologist. On the contrary, a duty-observing victim recognizes only a limited number of threats, namely, those that go against his norms and duties. These can of course be fairly abstract and cover a lot of ground, like the universalized maxim "you should not kill, regardless of the circumstances," or detailed and restricted, like "never tell a significant lie to the female members of your own clan."

What the coercer can do against such a deontologically thinking victim is, first, to check what duties the victim recognizes and, second, to threaten to make him break them. These may concern the victim himself ("take care of your own physical health"; "do not eat meat") or someone else among the victim's reference class ("protect your family at any cost to yourself"). If the coercer is able, say, to force his victim to eat meat or if the coercer can harm the victim's family, he has an effective threat position available against the victim's interests.

Nevertheless, no single combination of the victim's norms and duties can be equally all-inclusive as, say, "whatever you do, act in such a way that your action rule will be such that it maximizes utility in the long run." And some duties cannot be used by the coercer to create threats. Norms and duties as individual principles have a limited area of application, despite the possibility that they are universal: they concern only given action types and principles. This holds also for any group of them, but utilitarian maxims cover all actions and action contexts at once. Therefore, if the coercer is dealing with a consequentialist, he has more degrees of freedom to plan his threats. In the deontological case, he must notice that some contexts are devoid of any threat positions that exploit ethics. What could a highwayman say to his deontologically thinking victim?

Moreover, "never let yourself be coerced" makes perfect sense as an unconditional duty, but can hardly be understood from a utilitarian point of view. In fact, many duties seem to be such that they do not permit a victim's obedience to the coercer, who has no right to demand it. Just the opposite; the victim may have a duty not to obey.

So in spite of the fact that norms and duties provide a possible basis for coercive planning against the victim, an antiutilitarian victim may as well offer resistance on the basis of his duties. To the coercer this negative aspect more than shakes the idea that such a deontological opponent might be a systematically desirable one. Possibly the most damaging situations in social life, outside war, famine, and exploitation, occur in cases in which the coercer has no authority whatsoever over the victim who is a strict believer in duty.

With respect to the victim's thinking in terms of rights, the situation is not quite such a cul de sac. The victim may think that his money and papers are his private property to which he has an unconditional natural right of ownership. He can, however, alienate this right without breaking any moral rules. The coercer's demands are immoral, but the victim may comply in the case of his own rights whenever he thinks that it is not sensible to resist. The victim may become prudently suspect, but from the point of view of his rights, the case is unproblematic: the victim may give away what is his own. Nevertheless, the victim's rights give him good and sensible ground for resisting even after the coercer's threat exceeds the dollar value of his money and papers. Such a victim is bound to be quite unpredictable. He can make his own decisions in this case. It is not clear, however, what factors should determine his decision to yield or resist. In the case of pure utility calculations, the decision rule exists, unlike in the case where utilities are mixed with rights. Rights make the victim's decision to resist difficult to predict. He may resist on the basis of his rights as long as he likes, depending only on the subjective importance of these rights.

Duties, on the contrary, tend to make the victim vulnerable to accusations of immorality independently of his subjective opinion and initial resistance, if he ultimately yields. Duties are other-concerning principles, and thus the issue as to whether to break them or not cannot be the victim's private affair. In the paradigmatic cases, he has a duty because of another person's corresponding rights. Therefore, to act against his own duty is to violate another's rights. Threats against duties are most serious moral infringements.

Resistance against coercion may, therefore, be extremely high if the victim is strictly duty oriented. As a social self-defense of some minority groups and persecuted ideologies, religious and political, this has had considerable social and historical importance. Small groups who see themselves in danger emphasize customs, identities, traditions, virtues, and duties as absolute moral values, outside all compromise or negotiation as to their implementation. Such factors constitute their identity. Who can say that those people are not perfectly sensible in doing so? Their attitude makes the social cost of power exercise very high. But it is high for all relevant parties.

Serious conflicts arise when a collective victim emphasizes the members' freedom and welfare rights to such an extent that they now assume the role of survival rights. As Alan Gewirth so strongly argues, all people, if they are logically rational, will necessarily claim a right to freedom and welfare for themselves.[2] This is simply because these are necessary components of all action plans. Without freedom, one cannot act; and welfare is the goal common to all action. But an even more basic right is the right to survival. One cannot act at all, if one does not survive. Freedom and welfare, which are presupposed in action, themselves presuppose this.

However, in the case we are discussing now, the victim tends to see his freedom and welfare as being so severely endangered that the main problem for him is no longer their realization in action but their basic existence in the near future. The victim's right claims are so urgent that their importance is roughly equal to duties. Survival rights cannot and should not be alienated. The coercer's plan of action against his victim becomes now problematic, and both rational players are at an equal level concerning their nonprudent motivation. Their respective mobilized norms are similar. The justifiability of coercive practices will then depend on these moral ideas: action against a victim's duties and rights is a more serious infringement than against his utility.

Is there a conceptualization of these diverse ideas that would allow us to formulate an ideal supertheory of morality so that the diverse rational requirements of institutionalized coercive policies would be derivable from it? This I shall discuss next.

As a preliminary point, the following argument from "missing circumstances of justice" shows why the standard universalizing ethics cannot work as a unifying principle across parties in conflict. Suppose Jack and Jill are traveling in a foreign country where several groups are waging war. Now they are trapped among the rocks on a mountain, waiting for the final assault by the Reds. Jack and Jill are absolutely certain that they will be killed. No help is coming. The Reds think that they are the Blacks' spies. Should they commit suicide or fight? Prudent thinking advises them to kill themselves; otherwise they may be tortured. Certainly they should not fight — they should minimize harm in the situation. And if Jack and Jill universalize their personal motives, they will notice that killing that does not serve any purpose cannot be justified according to any universal rule of ethics. The enemy is human, and their lives should be respected. The right to self-defense does not apply either. They cannot defend themselves. If they cannot defend themselves, their only motive to kill would be personal aggression and hatred. They could only want to kill as a revenge, to harm the enemy. This is an egoistic and nonuniversalizable motive.

Of course, Jack and Jill cannot be demanded to commit suicide. They are entitled to fight back. Such a conclusion does not rest on moral grounds. Needless killing is always wrong. Therefore, at least in some conflict situations, the parties cannot agree on moral views. Both parties must act on prudent and nonuniversalized grounds. Yet Jack and Jill may refer to their entitlements regarding the situation. The case is not without prescriptive content.

Moralities in conflict?

Many complexities at which I have tried to hint lurk behind the simple framework we have been using up to this point. It may well happen that an institutional coercer, whose role presupposes his personally internalized norm and duty orientation, is at the same time an object of functionally important coercive activity. In this case, he is a victim. Or, to put it more accurately, his social position is characterized by those demands and pressures directed at a coercer as well as by those directed at a victim. We may suppose that the situation is one of cognitive conflict and tends to lead to a kind of normative schizophrenia when our coercer/victim is required to alternate between his deontological and consequentialist moral moods. He has certainly a good motive to try to combine them. He is, after all, supposed to believe in both these ideologies in earnest. Can one accept two moral codes at the same time?

Nevertheless, most persons seem to be able to live that kind of double moral life, if they have to. Many of us assume combinations of different roles in family, business, in the service of the state, as well as in our innumerable relationships with strangers. Typically, we live in many worlds, with at least partially conflicting ideals.

Psychologically, there is nothing surprising in this schizophrenia. It need not disturb us. As F. G. Bailey puts it, everyone of us is a "colony of selves."[3] Yet, the recognition of this truth leads us toward an important philosophical point: institutional coercive power has its typically hierarchic structure; and hence, the two moral perspectives, one conceptualized in terms of rights and duties and the other in terms of utility, cannot in actual practice be unified into one single overarching ideal moral code—speculation is, of course, a different matter altogether. As I have already argued, systematic coercive success requires the existence of two broad types of morality. My question is the following: Can they be unified into one single and all-embracing moral ideology or into some rational method we could, in principle, implement in social life? The solution should also be motivationally effective. Certainly, it would be neat if we could answer in the affirmative. A negative answer may imply that moral subjectivism is a chaos of opinions.[4] But we seem able to avoid the worst alternative. Moral principles may be subjective, but they do not collapse into chaos. Their main outline has a social function, which, of course, allows for an almost endless variety of social details and individual styles.

To see that this is indeed the case, we may consider the following possibility. Two actually supported moral theories exist: (1) deontology reinforced with rights; and (2) consequentialism. Their respective roles and effects in social life are often (though not always) different. They serve mutually incongruent purposes.[5] There is no question that the social functions of deontology and consequentialism are really different. The coercer's and the victim's roles are actually converse in the sense that one person's success is the other's defeat. (This is rather ironic, however, because in a coercive situation the victim can never actually win in the sense that he could gain something positive.) In order that a coercive system function properly, the coercer must be deliberately rigid in his decisions and actions and he must not start any social exchange with the victim. The victim, in his turn, may lapse into s-irrationality when he tries to avoid the coercer's undesirable influence. But if this is indeed irrational behavior, the victim's acceptance of consequentialism shows exactly why he is irrational and why he should not be so.

According to consequentialism, it is either inadvisable or morally questionable to resist the coercer beyond certain limits. If the victim supported deontology, the resulting social conflict would be more serious, and of a qualitatively different kind than in the case where he supported consequentialism. The style and success of a coercive exchange depend on its moral background. Therefore, at least two different moral views must exist in any properly organized and sufficiently complex social system. If they are too similar, the ideological basis of controlled coercive policies will be disturbed. The underlying lack of consensus of values then becomes necessary to guide the coercer's and the victim's choices of action. Therefore, the main social goal of ethics—the advancement of social peace and stability[6]—can be reached only if there are at least two different moral theories accepted in the society. The point is that a change of role may imply a change of moral code and its associated principle of individual rationality. Morality need not be an internally inconsistent— but only a very loose—form of life. It has no hard core. Yet, within a given situation, and case specifically, morality binds either agent.

Moral theories can be harmonized. I mean this in the sense that we subjectively admit the necessity of rationality and of doing only what is good and right. But we do not pay much attention to the origins of those deeper reasoning processes that produce our knowledge of these matters. Such a hazy supertheory is certainly possible. Nevertheless, at the level of more critical reflection, consequentialism and deontology are destined to be mutually exclusive. We can try to unify them by, for example, reducing one to the other; but, as their social uses are so glaringly different, our effort in the direction of ultimate unification is doomed to be a philosophical failure, as I have already tried to show. Moral theory and practice would then form an unhappy and anomalous combination within the limits of the suggested consequentialism + deontology theory. And certainly there is no reason to be surprised that consequentialism and deontology are two separate theories, since this very idea reflects the further fact that below the smooth surface of social life there always exist aggression, perversity, contradictory values, mutually inconsistent desires and goals, zero-sum games, severe shortages of resources, and cognitive irrationality, all of which combine to make it impossible to create the kind of just and free society in which coercion would never be needed.

We then come to a warning concerning my arguments and their conclusions. I have claimed that real coercion exists, independently of other types of social power. I have said nothing about the further empirical question concerning the importance and frequency of coercive efforts in social life. And, therefore, if it is not the case that coercion is a widespread and important ingredient of control and planning, it is also possible that my distinction between the respective roles of consequentialism and deontology does not explain much about the actual diversity and controversy concerning moral notions and ideologies. That is an empirical question, though.

Let me finally provide an argument to the effect that consequentialism and deontology cannot be expected to become unified at the level of relevant and effective ethical theory. We suppose that the consequentialist theory, which the victim ideally should support, has its positive value or is only indifferent to the victim. Moreover, consequentialism should contain a proviso that guarantees certain strong rights to the victim, as these are positively valued by him. This means simply that the victim is supposed to take care of the consequences of his own actions, given that his strategy of action does not infringe on his own basic rights, like political liberty. It is easy to grant this much to the victim, as we need to think of his rights as Nozickian "moral side constraints" that the coercer may not touch.[7] Empirically speaking, we should realize that such limited consequentialism forms a core element of ordinary morality.

The coercer's perspective is different, and any society where power is exercised must try to provide moral education for its members so that this fact is recognized. It follows that a coercer must have a definite power advantage over his victim. Notice also that the value of prudent rationality is negative to a coercer, personally, although the relevance of utilitarianism is not quite clear. Some kind of basic utilitarian proviso must be guaranteed to the coercer, simply for psychological reasons. If he takes no notice of the general consequences of his actions, he is either a monster or a machine. What is required is only that deontological considerations overcome in importance

those of consequentialism. Thus deontology dominates over consequentialism in the case of the coercer.

Can we formulate such an ideal combination of both (1) consequentialism that entails the rights proviso for the victim and (2) deontology that dominates but does not strictly exclude consequentialism in the case of the coercer? That does not seem to be possible.
The following (invalid) ideal principle might be suggested, contrary
to my thesis that consequentialism and deontology are different. P:
*If a person is in a distressing situation, he may put personal inter-
ests before social duty; and if a person is not in such a situation,
he should always put social duty before personal interests.* This principle can perhaps be applied to coercion: the victim is in a distressing
situation, but the coercer is not. And if P is itself judged to be a deontological thesis, deontology dominates over consequentialism.

Certainly P cannot be accepted. It is enough to notice that (1) a
coercer may coerce because of some personally or socially distressing motives; and (2) the victim's subordinate position in relation to
the coercer might depend on the fact that someone else besides him
is in a very distressing position. Therefore, it sems that P builds too
close a connection between coercion and the regulating moral principles. The relative distribution of a person's duties and preferences
seems to depend mainly on whether he is in the position of a (superior) coercer or a (subordinate) victim.

We cannot deal with the present issue any further without sketching
some features of a metaethical theory. I shall point out what is needed
if we hope to understand the ethics of coercion. I shall first draw a
distinction between (1) moral justification by means of "ideologies
of legitimation," to use a sociological jargon expression; and (2) the
application of a justification within the actual social life world by
means of some bridge principles, or "ideologies of implementation."
Second, I shall once again emphasize the difference between moral
justification and motivation. To do this, it is useful to start from
John D. Hodson's recent book *The Ethics of Legal Coercion,* which
is a serious attempt to say something about the justifiability of coercion.[8] But Hodson's attempt is marred by his inability to see the
peculiar nature of "bridge laws." Let us see what this means.

In a fashionable manner, Hodson accepts the Kantian thesis to the effect that it is our overriding duty to respect persons or so to act that no one is treated as a mere means but always as an end in itself. This is a familiar and prima facie valid principle of moral justification: we cannot be blamed if we (always) treat human beings as intrinsically valued persons. Hodson then gives the following definition of coercion:

> The concept of coercion may be usefully explicated by means of the idea of a "declared unilateral plan." . . . The person's declared unilateral plan is what that person declares that he or she will do if the second person fails to cooperate or comply. . . . Coercion is the attempt to secure compliance by means of a declared unilateral plan which is *prima facie* immoral, whether by the mere declaration of the plan or by its actual performance.[9]

Certainly this description of coercion is only partly consistent with the one I explicated above. It may also confuse threats and offers. Sometimes I give money to another person without asking first whether he wants it or not. I say that I shall send the money in mail if he does not collect it personally. And such offers may not be immoral.

Hodson's problem is that he provides us with such weak necessary conditions of coercion that they are scarcely illuminating. The crux of the matter is that the victim of coercion must have some plans of his own if he is going to act intentionally and respond to the coercer's "unilateral" plans. The mere use of force to overpower the victim is not yet coercion. And the same is true of verbal manipulation. We have already discussed the idea of distinguishing between mere force and real coercive threats. The result is that the victim must have his own well-founded goals, if the coercer is supposed to be in principle able to get what he wants from his victim. I take up this issue once again because it has certain important implications concerning Hodson's justification of coercive legal interactions.

Next, let us check what acts of legal coercion may be morally justifiable from the victim's point of view, forgetting all the tricky demands on the coercer. "It is not a violation of the principle of respect for persons to use legal coercion to require persons to aid others, provided that what is required is . . . vital to the personal functioning . . . of those aided, and provided that the burden of bringing aid is fairly distributed and does not impose a major sacrifice on anyone."[10] This welfare principle is just one of the several specifications of Kant's maxim discussed by Hodson.

We have here what we might call a specified principle of respect for persons applied to coercion (call it SP). It says that *one person may coerce a second person (the victim) to help a third person, provided that the third person really needs help, the victim is treated fairly, and his interests do not suffer too much.* The key provisos embedded in SP seem to work like bridge principles, allowing us to apply Kant's basic maxim to real-life situations. We thus have a maxim, a description of a coercive interaction, and a specification of the features of the interaction that makes the maxim apply to it.

Notice next that if a coercer wants to justify some forms of coercion by means of SP, he should guarantee that the victim's evaluative and prescriptive attitudes toward the interaction are of the right kind. As we know, the victim should (functionally) be a consistent utilitarian (both prudently and generally). If the victim strongly emphasizes his own rights or the value of his personality, SP is prima facie not satisfied, however mild the threat might initially look. In this case, the violation of his rights implies a "major sacrifice of someone" (the victim), and thus the threat cannot be accepted. Only if the victim is a utilitarian can this key condition of SP make sense. But then there is no Kantian maxim to be satisfied. On the contrary, SP says, simply—and in a utilitarian fashion—that threats should not be too expensive to the victim. But this is not enough: if the third person's predicament is not (causally) the victim's fault, the fact that helping the third person is not expensive cannot alone justify the threat. To avoid vacuous utilitarianism, the coercer needs to show that the victim has a duty to help the third person in the given situation. But SP says nothing about this.

Let me illustrate the problem I have in mind. According to SP, almost any citizen of Finland can be coerced to help the people in the developing countries. At least 10 to 20 percent of an average salary should be surrendered. Such a coercive policy would not violate SP, as formulated by Hodson. Yet it seems that the whole idea is strictly unacceptable. Extra taxes cannot be created on a coercive basis just because someone needs my money more than I do.

If a coercive agent hopes to justify his policy, he should at least be able to show that there are some deontic normative requirements that apply to the victim, even if those requirements are such that the victim will not consider them. Otherwise, no coercion is needed. He should also show that the victim's personal losses will be neither unfair nor excessive compared to social benefits. Unfairness is a deontological idea, however, and thus we cannot suppose that the victim takes it too seriously while under coercive threats. Therefore, the applications of SP seem to hinge on the "major sacrifice" idea, which, again, means that the victim is supposed to be a prudent utilitarian agent.

The whole business of the justification of coercion in terms of SP is a questionable affair, simply because the victim cannot be supposed to be able or willing to use a part of SP to evaluate his own role in the interaction. SP does not provide a shared moral motive, even if it provides an occasional moral justification. Such an incongruence entails that the victim will be coerced to be moral to fulfill his relevant duties. This reinforces my original claim that there cannot be one unified ethics of coercion. The victim does not and cannot accept the same principles as the coercer. Hodson himself assumes the coercer's position.

What seems to happen in the typical evaluations of coercion is that the divergent moral pressures on the coercer and the victim make it impossible to use and implement a solid and unified principle like SP. To use our former conventions, consequentialism and deontology are in conflict in coercive interaction, and they cannot both be applied at the same time to justify or condemn an instance of coercion. An attempt in that direction will be a motivational failure. The bridge principles are social in the sense that both agents are supposed to know "their station and its duties" and to apply suitable normative methods.[11] Otherwise, no coercion obtains. And a part of those social bridge principles is that they demand that the coercer and the victim use different moral ideas.

Now, these moral ideas that the coercer and the victim are supposed to use, consequentialism and deontology, cannot be combined, because they are also used to motivate and not only to justify the interaction. If we want to justify or to condemn the interaction as a whole, we need an external perspective from which something like SP can be applied. It is rather paradoxical to maintain that the moral thinking that may justify or condemn a coercive interaction is not applicable within the interactive process itself as a principle that motivates both the coercer and the victim. Normally, we think that moral justification is a prescriptive process, which should and can motivate the agents in question. An ideal moral person is supposed to be a well-informed and logical agent, who is also motivated by the idea that his goals and methods are morally justified. But as we have seen, in coercive interaction the coercer cannot think that the victim is such a person. Actually, SP logically entails that the victim cannot understand SP; that is why he is coerced. The coercer, as the user of SP, may assume the position of a morally superior agent.

My conclusion is that the coercer and the victim must follow different principles of moral reasoning, if their coercive relationship is going to make sense at all. A unified moral theory can be used to explain the justification of coercion, but no such theory applies to its prescriptive or normative motivation.

If, however, *ought* implies *can*, the victim may forget the whole moral issue. He cannot apply it to his own case, and therefore he need not obey its directive norms. Because the victim cannot be required to agree with the coercer's justification due to the genuine conflict between them, the only thing that can be expected from the victim is that he make coercion as easy as possible for everyone involved — for instance, by not seeking revenge later. This implies prudent behavior on the victim's part. And certainly the victim himself may agree to the norm that he should be prudent in certain types of conflict and not pay attention to his deontological commitments. Such a prudent approach makes sense exactly in those cases in which coercion is "objectively" justified, say, by means of SP. But neither Hodson nor I have been able to prove anything like that to be the case.

The personal responsibility of a deterrent agent

An antiutilitarian, like John D. Hodson, says that moral choice logically presupposes that the choosing agent respects the rational freedom of those whom he sees to be under the influence of his choices (this group includes the agent himself). Respect for genuine freedom is a necessary condition of moral action. Notice that according to traditional views, not all freedom qualifies for this morally crucial role. The whole Kantian idea of respect for freedom tends to be extremely vague in the sense that its bridge laws are difficult to specify. Even slaves are treated as human beings in some minimal sense; is this enough? The most respectful treatment of one's friends may require an infringement of their perhaps questionable rights; is this immoral?

It seems very difficult to specify the empirical limits of the Kantian moral maxim, important as it is. It may be true that the lack of respect for a person's freedom logically entails that the intervening agent's actions are not morally good. However, a person's social obligations and other commitments may cause trouble in connection with such an individualist interpretation. Social reality has its own normative demands.

Imagine a prison guard in modern democratic society. I shall try to show that certain demands of the guard's characteristic social position present a relevant example in the following sense: the guard's behavior is contrary to the moral requirement of respecting another person's freedom—even if it is hard to see, in the social perspective, why this should make his action immoral. This discussion is needed for the justification of a nonanarchistic social theory.

Let us start by supposing that the guard thinks that the society he is a member of is perfectly just (otherwise he would leave his job and believe that no one should replace him; and in fact should try to eliminate his job). Thus the guard thinks that his job, too, is morally justified. He has one basic way of supporting this positive idea; that is, by first referring to the allegedly just nature of the society and then applying the universalizability test to his own action. It seems that the guard must indeed rely on the ultimately just nature of the social order if he wishes to maintain his conviction that he should not resign from his job. He simply says that his individual behavior cannot be immoral because the social order is just. In what follows, I shall try to show that this line of argument leads us to recognize some interesting problems.

It should be clear that the familiar Kantian maxim EI (*to treat all humanity as an end in itself*) does not apply smoothly to the case of the guard's social role. He is unable to respect the prisoner's rational freedom, because he himself is not free to make any decisions in the situation. In other words, he does not possess personal decision-making power. He is not free with respect to his reactions to the prisoner's challenges. Yet the prisoner's life is restricted by the guard's presence and by his typical deterrent capacity. The guard will react mechanistically, or in a socially deterministic and alienated manner. To him, the prisoner is a nonperson. But this is to say that the guard makes himself a nonperson, as well, in the relevant aspects of his life. He allows his own decisions to be rigidly deterministic reactions to the other man's behavior, even if they were designed to diminish the prisoner's—and only his—basic welfare.

We can argue that the guard cannot possibly satisfy the personal demands of EI while staying within the limits of his social role. However, let me note one essential fact: we are really exploring the demands of the guard's role, or his position within a social substructure. This means that we are not interested in the guard's personal features but only in the code of official demands.

Let me next specify why I think EI does not apply to our master example. Within the limits of the social structure, the guard has no possibility of compensating for his deeds and their consequences on the prisoner's welfare. His noncompensatory role is in a certain sense authoritarian, since he is supposed to think that his deterrent role, which is also his power against the prisoner, is legitimized through the structure of law enforcement, which is, again, a part of a still larger social order. The guard, so to speak, represents some genuine decisional power sources, although he himself certainly does not possess personal power to do anything relevant. In other words, his power over the prisoner can be explained by pointing out that the guard passively represents an authority that belongs to a different structural level and to its positions; there, power is linked to the freedom to make decisions concerning the prisoner's welfare. And certainly the guard is supposed to accept the fact that his action causes welfare effects for which he, nevertheless, cannot compensate in case such effects are inappropriate.

There are at least two possible sources of error with respect to the guard's action against the prisoner. If the state is just, its directives will be unquestionable. Nevertheless, first, the orders the guard gets might become confused and distorted because, say, of some misinterpretation of information. Second, the guard may make a personal mistake by, say, exaggerating his anticipatory reaction to the prisoner's action. Both cases are independent of any questions of justice. Now, the main point is that the guard may hurt the prisoner in a situation that later he will consider not to have warranted the use of such extreme measures. Yet, whether what he did was right or wrong, appropriate or not, its evaluation is not dependent on his own judgment. In other words, he is not supposed to compensate the prisoner for it. The matter of compensation is examined by authorities in the same way cases are examined in the law courts. The decision concerning any action against the guard and in favor of the prisoner belongs to authorities superior to the guard. They may consider the guard's deeds as unjustified or as misrepresenting his degrees of freedom with respect to the prisoner. And, therefore, *they* may offer compensation for these errors to the prisoner. The main point is that the guard's action and its consequences are indeed compensated for in a just society, but independently of the guard's own ideas of what is to be done with respect to its retrospective correction. I call this moral alienation.

The essentially authoritarian aspect of the guard's position is reflected in the fact that he brings about certain effects whose risks he is not supposed to correct. He may, therefore, be supposed to act against his own factual beliefs, normative ideas, preferences, and values. There are cases where he must punish the prisoner, although he knows the latter is innocent and he himself does not accept the form of punishment. He can only hope that the social system (which he takes, with good reasons, to be just) will ultimately compensate for the wrongs committed against the prisoner in a manner that corresponds to the guard's own values and that satisfies his normative requirements. His ethics is based on social trust.

Notice that, from a practical point of view, the denial of a direct case-to-case personal compensation function and the resulting discharge of accountability, even if the social order is just, cannot possibly be anything like the ideal state of moral affairs. The main problem is that the guard's sole justification for his action is based on his warranted belief that the society is indeed just. Yet there is nothing in the guard's position that would make the subjective justification of his particular deterrent actions depend on his own deliberate execution of just procedures. This means that, from his own point of view, nothing needs to change visibly with respect to his duties even if the social order became gradually more corrupt. He is not forced to see any differences, and he need not do so. In fact, the behavioral aspects of the guard's job may be similar both in just and in moderately unjust societies. He may fulfill his duties in a similar way in both, presupposing that the unjust order does not alter too radically the whole prison system. This would not be the case if the guard were working under the principle of direct personal compensation, so that his actions would be directly relevant to the realization of social justice. The injustice of the system would imply direct losses to the guard, if he were a fully moral person.

I do not wish to overemphasize these ideas. It is after all a utopian suggestion that all authoritarian positions must be eliminated from just societies. It is implausible to think that we could transform our society in that anarchistic direction, or that such a nonauthoritarian system could take care of the various administrative and executive tasks necessary in any complex, real society. The theory of justice ought to be practically relevant, which is to say that it must not be alienated from historical social reality. Mere utopias do not help.

A quest for justice

We shall turn to moral epistemology. We may think that the case of the guard is an example of the fact that social justice may allow for prima facie individual immorality. This presupposes that we have a clear intuition concerning this thesis. But do we really have such intuitions about social structures and the effects of threats? We do seem to think that some social relations are insignificant, but I do not believe that we can say the same about the case of the guard and the prisoner. The guard's case qualifies as a genuinely moral context, which makes the guard immoral; but we also seem to be ready to admit that this is too strong a conclusion. The guard's position is a normally accepted job with which we all are familiar. There are other similar jobs, and we feel that there is no way to eliminate all authoritarian positions. We may be somewhat uncomfortable with them, and we certainly think that they are potentially, both socially and individually, dangerous jobs. But if we take care of the general justice of our penal system and guarantee compensation to prisoners in case of mistakes, we are morally permitted to forgive their implementation in society. In other words, these structural positions are dangerous but necessary and even acceptable.

Now, if we focus on the ethical method of universalization, we see clearly how difficult it is to fix our intuitions concerning the present problem. In short, the guard argues that anyone, including the prisoner, could accept the position and duties he has. There is, nevertheless, one counterargument, which makes the guard's proposed line of argument apparently ineffective. If the prisoner accepts the universalizability of the guard's positional duties, he must think in the following way: "If I were a guard, I would prevent everyone's escape, even if they were in a situation identical with my present one," and find all this personally convincing. The prisoner is actually saying that the guard's job is to keep convicts in prison; and if someone is to be blamed for what he is doing, the whole legal system in general must be accused. In other words, we are driven to suppose that the prisoner accepts the guard's superior structural position in the sense that the prisoner believes that any convict gets what he deserves (he himself brings about his present status), and if he does not, adequate compensatory measures will be taken promptly. But this global perspective misses the real point: the prisoner may also think that if he himself were a guard he would not apply the rules that guide the guard's action in such-and-such a manner—in, say, a rigorous way—since such an interpretation is bound to hurt the prisoner's individual rights at some point.

A real problem exists at this level. If the guard is rigorous and, say, prone to use violence, the prisoner may, naturally enough, support a looser approach. If he wants this approach, he cannot accept that everyone should act as the guard acts. And certainly the prisoner should insist on some direct compensation principle. This whole standpoint is at least partly independent of considerations of social justice, since it concentrates on the prisoner's individual rights in some fully specified situations. I mean that the controversial minor issues here are tied to the guard's and the prisoner's personal understanding and interpretation of certain structurally determined guidelines for action. It is, moreover, predictable that no complete agreement can be reached. The interests of the two parties are so different. It seems to be the case that the results of universalization are rather dubious in our master example: the results depend either on (1) subjective factors or (2) a prior consensus concerning the overall justice of the social system in question. In the former case, positive results can scarcely be expected; but in the latter case, the whole issue simply moves back from the area of ethics proper to that of social justice. This result supports my claim that the guard's position is acceptable if and only if his social position is located within a just social order.

This shows, it seems to me, that the guard's case is not a mere illustration of our intuitions concerning nonmoral contexts of action. It provides new epistemic evidence to confirm the hypothesis that there really exist social cases that are not immoral but are excusable, in spite of their problematic nature. The key element of this explanation is our attempt to show that the reason why we should not be individually worried or why the social context in question is not a personally significant moral one is that the society is just: the prisoner gets exactly what he deserves. In such a social structure, the noncompensation principle and the related discharge of personal accountability would not matter. They apply only in personal face-to-face interaction. In short, the satisfaction of the demands of social justice could be used to explain why some authoritarian prima facie violations of the EI principle are not really relevant. The guard's case provides supporting evidence in favor of our conclusion that such an explanatory principle exists in the realm of practical and applied ethics.

But now a serious conceptual problem arises. If we have no independent intuitions concerning the moral acceptability of the guard's personal position, we are in trouble. This is the case, because we know, as Alan Donagan has said, that no social order, just or unjust, can justify immoral choices and actions.[12] For example, no laws or "democratic" decisions can make slavery morally acceptable. No social order with its laws, traditions, values, and economic institutions can alone make a prima facie immoral action acceptable in the prescriptive perspective. But now, if the guard's personal position with its typical action possibilities is a morally suspect one, this logically entails that the respective social order is unjust, because it allows for such structurally determined authoritarian actions. This is to say that the society is just only if the guard's position is not immoral.

It therefore follows that we do not really know whether society is unjust or not before we get to know whether the guard's position is immoral or not. This means that we cannot use our ascriptions of social justice to legitimize an authoritarian position if the two things are not mutually independent; and one may suggest that justice and structurally determined action are conceptually connected. We are discussing the guard's role, which then implies his personal decisions.

Perhaps we cannot be required to show that a social order is just, if that is supposed to be done without having recourse to something like the normative status of authoritarian personal positions. The question now is whether this kind of independent proof of justice can be expected to emerge. In fact, the guard's position seems to constitute an important, and perhaps even crucial, test for the alleged punitive justice of any social order. One might think that, if these tests are not available, we cannot decide whether the social order is just or not.

There is really something strange in the idea that the guard's position is moral only on condition that the social order is just, since in this case we may try to justify an otherwise possibly immoral practice by referring to a social order that makes apparently immoral actions moral. But how is it possible that a violation of a person's rational freedom in a seemingly moral context turns into an innocent nonmoral deed if the society is just? Neither the practice itself nor the guard's action changes if we move from a just to an unjust order. This type of justificatory miracle is needed, however, if one hopes to save the guard's authoritarian position from accusations of immorality. We need a proof that the guard's situation cannot be judged without paying attention to its institutional setting. I do not know what that proof would be like.

The following seems to be true: (1) practical applied ethics requires much theoretical background work (theory of justice); (2) some formulations depend on our personal tastes (one may be utopian minded, practice oriented, or a rigorous theoretician); and, in addition, (3) the method and vocabulary we use to describe our examples and formulate our problems may be crucially important to our conclusions. Finally, (4) the simple Hegelian demand, the core of social ethics, to fulfill the duty of our position is relatively independent of both social justice and personal morality.

The point concerning (4) is this: social life must be organized in some way; otherwise we all shall suffer. The organization presents unavoidable but suspicious demands on its individual placeholders.

But we also must take considerations of justice into account: we entertain the idea of an ideal social order. There emerges a gap between the real and the ideal order and between the independently justified respective prescriptions. Justice alone cannot guarantee the individual morality of anyone's personal decisions. Therefore, justifiable demands are conflicting and leave room for personal accusations of immorality. No way out exists, as the duties and norms of the makeshift social morality are backed by one powerful idea: security and ultimate physical survival exemplify a basic natural right for us all.

At the most general level, my conclusions come to this: there are many useful moralities, including ideas of value, right, duty, and rationality. But there is no existing ideal of a supermorality that could unify all the codes and ideas. The level of the generality and rigor of moral discourse may be raised more and more, but no final ceiling will be found. Morality is ultimately open-ended.

The implications of injustice

Having considered a case wherein the exercise of power in a just context causes moral problems, let us examine some cases of unjust exercise. Robert E. Goodin's book *Manipulatory Politics* is a good source.[13] He defines manipulation as social power in morally negative terms and maintains that all uses of manipulation are unacceptable, a thesis he seems unable to support when he deals with some realistic social examples. Even if the definition of an interactive strategy is given in morally negative terms, it must be evaluated also by its consequences, and nothing can have only bad consequences. In some unjust situations, consequences of manipulation are simply so desirable that the wicked character can be neglected. It is impossible that all the actual uses of manipulation will have a surplus of harmful and unjust consequences. We have here a familiar dilemma: a given interactive policy is at the same time immoral and perfectly excusable. Individual morality is once again dominated by social considerations.

Let us see how Goodin gets himself trapped. He defines manipulation thus. "It is power exercised (1) deceptively and (2) against the putative will of its objects. Each of these aspects is morally objectionable in its own right. Together, they guarantee that manipulation constitutes the evil core of the concept of 'power.'"[14] He also says that manipulation is the "nastiest face of power."[15] It is problematic why exactly this should be the case. Goodin does not discuss any systematic ceteris paribus clauses, which would allow him to specify what kind of social worlds are better places if manipulation is not used in them. For example, about rhetorical trickery Goodin says that it "is a mode of manipulation, and as such it is *prima facie* immoral."[16] On the one hand, it may appear that Goodin is arguing that manipulatory contexts are intrinsically unacceptable, regardless of their consequences in specific cases. On the other hand, mere prima facie problems can hardly be sources of moral despair.

As a consequentialist, Goodin writes as follows: "Rhetorical tricks for implicit argumentation are therefore peculiarly useful to oppressed groups. They must hide their meaning if they are to express it at all."[17] The American black slaves in the antebellum South provide an example. They developed a special communicative language in order to mislead their masters into believing that they had nothing to hide, or to say. This deception was a life and death affair to the slaves and their welfare interests. This is as good a case as anyone can find to show that manipulation may be a good thing. In a slave society, rhetorical manipulation by the slaves is a desirable thing, ceteris paribus.

We now focus on such cases where the distribution of power is so uneven that the weaker party must resort to methods whose justification in a case where power is more evenly distributed would be impossible. The weaker party should not make his own situation still weaker by using only such methods appropriate in balanced situations, which definitely do not obtain. Goodin's problem is that he starts from the modern-day democratic decision-making climate, within which it is indeed true that all kinds of manipulation should be minimized. Yet, the same normative idea does not apply across all power distributions and mechanisms. For instance, if the objects of manipulation have no moral right to do what they are doing, it may well be that we are entitled to manipulate them. Manipulation, just like coercion and deterrence in the service of moral good and right, will become morally indifferent, as Goodin himself concludes in the case of the slave language. And if such a morally indifferent effect is possible, it is simply false that, other things being equal, any social context without manipulation would be preferable to one including manipulation. Since the institution of slavery is undesirable to the slaves, it will not do to say that by rejecting manipulatory slave language the world would become a better place to live in.

In this way, Goodin's claims that manipulation is always undesirable is unfounded. Accordingly, let us also resist the temptation to evaluate social power and its uses before we are clear about their basic analytic descriptive features. Intuitions do not help much here. The real moral problem with power is the conflict between institutional (punitive and corrective) justice and the dubious requirements it imposes on individual agents, seen as private persons. Paradoxically, an agent's position in a just context may be more difficult to understand than his position in an unjust context. Injustice makes some immoral countermeasures excusable. This may be common wisdom. It is, however, more surprising that justice can make some immoral practices excusable.

The reality of morals: explanation as an existence test

Coercion, authority, and related forms are complex and ambiguous, and yet each have their respective constitutive roles in social life. Therefore, their evaluation is not straightforward. And many of the definitions of social explanatory terms by means of such moral ideas as rights make the normative use of these terms a trivial matter. The use of some global moral criteria in connection with coercive power makes the task of moral critique all too easy. Typically, we can either lapse into a gross rejection or take a partisan standpoint. Coercion, especially, is an elusive target, as it seems to be necessary, demanding, repulsive, and useful; in fact, everything at the same time. Perhaps nothing interesting can be said about coercion and authority from the most general evaluative perspective. Those forms of social action are in some cases morally laudable; they may be duties, and sometimes they qualify as supererogatory acts. They may be components of tyrannical and repressive policies, too. But no clear-cut moral pattern should be expected to emerge.

It is more advisable to focus on the functional roles of the power notions in moral life and their reflection in moral theory. Some advantages will become apparent. Actually, what we have been studying is how social life and institutions necessarily interact through moral ideas and their implementation. If human morality is not all fictional, it must be at least partially dependent on social praxis. This is indeed a broad thesis, but yet its explication seems worthwhile.

We can put the idea thus: (1) any existing morality is supervenient on social life; and (2) no philosophically critical and ideal moralities can be sensibly formulated independently of their humbler ancestors. Taken together, these two points entail that normative and ethical attitudes toward social life are themselves part of that very realm of existence. Otherwise, ethics is just a genre of fiction. It is one of the philosopher's tasks to indicate how social life explains morality and its main identifying features, such as prescriptivity, rationality, and overridingness; or its alleged objectivity versus its emotive efficacy. Not before such explanations are in hand can the moralists say that they indeed have something real at their disposal, referring to their own conceptual tools, which they can try to employ on human social life in order to criticize and guide it.

The following idea has been implicit in all that I have done in the course of my main argument: moralities are explicable through social variables. As an extension of this, I shall argue that no alleged morality that is not so explicable through social variables can possibly be real. My point is a logical one: the idea about the explanation of moralities provides us with a criterion of the existence of a morality only because the very meaning of existence in connection with morality is anchored to this idea of explanation. Otherwise, we would not know what it means to ask whether a moral system exists or not. The problem arises because morality is not a matter-of-fact or perceptible quality of things, however nonnatural such Moorean qualities might be. Morality as a whole is a peculiarly practical, evaluative, and prescriptive ideal entity, whose existence conditions may well be supposed to be different from those of empirical facts or of logical and mathematical truths.

It is simply not enough to say, as we may be instinctively inclined to do, that we believe that moral prescriptive considerations both motivate and direct our decision making. Such an idea suggests that morality explains both social life and individual decisions: things are as we make them, and we are supposed to be guided by our moral codes. But human motivation is a complex affair, so that we always have more than one motive to which to refer as an explanation of our actions. Even if one of them is merely a fictional entity, like morality might be, no damage to our overall action explanation would be done. Psychological explanations are strongly overdetermined, anyway. Furthermore, we can explicate our own decisions and actions both privately and publicly in terms of some traditional moral notions but fail to see that these explanatory considerations are subjective and perhaps even controversial and idiosyncratic, in such a way that they really have the status of an explanandum rather than the intended explanans. Subjectively grounded morality certainly affects the agent, but its initial adoption and its specific validity each require a new and separate explanation.

We possess no such a priori arguments that show that moralities and moral ideas exist and can be used to explain our lives. We have philosophical theories, but they are full of difficulties. One possible candidate for an empirical argument is the proposition that morality actually explains our decisions. Is morality an explanans? If morality is a controversial social factor, nothing is achieved by explicating our actions by means of it alone. In doing so, we would employ a tool that is so indeterminate that whatever results emerge may be explained by means of it. In fact, a theory of morality is needed before we can use moral ideas to give an account of our actions. But then whether the main terms of this moral theory refer or not becomes the central question. For instance we may ask, Is it a fictional construct fit only for rhetorical persuasion and manipulation?

Now we come to the pragmatic stage of the discussion. It is natural to suggest that if action explanations in terms of beliefs in and commitments to moral values and norms are successful—or in other words, if people act as they "should" whenever they can be seen to have the relevant moral code available to them—then morality is indeed real. The basic intuition is acceptable, namely, that if people successfully realize their moral ideas and turn their moral ideals into reality, morality also exists in social life. Nevertheless, this argument can be better used to refute the existence of morality than to verify it. People report that they have moral codes but fail to act upon them. No basis exists for the claim that a moral ideology will be turned into action in a lawlike manner and that this happens so regularly that the effect could be best explained by referring to the moral principles adopted by the agents. On the contrary, the observable effects of morality on power exercise and conflicts are often so negligible that other action explanations will apply equally well.

These theses can be illustrated by means of an empirical sociology of morals. It is evident that people's explicitly declared moral convictions have not much to do with their observed behavior. Francesca Cancian writes as follows: "Norms do not concern behavior that is measured 'objectively' without reference to its meaning to the group. Therefore, if a researcher measures behavior in terms of a category system that is not shared by the group, we should not be surprised if the data show a low correlation between norms and behavior."[18] The most important "meaning to the group" is said to concern the person's social identity, or his location within the center of expectations and beliefs of the members of the group. In order to find a correlation between norms and behavior, an extra variable must be introduced, that is, the person's social identity description. In the moral realm this cannot mean that, in order to find a correlation with a person's ethical behavior, the researcher should know what the person thinks about morality, in the sense of his own moral commitments. This would put the cart before the horse. We cannot presuppose the effectiveness of some given personal and prescriptive beliefs. What happens is that a person's moral behavior is explicable through other people's beliefs about that given person and his role, according to some moral prescriptions.

But what are those prescriptions? How can we decide what role expectations are in fact identity constituting? Again, we must presuppose knowledge about actually effective ethics. The questions are, What moral beliefs can be supposed to explain social identity? What is the existing morality? In order to show that morality affects behavior, we must show that a moral system exists. This fact will be inferred, say, from verbal reports. The research moves in a circle.

I feel quite comfortable with the following set of theses. First, we must take the idea of morality seriously and not confuse it with that of any other type of directive code, such as social mores, religious prescriptions, or plain manners. It is not always easy to distinguish between those nonmoral and moral ideas. It is not questionable, however, whether we can separate the moral from nonmoral factors in action explanation. Second, most people use several different and incompatible moral codes, in addition to their nonmoral sources of directives, in a highly confusing manner. I want to suggest that it is a false social psychological hypothesis that an agent typically cannot make a decision concerning the issue of whether he should act or refrain from acting if one element in his set of moral prescriptions pulls in one direction and the other pulls in the opposite direction. Conflicts do not prove anything. An agent may make decisions on the basis of some such conservative rule as *if any moral considerations clearly condemn a course of action, do not do it.* Alternatively, he might be a moral liberal and maintain that *if at least one moral code allows for action, it is right to do it.* A different possibility is to arrange alternatives in a priority order according to the nature of the problem area — saying that, for instance, in medical ethics social utility overrides rights but in ecological questions rights override utility. It seems that "ordinary people" may be capable of doing these tricks successfully with their normative conceptual apparatus.

Actually, it seems that no strictly prescriptive ethics makes sense in the empirical social world. Moral authority and its commands are void. Morality is an ideal in the standard normative sense of the term *ideal.* Morality says what we should do and would do if we were rational, benevolent, impartial, well informed, and so on. They may have no explanatory effect concerning our actions; and still it is the ideal morality that is worth studying and using. It says what we should do — and if we are unable to take notice of it, the worse for us. We should have followed those moral prescriptions anyway. The only thing that matters is that it is not impossible to be moral.

In this way it seems that if the sense of the claim that a given morality exists is given through the idea that morality should explain people's behavior then the expected results will verify the nonexistence of morality rather than its existence. Yet, people in general believe in morality.

The sense of the claim that morality exists must be given in another way. I have already suggested that we should take morality as an explanandum and try to handle it in such a delicate manner that we shall also find out why exactly morality is so inefficient a factor in social life.

Analogies to Marxism

Logic provides a weak existence demonstration: normative systems seem to allow for a coherent systematization in an axiomatic form. One necessary condition for their existence is thus satisfied. Sociobiology focuses on some relevant issues, but we cannot deal with these in the present context. Anyway, sociobiology dismisses some rationality considerations crucial to our present purposes.[19] It has been shown that some biological phenomena are at least analogous to the real "moral facts," such as altruism, but it is questionable whether anything more can be said. Biology is an empirical science; but in morality, rationality and prescriptivity are the key issues. For example, sociobiology may show that altruism is an evolutionary functional behavioral tendency. One cannot show in a similar way that it is rational or advisable for a human agent to adopt such altruistic policies. Sociobiology alone cannot give us the necessary or sufficient conditions of rational acceptance of values and prescriptions, even if it could describe some analogies to them and their genetic evolution in nature. From the sociobiological point of view, all analogies to moral systems are equally desirable. However, some of the biological systems seem to bear a certain resemblance to those values that the sociobiologists themselves recognize as their own.

Certainly, Marxism and its well-known attempts to show that all moralities are ideologies based on economic class interests and tied to some definite periods of man's history resemble my present attempt to explain morality. Marxism explains the existence, effectiveness, and content of moralities by means of their economic function in class societies. One class dominates the others, but it cannot reach its goals without the help of an invisible hand; this implies some such normative devices that make it possible to control subordinate agents without violence or explicit coercive power and policies. Morality establishes an apparent (false) social consensus concerning the large-scale aspects of life and makes social order possible. This also justifies the legal enforcement of the consensus. Moreover, such acceptance has severely biased distributional effects. One class dominates the distribution. It is the main point of social ethics to provide an overriding and autonomous justification for the economic system, which embodies certain legally enforced norms of partiality.

According to this Marxist view, genuine morality has its non-moral "material" roots in economic history, and its effects are to be found in all such patterns of distribution that have a biased function in the nonmoral economic area. Moralities serve a latent purpose different from all the explicit formulations of moral goals and whose real point is outside the area of moral prescriptions. Any claim concerning right or wrong has its own apparent validity. Norms and values may be motivationally effective, but only so far as they do not go against the grand historical purpose. That alone makes morality a persistent feature of the social world during a given period of history.

It follows that no one who knows what morality is will be constrained by moral propositions without having some additional reasons. He must know both what the particular moral codes demand and what the historically established status of that code is. To focus only on the first aspect is to remain within the bounds of a false ideology; not before he checks the second point can he be a free person. A morally rational person must know the direction of history toward a goal and, at the same time, its nature as a lawlike economic process. The principal features of the dominant future morality can be inferred from this information. The ultimate moral agent acts ahead of his own time.

However, if this idea implies personal requirements, it must come very close to supererogation: the agent is supposed to act against his own dominating morality, which is still valid because it serves the purposes of economic history. Therefore, even in periods of drastic social change, real morality is reserved for intellectual elites, in the sense that a small group of people is able to sense the direction of change, and thus their moral principles override those of their contemporaries.

The general Marxist approach to morality is both speculative and problematic. Moreover, in its rougher forms, it is certainly false. The Marxist economic perspective explains morality as a nonmoral discourse. Thus it seems questionable whether Marxism can show that morality exists—or not at least in the standard philosophical sense. Something like morality exists, but it is not clear that it is the right type of social fact. One comes very close to explaining morality away, because knowledge of economic history takes the place of morality in providing the ultimate guide to socially laudable action. Knowing exactly what the historical processes of society are like would eliminate any need to use moral notions to direct one's own life among the elite. Because such cognitive liberation cannot in general be achieved, one must continue normative discourse and the use of moral language.

Not everyone can come to know the true nature of morality, because that would destroy one of the necessary functional conditions of historical progress, or its driving force: moral anger and justified dissatisfaction. Morality is needed for sociohistorical purposes; but because the full knowledge of this fact is destructive to moral ideas as we know them, not everyone should come to comprehend the truth. This fact explains why some people indeed believe and also why they should believe in the validity of moral prescriptions. Nevertheless, some kind of morality is real even in the Marxist perspective: morality is real as an essentially distorted idea of what is demanded from a typical, or representative, social agent.

Of course, the historical goal of social progress is a value in itself, and as the limit value of moral development we may find some kind of a universally valid moral system. In utopian communism, all moral prescriptions and values are objectively true; this is one possible "soft" interpretation of Marxism. But then we are driven back to our former considerations of ideal morality in the role of a social explanans. In actual fact, it seems that no morality is needed. It will not even be mentioned in the final ideal society, which works without moral constraints. In the communist utopia, the social order is such that no normative problems occur and no skeptical thoughts may be sensibly entertained. Its institutions, including education, are such that their justification becomes evident from history alone. Everybody behaves in the absolutely correct way. No controversies emerge, except perhaps trivial ones. Morality has nothing to do, and it explains nothing, as it seems to me.

This is what we learn from Engels's *Anti-Dühring:*

Our ideologist may turn and twist as he likes, but the historical reality which he cast out at the door comes in again at the window, and while he thinks he is framing a doctrine of morals and law for all times and for all worlds, he is in fact only fashioning an image of the conservative or revolutionary tendencies of his day—an image which is distorted because it has been torn from its real basis and, like a reflection in a concave mirror, is standing on its head.[20]

He writes also as follows: "A really human morality which stands above class antagonisms . . . becomes possible only at a stage of society which has not only overcome class antagonisms but has even forgotten them in practical life."[21] It indeed seems that Engels postulates the reality of objective and absolute moral truths in the latter quotation, but this is not quite true: morality is always derivative of social life, and if the life conditions are perfect, so is morality and justice. It is, therefore, easy to see that absolute morality is an insignificant conceptual addition to the material conditions of utopian life.

For instance, according to Engels's own example, "Thou shalt not steal," becomes void, as he states, when private property ceases to exist. It seems to follow that all the known moral prescriptions, like those of honesty, must disappear from the classless society and at the point of nonantagonistic life. Morality will have no function at all. It is ultimately and at its best simply useless. All that will be needed to regulate human life will be a set of simple and unproblematic codes of manners.

I have tried to give an account of the existence of a somewhat stronger form of morality than that constituted by the Marxist ideologies. Social power implies moral codes in an agent-internal and genuinely prescriptive perspective. Some features of moral codes are inescapable in any advanced society. Such a society requires a complex morality. Yet I am not saying that morality would serve only an external function, like manipulation or mere mental hygiene. Instead, morality serves an intrinsically moral function: we live a social life, and that is something we desire and cannot help desiring. Therefore, social power, which partly but necessarily constitutes our social life, is to be desired as well. If we want to continue structured social existence, however truncated, we need power. As an essential counterpart of the exercise of power we get moral rules, values, and principles. We need prescriptive ethics. Descriptive ethics does not suffice.

We justify the proposition that moral codes exist by saying that otherwise social life could not exist. Furthermore, we can show how several incoherent-looking details of those codes come together to constitute a coherent functional structure of, say, interlocking coercion and authority.

If we are able to show that some forms of concrete and visible social power help explain moral notions and their relations, we can also plausibly conclude that morality is a real phenomenon in our social universe. Conflicts tend to be so serious that their regulation necessitates a suitable distribution of quite special ideas, that is, normative notions. How should we formulate these explanations? The answer can be seen among the results of the present study: the everyday phenomena of social power point to the need to identify such a social morality whose relation to individual prudence cannot be understood without certain structures and functions of the coercive and noncoercive forms of power. Actually, we may be able to show exactly who some aspects of real moralities are so epistemically elusive, conceptually open-ended, and practically ineffective. Nevertheless, it is also true that social-power-related explanations of the moral phenomena cannot alone prove conclusively the reality of morals.

An immediate relativist corollary of my basic position may now be recognized: certainly, if no power phenomena occur in some, say, primitive or anarchistic cultures, we cannot explain morality in the same way as we did above. Is it then sensible to speak about morality in connection with such a culture at all? If we cannot, is this not a highly implausible conclusion? Thus we can speak about morality, but we cannot establish the existence of morality in the present way. There are other ways, though. The social institutions of these cultures give rise to a different type of moral relation. But then we cannot give exactly the same meaning to the question of the existence of morality in their society as we gave to it in ours. Their morality is not quite like ours. This radical proposition does not, nevertheless, imply that their practical action-constraining code could not be called morality. There can be no fixed set of necessary and sufficient conditions for being a moral code. Moralities are many things, as we know when we try to understand a foreign cultural life and its norms.

Hegel says in his *Philosophy of History* that cultures that have no state structure are impossible to grasp.[22] We may well fail to understand their practical logic. This is still quite consonant with the idea that there is such a logic. If one exists, it need not be like ours. My own position requires only that, if we know a form of social life well enough, we can identify some functions, like power, that can be used to explain the role of some analogies to moral ideas. I say merely that something can be found that makes the ultimate prescriptive ideas in a culture understandable from a pragmatic point of view.

Notes

1 Focus on Power

1 C. Fried, *Right and Wrong* (Cambridge, Mass.: Harvard University Press, 1978), p. 1.

2 See especially J. Mackie, *Ethics: Inventing Right and Wrong* (Harmondsworth, Middlesex: Penguin, 1977); see also J. Mackie, "Morality and the Retributive Emotions," *Criminal Justice Ethics* 1 (1982): 3–10.

3 See T. Airaksinen, "Moral Education and Democracy in the School," *Synthese* 51 (1982): 117–34.

4 See T. C. Schelling, *The Strategy of Conflict* (Cambridge, Mass.: Harvard University Press, 1980).

5 Perhaps this applies to the idea of fanaticism in R. M. Hare, *Freedom and Reason* (London: Oxford University Press, 1963), pp. 157ff.

6 *Hegel's Philosophy of Right* (Grundlinien der Philosophie des Rechts), trans. T. M. Knox (London: Oxford University Press, 1967).

7 K. R. Popper, *The Open Society and its Enemies*, vol. 2 (London: Routledge and Kegan Paul, 1966).

8 *Hegel's Philosophy*, nos. 232 and 234.

9 Ibid., nos. 241 and 244 Zusatz.

10 Ibid., nos. 246–48.

11 R. Nozick, *Anarchy, State, and Utopia* (New York: Basic Books, 1974).

12 *Hegel's Philosophy*, nos. 325 and 328.

13 Ibid., no. 324.

14 Ibid., no. 327.

15 Ibid., no. 326.

16 Ibid., no. 261.

17 Ibid., no. 291.

211

18 Ibid., nos. 202–03.
19 B. Russell, *Power: A New Social Analysis* (London: Unwin, 1975), p. 25.
20 D. Wrong, *Power: Its Forms, Bases and Uses* (Oxford: Basil Blackwell, 1979), p. 2; my italics.
21 M. Weber, *Economy and Society* (New York: Bedminster, 1968), vol. 1, p. 224.
22 Russell, *Power*, p. 11.
23 S. Lukes, *Power: A Radical View* (London: Macmillan, 1974); S. Lukes, *Essays in Social Theory* (New York: Columbia University Press, 1977); S. Lukes, "Power and Authority," in T. Bottomore and R. Nisbet, eds., *A History of Sociological Analysis* (London: Heinemann, 1978); A. Goldman, "Toward a Theory of Social Power," *Philosophical Studies* 23 (1972): 221–68.
24 A. Giddens, *New Rules of Sociological Method: A Positive Critique of Interpretative Sociologies* (London: Hutchinson, 1976), pp. 111 and 113; italics deleted.
25 Ibid., p. 110.
26 Ibid., p. 161; italics deleted.
27 E. Canetti, *Crowds and Power* (Masse und Macht), trans. C. Stewart (New York: Continuum, 1981), p. 448.
28 C. C. Ryan, "The Normative Concept of Coercion," *Mind* 89 (1980): 481–98.
29 Ibid., p. 483.
30 Ibid., p. 485.
31 Ibid., p. 488.

2 Threats and Personal Coercion

1 A. Huxley, *The Devils of Loudun* (London: Granada, 1977).
2 T. C. Schelling, *The Strategy of Conflict* (Cambridge, Mass.: Harvard University Press, 1980), p. 196.
3 Huxley, *Devils of Loudun*, p. 209.
4 G. Orwell, *1984* (New York: New American Library, 1961).
5 Ibid., p. 232.
6 J. P. Day, "Threats, Offers, Law, Opinion and Liberty," *American Philosophical Quarterly* 14 (1977): 257–72.
7 Ibid., p. 259.
8 Ibid., p. 269.
9 D. Miller, "Constraints on Freedom," *Ethics* 94 (1983): 66–86; p. 77.
10 Ibid.
11 Ibid., p. 70.
12 *Hegel's Philosophy of Right* (Grundlinien der Philosophie des Rechts), trans. T. M. Knox (London: Oxford University Press, 1967), no. 91.
13 D. Gauthier, "Deterrence, Maximization, and Rationality," *Ethics* 94 (1984): 474–95.
14 Ibid., p. 483.
15 Ibid., p. 488.
16 M. Taylor, *Community, Anarchy and Liberty* (London: Cambridge University Press, 1982), p. 19.
17 Ibid., p. 20.

18 H. Frankfurt, "Coercion and Moral Responsibility," in T. Honderich, ed., *Essays on Freedom of Action* (London: Routledge and Kegan Paul, 1973), p. 75; see also p. 77.

19 J. Galtung, *Peace: Research, Education, Action*, vol. 1, *Essays in Peace Research* (Copenhagen: Christian Ejlers, 1975), pp. 110–11.

20 R. Audi, "Violence, Legal Sanctions, and Law Enforcement," in S. M. Stanage, ed., *Reason and Violence: Philosophical Investigations* (Totowa, N.J.: Littlefield, Adams, 1974). See also B. Harrison, "Violence and the Rule of Law," in J. Shaffer, ed., *Violence* (New York: David McKey, 1971).

3 Types and Meaning of Repression

1 M. Laver, *The Crime Game* (Oxford: Martin Robertson, 1982).

2 R. Nozick, "Coercion," in P. Laslett, W. G. Runciman, and Q. Skinner, eds., *Philosophy, Politics and Society*, fourth series (Oxford: Basil Blackwell, 1972), pp. 115–16.

3 D. Golash, "Exploitation and Coercion," *Journal of Value Inquiry* 15 (1981): 319–28; p. 324.

4 H. Steiner, "A Liberal Theory of Exploitation," *Ethics* 94 (1984): 225–41; p. 233.

5 M. Fowler, "Coercion and Practical Reasoning," *Social Theory and Practice* 8 (1982): 328–55; pp. 331–32.

6 Ibid., p. 350.

7 H. J. McCloskey, "Coercion: Its Nature and Significance," *Southern Journal of Philosophy* 18 (1980): 335–51; p. 342.

8 Ibid., p. 348.

9 D. Zimmerman, "Coercive Wage Offers," *Philosophy and Public Affairs* 10 (1981): 121–45.

10 Ibid., p. 133, italics deleted.

11 Ibid., p. 136.

12 D. Lyons, "Welcome Threats and Coercive Offers," *Philosophy* 50 (1975): 425–36; and D. Lyons, "The Last Word on Coercive Offers?," *Philosophy Research Archives* 8 (1982): 1–22.

13 Lyons, "Welcome Threats," p. 433.

14 Ibid., p. 434.

15 Ibid., p. 435.

16 Ibid., p. 436. See also Lyons, "The Last Word on Coercive Offers," pp. 14ff.

4 Coercive Institutions

1 See S. Bok, *Secrets* (New York: Pantheon, 1982).

2 R. Nozick, *Anarchy, State, and Utopia* (New York: Basic Books, 1974), pp. 14ff.

3 R. Tuck, *Natural Rights Theories* (London: Cambridge University Press, 1979), p. 56.

4 See, for example, J. Mackie, *Hume's Moral Theory* (London: Routledge and Kegan Paul, 1980), p. 84.

5 See also J. Rawls, "Two Concepts of Rules," in P. Foot, ed., *Theories of Ethics* (London: Oxford University Press, 1967).

6 R. M. Hare, "Utilitarianism and the Vicarious Affects," in E. Sosa, ed., *The Philosophy of Nicholas Rescher* (Dordrecht: Reidel, 1979), pp. 146ff.

7 J. Rawls, *A Theory of Justice* (Cambridge, Mass.: Harvard University Press, 1971).

8 Compare R. A. Brandt, *A Theory of the Good and the Right* (Oxford: Clarendon, 1979), pp. 113ff.

9 Rawls, *Theory of Justice*, p. 5.

10 A. Flew, *The Politics of Procrustes* (London: Temple Smith, 1981), p. 90; see also p. 85.

11 Rawls, *Theory of Justice*, p. 491.

12 Ibid., p. 213.

13 P. P. Hallie, *Cruelty* (Middletown, Conn.: Wesleyan University Press, 1982).

14 E. A. Poe, *Complete Tales and Poems of E. A. Poe* (New York: Vintage, 1975), p. 281.

15 Hallie, *Cruelty*, pp. 37ff.

16 Ibid., p. 82.

17 J. Rudnianski, "Men of Science and Men of Power: Some Similarities and Differences," *Science of Science* 3 (1983): 379–88; p. 381.

18 See, for example, E. D. Watt, *Authority* (London: Croom Helm, 1982).

19 J. Raz, *The Authority of Law* (Oxford: Clarendon, 1979), p. 18.

20 Ibid., pp. 18 and 19.

21 Ibid., p. 23.

22 R. Flathman, *The Practice of Political Authority* (Chicago: University of Chicago Press, 1980), p. 130.

23 Ibid., p. 164.

24 Ibid., p. 150.

25 R. P. Wolff, *In Defense of Anarchism* (New York: Harper and Row, 1970), pp. 4ff.

26 Raz, *Authority of Law*, p. 24.

27 S. Milgram, *Obedience to Authority* (New York: Harper and Row, 1974).

28 Ibid., p. 5.

5 The Requirement of the Diversity of Morals

1 See, for example, W. H. Riker, *Liberalism Against Populism* (San Francisco: W. H. Freeman, 1982).

2 A. Gewirth, *Reason and Morality* (Chicago: University of Chicago Press, 1978).

3 F. G. Bailey, *The Tactical Uses of Passion* (Ithaca, N.Y.: Cornell University Press, 1983), pp. 42ff.

4 See A. MacIntyre, *After Virtue* (Notre Dame, Ind.: University of Notre Dame Press, 1981).

5 See also J. Rawls, "Two Concepts of Rules," in P. Foot, ed., *Theories of Ethics* (London: Oxford University Press, 1967).

6 See G. J. Warnock, *The Object of Morality* (London: Methuen, 1971), p. 26.

7 R. Nozick, *Anarchy, State, and Utopia* (New York: Basic Books, 1974), pp. 28ff.

8   J. D. Hodson, *The Ethics of Legal Coercion* (Dordrecht: Reidel, 1983).

9   Ibid., p. xiii.

10 Ibid., p. 73.

11 F. H. Bradley, *Ethical Studies*, 2d ed. (London: Oxford University Press, 1927), essay 5.

12 A. Donagan, *The Theory of Morality* (Chicago: University of Chicago Press, 1977), p. 97.

13 R. E. Goodin, *Manipulatory Politics* (New Haven, Conn.: Yale University Press, 1980).

14 Ibid., pp. 8–9.

15 Ibid., p. 7.

16 Ibid., p. 111.

17 Ibid., p. 115.

18 F. Cancian, *What Are Norms?* (London: Cambridge University Press, 1975), p. 146.

19 See P. Singer, *The Expanding Circle* (Oxford: Clarendon, 1981).

20 F. Engels, *Anti-Dühring* (Moscow: Progress, 1969), p. 117. See also S. Lukes, *Marxism and Morality* (New York: Oxford University Press, 1985).

21 Engels, *Anti-Dühring*, p. 115.

22 See T. Airaksinen, "Social Time and Place," *Man and World* 18 (1985): 99–105; and G. W. F. Hegel, *The Philosophy of History*, trans. J. Sibree (New York: Dover, 1956), p. 61.

Index